EXPLORING NATURE IN ILLINOIS

EXPLORING NATURE IN ILLINOIS

A FIELD GUIDE TO THE PRAIRIE STATE

MICHAEL JEFFORDS AND SUSAN POST

UNIVERSITY OF ILLINOIS PRESS
Urbana, Chicago, and Springfield

Manufactured in the United States of America
P 5 4 3 2 1
∞ This book is printed on acid-free paper.
Library of Congress Cataloging-in-Publication Data
Jeffords, Michael R.
Exploring nature in Illinois : a field guide to the
Prairie State / Michael Jeffords and Susan Post.
pages cm
Includes index.
ISBN 978-0-252-07990-0 (paperback : acid-free paper)
ISBN 978-0-252-09626-6 (e-book)
1. Natural history—Illinois.
2. Natural areas—Illinois—Guidebooks.
3. Parks—Illinois—Guidebooks.
4. Wildlife refuges—Illinois—Guidebooks.
5. Illinois—Guidebooks.
I. Post, Susan L. II. Title.
QH105.I3J44 2014
508.773—dc23 2013032195

We dedicate this book to the Illinois Natural History Survey, our intellectual home for more than thirty years, and the source of limitless opportunities to explore the landscape we call Illinois.

CONTENTS

NORTH

CENTRAL

SOUTH

FOREWORD

IT BOGGLES MY MIND to think about the progress of humans since 1818, when Illinois became a state. Our advancements continue to stagger the imagination. Yesterday's technological dreams are not just today's realities; they are today's necessities. But no matter how you cut the deck, we nurtured our innovation and achieved our inventions by forever altering the very landscape that attracted us.

Today, archeologists work hard to discover trace evidence of hundreds of generations of human beings that once inhabited Illinois. Through artifact fragments, scientists can only wonder about those ancient people, how they lived and how they perished.

I do not think archeologists of tomorrow will have as much difficulty figuring us out, given the amount of "artifacts" we currently are producing. It is with amazing speed and often reckless accuracy that a mere handful of recent generations changed our landscape forever. It is unfortunate but true, only a fraction of the pre-settlement Illinois landscape exists that has not been plowed, fenced, dug, drained, or cleared.

Thankfully, what you are about to learn in *Exploring Nature in Illinois* is that remnants of what once was the original landscape of Illinois still remain. With this beautifully assembled poetic nudge from Michael Jeffords and Susan Post, you are now tooled to discover for yourself what is out there. I must warn you, however, *Exploring Nature in Illinois* is a low-tech endeavor. All this journey requires is a desire to explore and an eagerness to discover.

Illinois harbors millions of acres of row crops, on which so many of us rely. But tucked into and around those fields of green are magnificent natural features hosting a remarkably diverse array of plants and animals. From bird's-eye primrose clinging to the cliffs of Apple River Canyon to prothonotary warblers nesting in Cache River cypress-tupelo swamps, Illinois is an explorer's paradise.

When T. S. Eliot wrote about the end of life's journey, he said we would arrive where we started, "and know the place for the first time." With *Exploring Nature in Illinois* in hand, it is my hope that you now begin your trek to discover Illinois for the first time. She is out there waiting for you, and I will wager her secret places offer your spirit enlightenment beyond all that is technologically possible.

Happy Exploring,
Tom Clay, Executive Director
Illinois Audubon Society

PREFACE

A Hint of Wildness

"This is the most beautiful place on earth.
There are many such places."
—Edward Abbey

EACH FALL WE ARE AMONG the many who eagerly await the release of the coming year's nature calendars, each brimming with photographs of pristine landscapes and the world's "charismatic megafauna"—lions, cheetahs, bears, and wolves. We also continually pore over images in nature magazines and on websites and marvel at the natural beauty of the earth. During recent years we have adventured widely, visiting southern Africa, Alaska, Peru, Australia, Mexico, and Brazil in search of wild creatures that call these landscapes home. We are biologists (entomologists to be exact) and native Illinoisans. The former makes us realists when it comes to the actual state of the earth; the latter means that we have come to appreciate not necessarily the wilderness of our state (there is little or none of that left), but the wildness. The difference between the two lies only in perception. Unfortunately, Illinois ranks an unenviable forty-ninth among the fifty states with regard to land that remains in relatively natural condition—in other words, land with its pre-European (pre-1800) settlement component of native flora and fauna. Only Iowa has less. Fortunately, Illinois was and is a very diverse expanse of land, and "threadbare patches" of nature occur in the blanket of development that has covered 99.93 percent of Illinois over the past two hundred years. These patches are windows to the past. Biological hotspots in Illinois range in size from a few square feet to several thousand acres and contain representative samples of the nearly one hundred different habitat types and more than fifty-four thousand species of organisms. Remnant landscapes, some protected as nature preserves and state or national landmarks, others existing merely as forgotten corners at the edge of an agricultural field, corridors along rail lines, or in pioneer cemeteries, all hint at the wildness of Illinois.

Perhaps it is the contrast these areas present to the uniformity of most of Illinois that makes them stand out as exquisite examples of nature. It is also likely that most would not stand up to a test for "true" wilderness areas, such as those that exist in the western United States. For example, during summer we can stand on the highest hill (an interstate highway overpass) near our home in central Illinois, look in all cardinal directions, and see predominantly two species of plants, corn and soybeans, laid out in a green-on-green, corduroy tapestry. This is a true biological desert. In reality, to find the wildness of Illinois requires a bit of searching, some biological detective work, an *Illinois Atlas & Gazetteer*, and knowledge of what "wildness" really is. To us, wildness can be a persistent compass plant growing along a fence in our front yard (a native plant from the twenty-one million acres of prairie that once covered 60 percent of Illinois), a native Illinois stinkbug waiting for prey in an oversized flower head of a garden cockscomb (originally from the Old World Tropics), or a few acres of wet meadow remaining at the base of an old glacial moraine. Even in the tamest, most formal of gardens, agricultural, or urban landscapes, nature will not be denied her wildness! Over the years we have traveled extensively and been exposed to much of North America and the world, but we continue to live in Illinois, and most of our photographic images are from the state. How does nature in Illinois stack up against the rest of the continent? In area and extent of wilderness, it's not even in the game. In wildness and diversity of species and habitats, it holds its own.

In experiencing natural landscapes, we find ourselves comparing what we find in widely divergent areas of the country to our own Illinois landscape. This leads us to conclude that while the nuances of natural habitats are infinite and their species diversity immense, many share remarkable structural and aesthetic similarities. We call these "perceptual equivalents." For example, foam flowers in an Appalachian cove forest are the perceptual equivalent of wild hyacinths in an Illinois prairie. Wildflowers in an upland meadow in the Grand Tetons are the perceptual equivalent to spring wildflowers residing on a gentle slope along the Sangamon River in central Illinois. Over time, we have come to realize and appreciate that Illinois, while still and likely to remain a corn and soybean desert, has more than its share of nature's "perceptual equivalents" and that these can and do provide numerous glimpses into the wild heart of Illinois.

Within the pages that follow we gladly accept the challenge of acquainting readers with the natural wonders of Illinois and fully expect to change the way you look at, think about, and experience the state. As biologists, we have explored Illinois for most of our lives and are aware of its dusty corners, nooks, crannies, and other forgotten places in the landscape that still reflect Illinois in its natural state. These relatively undisturbed waysides, containing elements of nature, are the building blocks or templates on which to build your own impressions of the nature of Illinois.

ACKNOWLEDGMENTS

AS WE EXPLORED THE STATE, many people made the job easier. Our thanks go to all the staff members and volunteers at nature centers, state parks, and forest preserves for answering our innumerable questions and providing maps to their sites. Several friends went beyond just answering questions and either took us directly to sites to see what was going on or provided additional access: Molie Oliver at Cache River State Natural Area, Stacy Iwanicki at Volo Bog State Natural Area, Terry Esker at Ballard Nature Center, Mike Brown and staff at Cypress Creek National Wildlife Refuge, and Randy, Angela, and Jill at Sugar Grove Nature Center. Jim Waycuilis at Cache River State Natural Area and Liz Jones at Cypress Creek National Wildlife Refuge went above and beyond mere maps and information. They welcomed us with southern Illinois hospitality and friendship.

Randy Nyboer provided access to and information about northwestern Illinois sites; Fran Hardy provided maps, information, and blooming times for the Kankakee Sands area. Jan Sundberg shared her observations on Cedar Lake, while Jane Ward provided updates on waterfowl and dragonfly happenings at Emiquon. Jim Wiker provided butterfly identification, information on where to find certain species, and accompanied us into the field on several occasions. Le Ann Benner, retired from the Illinois State Geological Survey, always had the right topo map or geological publication for our explorations. The Prairie Research Institute library staff provided access to much needed, often obscure reference materials, and were always ready to find information for us.

While all of our Illinois Natural History Survey colleagues are willing to share information and help identify specimens, we must single out a few special individuals. Dave Enstrom provided the initial impetus for the project. Diane Greer and Diane Szafoni created the location maps. Jamie Ellis used his expertise as a technical editor for the manuscript and Connie Carroll Cunningham provided valuable insight into Vermilion County and was always ready to identify a plant. Charles Warwick was a copyeditor for the book, Danielle Ruffato helped us with indexing, and Jen Mui contributed her expertise on all things reptile and amphibian, and accompanied us on several forays. Patty Dickerson scanned and sized many photos, was always curious about what we saw, and offered many words of encouragement. Patty, and her son Neil, also cared for Lark during our absences. And finally, thanks to Lark (our guinea pig), who always had "wheeks" of encouragement.

INTRODUCTION

A Brief Natural History of Illinois

> Two hundred years ago Illinois was one immense natural area, dotted with islands of human development. Today, Illinois is an almost completely developed landscape with islands of natural habitat occurring across the state.
>
> —Michael Jeffords, 2003

BEFORE WE BEGIN TO EXPLORE the nature of Illinois, we must take a brief, analytical view of our state and look at it in a new way. Historical accounts of Illinois noted huge trees, vast grasslands, and extensive wetlands. The state was chiefly a combination of flat, "marshy" prairies and forested, hilly country. Interspersed among these prairies and forests were a great variety of other habitats, including sand dunes, bogs, fens, sedge meadows, marshes, savannas, and swamps. Before European settlement, Illinois was approximately 60 percent prairie (ranging from very wet to very dry) and 40 percent forest of various types. The unique location of Illinois on the North American continent allowed for considerable habitat diversity and an unusually large number of species.

To understand the landscape of Illinois we must look not only at the surface but also at what lies below. Illinois has a rich, complex geological history, most of which goes beyond the scope of this book. However, two recent geological events (glaciers) have greatly influenced what we see today. Most of Illinois has been glaciated, and these masses of moving ice almost entirely covered Illinois with glacial *till*, a deposited mixture of gravel, sand, silt, clay, and boulders. Glaciers scraped, kneaded, and dropped materials on the land as they repeatedly advanced and retreated. The two most recent glaciers were the Illinois Glacial Episode, which melted around 130,000 years ago and covered 90 percent of the state, and the Wisconsin Glacial Episode, which melted around 12,000 years ago and covered the northeastern quarter of Illinois. The present topography, including various deposits of sand, was largely created by these glaciers and by the eroding effect of rivers and streams. As we explore Illinois, various geological terms and concepts will inevitably crop up, and we will endeavor to define them in the text.

Illinois is a long state. From north to south it extends over four hundred miles, and from east to west it spans more than two hundred miles at is widest point. Its borders are mostly defined by irregularly shaped bodies of water that make Illinois definable from space as a peninsula in the middle of the vast North American landmass. Illinois also spans the junction of several major ecological regions (often called biomes) that char-

Central Illinois agricultural landscape

acterize North America—the eastern deciduous forest, the western Great Plains, the southwestern Ozark uplift, the southern coastal plain, and even species found in the northern (boreal) forest. As a result, historically Illinois was a melting pot for plants and animals that are characteristic of these different biomes. Think of Illinois as the center of a very large Venn diagram, containing plants and animals representative of the species diversity typical of each of these major North American ecological regions. Each contributes to rich diversity of native species found in Illinois.

How do we know so much about the natural history of our state? In the early 1970s, state scientists described Illinois in terms of its topography, glacial history, bedrock, soils, weather patterns, and the distribution of its native plants and animals. Using all of these natural features, Illinois was divided into what scientists call "natural divisions." Fourteen distinctive areas were formally defined in a 1973 publication authored by then State Botanist John Schwegman and his colleagues. To quote Schwegman, "Natural divisions are geographic regions of a larger entity. . . . A division contains similar landscapes, climates, and substrate features like bedrock and soils that support similar vegetation and wildlife over the division's area. Natural divisions help conservationists classify land for purposes like protecting natural diversity." Over the years, the natural divisions within Illinois have proven very useful in the preservation of the state's natural areas, and they have helped biologists categorize the more than ninety habitat types in Illinois and the more than fifty-four thousand species of plants and animals that call Illinois home. For more details and a map of the state's natural divisions, see Appendix A.

Relatively few Illinois citizens, then and now, are aware of this classification system, and even fewer take note of the actual diversity of landscapes in Illinois. After all, one can take a summer drive from Chicago to Cairo, wheeling down I-57 at seventy miles per hour, and see little else but corn, soybeans, a few trees, and the occasional small town or city. Even the infrequent encounters with hills or deep valleys may go unnoticed in the eye-glazing zeal to reach our destinations—mostly outside of Illinois—a journey to somewhere perhaps more *interesting*.

Bridge on Heron Pond Trail invites exploration

What Are Natural Areas and What Is the Natural Areas Inventory?

Defining a natural area is not an easy endeavor. Each of us, operating in our hectic, stressful, day-to-day life, may have our own vision of a "natural area." To a child, it may be an overgrown, forgotten corner of the neighborhood, free of adult demands. To a business executive, it might be the gentle, rounded swells of the local golf course. To a parent, perhaps the quiet park bench under a spreading shade tree, close enough to keep the children in view but far enough away to be alone and relaxed, will suffice. None of these, however, captures the true biological meaning of natural area. What exactly *is* a natural area? The answer is not so simple. In its most basic form, a natural area contains relatively undisturbed terrestrial, wetland, or aquatic natural communities that have plants and animals that reflect, as nearly as possible, the conditions at the time of European settlement (ca. 1800). In addition, areas that have relict species (species that are widely separated from the rest of their population), endangered animal or plant species, or outstanding geologic features are considered natural areas.

In 1963, the Illinois General Assembly established the Illinois Nature Preserves Commission (INPC) to create a system of natural areas representative of the Illinois landscape. When natural areas are identified and protected *in perpetuity* by state statute, we call them nature preserves. Illinois has been a leader in the preservation of its natural areas. Ranging in size from one acre to more than two thousand acres, these lands are the last remnants of the Illinois wilderness. Without protection, many of these exceptional areas would be lost forever. This commitment to preserve the state's rare natural treasures made Illinois the first state

Fall colors at Little Black Slough Nature Preserve

to create such an innovative land-protection program. The INPC is now a national model. In 1992, the INPC received international acclaim when it was recognized at the Earth Summit in Rio de Janeiro as an "efficient and effective model of how to provide long-term protection for high-quality natural areas." Dedication as a nature preserve provides the greatest amount of protection that natural land can receive in Illinois.

Locating the last remnants of natural lands in Illinois so that they could be considered for protection was no easy task. During the mid-1970s, Illinois conducted the first statewide survey of natural lands. Called the Natural Area Inventory, its mission was to identify, evaluate, describe, and classify areas remaining in a natural state and little disturbed since the mid-1800s. This three-year project was completed in 1978. Scientists studied every acre of Illinois, using maps and aerial photographs; they visited and surveyed, interviewed knowledgeable citizens, and examined records. They gathered as much information as possible about each site.The words of a British paleontologist, although he was writing about fossils, sums up what the inventory was about and its accomplishments. He wrote, "These remains are just scraps, bits and pieces, odds and ends. . . . The skill of the scientist . . . lies in being able to identify small pieces of the whole. . . . Every morsel of the past is useful."

The inventory revealed that no more than seven-hundredths of one percent (0.07 percent) of Illinois land reflected the original natural conditions before settlement. For every million acres of black-soil prairie that originally existed in Illinois, only 39 acres remained. Of the 1,089 significant areas that were identified, only 610 were of the highest quality. While natural areas were found in all but 3 of Illinois 102 counties, they are not evenly distributed. It should come as no surprise that natural areas were mostly absent from the flat prairie land that is almost completely farmed. After all, some of the best soil on earth formed under Illinois's prairies. Most of the natural areas were concentrated in the hilly regions, along rivers, and, surprisingly, near cities. More than half of the natural areas occurred within fifteen miles of the boundaries of the state. The story is not over, however, as an Illinois Natural Areas Update was conducted beginning in June 2007, and it is just wrapping up as we write this book. Its goal was to further develop a list of high-quality grasslands, woodlands, and wetlands, using the latest scientific knowledge and technology. Thus, Illinois citizens may be privy to those last bits of information about its remaining natural lands. While every place featured in this book is not necessarily a Nature Preserve, protected by law, dedicated nature preserves do figure prominently in our discovery of wildness.

Natural Community Types within Illinois

Given the complexity of both the political and natural landscape of Illinois, dividing the state into natural communities may be helpful. We define the term *community* as a finite area consisting of groups of organisms that interact with each other and their environment. The communities found in Illinois include: forest, prairie, savanna, wetland, lake and pond, stream, cave, and a variety of others more difficult to clump under a single name.

Forest

The forest community includes lands dominated by trees (as one would expect), with an average canopy cover of 80 percent or greater. There are three different types of forests—upland, sand, floodplain—distinguished by their topography and soils. Each category has a relatively distinctive grouping of tree species. Illinois forests are predominantly oak-hickory, but elm-ash-sycamore, maple-beech-basswood, and oak-gum-cypress types are also interspersed across the state. Within these forests one can find more than 180 species of trees and shrubs.

Woodland

Distinguishing woodlands from forests may seem like splitting hairs, but the distinction is quite real. Woodland is a dry community (in other words, growing on well-drained soils) dominated by trees, grasses, and forbs (broad-leaved, nonwoody plants with showy flowers). Woodland tree height seldom exceeds fifty feet, and the trees, even though they are the same species found in forests, have a very different growth form. Trees here have a highly branched trunk with spreading limbs that allow enough light on the forest floor to support an abundant and diverse flora. Fire is extremely important in maintaining this community type.

Prairie

Prairies are largely treeless grasslands dominated by warm-season bunch grasses and broad-leaved, flowering plants (forbs) that depend on fire for their existence. Prairie grasses are not the cool-season, carpet-forming grasses of our yards. They grow during the summer in clumps and are often up to eight feet tall. Trees cover less than 10 percent of the land. Six types of prairies are recognized in Illinois, based on the materials on which they grow: tallgrass prairie on silt-loam soils (this ecosystem created some of the world's best soils for agriculture), sand prairie, gravel prairie, dolomite prairie, hill prairie, and shrub prairie. Further subdivisions may be made based on soil moisture and soil type, yielding a somewhat bewildering twenty-three prairie types in Illinois!

Egrets along Nippersink Creek

Savanna

Savannas have scattered, open-grown trees and are a transition landscape between prairie and forest. They have an airy, park-like look, and are dominated by oaks with a ground cover rich in tallgrass prairie species. Like prairie and woodland, savannas depend on fire to maintain vegetation diversity and structure. In early Illinois, these areas were settled first by pioneering families. Three savanna types—typical savanna, sand savanna, and barrens—are distinguished by soil types and the amount of soil moisture present.

Wetlands

Wetlands exist where the water table is at or near the surface. The soils are called hydric, having developed in low-oxygen conditions, and are occupied by plant species adapted to life in water or saturated soils. Wetland types are marsh, swamp, bog, fen, sedge meadow, panne, seep, and spring. These are recognized mainly by differences in water chemistry, soils, and vegetation. Wetland habitats figured prominently in the early colonization of Illinois, mostly in a negative way. They were treated as unnecessary "waste places" to be drained for agriculture.

Lake and Pond

Lakes and ponds are open, standing bodies of water. Ponds are small, less than twenty acres, hold water all year, and are shallow enough to allow rooted, aquatic vegetation to grow in most areas of the pond. Lakes are larger (greater than twenty acres), deeper, and have wave action that usually produces a semi-barren, wave-swept shore. Portions of the lake are too deep to support rooted aquatic plants. Lake types include the typical lake and the great lake (Illinois borders on Lake Michigan). Many of the lakes we are most familiar with in Illinois are human-created impoundments (for example, Rend Lake and Lake Shelbyville), but natural lakes also occur in selected parts of the state, primarily in the northeast.

Streams

Streams (either rivers or creeks) are natural communities with flowing water for all or most of the year. Creeks are distinguished from rivers by having watersheds of less than two hundred square miles. Individual streams are also described according to gradient (how steep a slope the stream is on, which determines how fast the water flows), and overall size. Illinois waterways range from small creeks to major rivers, such as the Mississippi, the Ohio, and the Illinois. As with wetlands, streams have had a long history of "human improvement"—channelization, removing the surrounding vegetation (riparian strips), and damming—and many have been irrevocably altered.

Cave

A cave is a natural underground cavity usually large enough for a human to enter, and it often has a section that receives no sunlight. There are two communities within the cave—terrestrial (basically air-filled cavities in the rock) and aquatic (cavities with pools, streams, and waterfalls).

Bedrock

Bedrock communities occur where the soil is thin or absent and the parent material (usually bedrock) is at or near the surface. These communities are in a perpetual state of change. Either natural disturbances or the bedrock itself never allows these communities to mature. The two subclasses of this community are glade and cliff. Glades are local areas in the forest where bedrock is at the surface. Vegetation is often sparse with large areas of exposed bedrock. Glades are categorized by their rock type—sandstone, limestone, or shale. Cliffs are vertical exposures of bedrock and can range in height from a few feet to about three hundred feet in Illinois. Soils are usually nonexistent and communities are again defined mostly on the basis of rock type—sandstone, limestone, dolomite, sandstone overhang, and eroding bluff.

Shore

In Illinois, the major lakeshore community occurs in northeastern Illinois along Lake Michigan. Wave action creates a zone of no vegetation, backed by a larger dune community that can have plants adapted for this ever-changing landscape. While the dunes that form here are not particularly high, they support a unique community dominated mostly by northern species of plants.

An Invitation to Explore

Aldo Leopold wrote in *A Sand County Almanac*, "The last word in ignorance is the man who says of an animal or plant, 'What good is it?'" The scientific value of the natural world cannot be questioned. It is a resource from which knowledge emerges or from which new knowledge can be derived. Nature serves as a reference for studies relating to air, water, and soil pollution, as well as many aspects of land management, and it is an indispensable outdoor classroom. Perhaps most important, nature provides limitless sources of beauty and inspiration, and it serves as a living, dynamic entity—the rich and diverse natural world from which our state and our country were created.

A. W. Herre, a botanist at Stanford University, spent part of his boyhood on a farm in Tazewell County, Illinois. "From the end of spring 1873, until the late summer of 1878, it was [his] privilege to see and enjoy life of a great tract of virgin prairie." Herre published his remembrances, titled *An Early Illinois Prairie*, in 1940 in the journal *American Botanist*. Through his eyes we begin to "see" a landscape that is relegated to the written memories of

Stink bug in garden cockscomb flowerhead

those fortunate to have experienced it firsthand. He concludes with, "What a pity that some of it could not have been preserved, so that those born later might enjoy its beauty also."

As you may begin to guess, much (but certainly not all) of the nature of Illinois we will showcase in this book exists in unique natural areas scattered throughout the state. They are often not easy to find and seldom promoted for their tourist appeal, as they are more "biological reserves" than roadside attractions. Additional places to see nature in Illinois include stretches along its major rivers, large ecological restoration projects scattered about the landscape, and even sites located in out-of-the-way places between highways and railways—sites where the buzz of rare cicadas may have to compete with the noise of roadside traffic. It may come as a surprise that the most daunting task associated with creating this book was not finding enough places to showcase nature, but in limiting our efforts to those we think the citizens of Illinois, and beyond, will most enjoy in their quest to see nature at its finest.

While we have never had the luxury of standing on a hillock or an old glacial moraine and viewing a limitless expanse of prairie or forest, thanks to Illinois's natural areas, other protected sites and the programs that define and protect them, and pure happenstance, we have remnants of these landscapes so that we and future generations may experience, through the natural wonders of these places, the essence of Illinois.

HOW TO USE THIS BOOK

Strolling through this woods after a
long, stressful month, the rounded, cool
smoothness of a tupelo fruit in one hand,
the felt-like texture of a pair of aged water
hickory nuts in the other, I am at peace.
—Michael Jeffords, Section 8 Woods, 2009

SOMETIMES IT'S EASIER to describe what something isn't than what it actually is. *Exploring Nature in Illinois* is not a complete field guide, nor an encyclopedic list of all the places in Illinois to see nature. Literally hundreds of such locations exist across the state. Even with the sixty-some sites we feature, do not expect a thorough trail-by-trail description of each place. Also, the sites are generally arranged from north to south to simplify (we hope) visits to multiple locations during a single excursion.

Our goal is simple. In the more than four decades we have traversed Illinois, we have seen and experienced some remarkable landscapes and wildlife spectacles. We feel these special places and events should not be missed by any Illinois citizen with an interest in nature and wild things. Thus, this book is designed to do one thing: entice our readers, through verbal descriptions and representative photographs, to visit each of the wild places we have chosen to showcase. Our maps and descriptions will get the traveler to the sites; our text and photos will highlight some of the reasons we think these places are special; but the exploration of each location is up to the traveler. Visit the local nature and visitors' centers, study the information from kiosks at trailheads, and wander around the area to acquaint yourself with the landscape. While we cannot guarantee that every trip to one of our favorite spots will yield a spectacular show of flowers (that is seasonal and weather dependent) or a sky full of waterfowl, or even plants cloaked with colorful butterflies, we can reliably predict that this book will provide you with the best chances for viewing some of the remarkable creatures and habitats that grace the Illinois landscape. While our sites should be the focal points for your investigations, remember that this book is far from inclusive. We urge you to keep your eyes open, your curiosity piqued, and you will find your own special corners of Illinois.

NORTH

CHAPTER 1

Apple River Canyon State Park

Perched precariously on a ledge,
I am up close and personal with the
primrose. I see ribbons of them, yet
I wonder, will they eventually wink
out, victims of global warming?
—Susan Post, April 2001

IF THE PHRASE "rotting dolomite of the Galena Group formation along the fast-flowing Apple River" excites your psyche, then Apple River Canyon State Park is your cup of tea. For a typical topography-starved Illinoisan, the prospect of exposed bedrock, sheer cliff faces, and a clear, gravel-bottomed stream in a remote location is nearly irresistible. Indeed, most visitors to the park in rural Jo Daviess County either enjoy a picnic in the shaded canyon carved by the river, try their hand at fly fishing, or indulge in a quiet wade in the cool water on a hot summer day.

Apple River Canyon is found in the Driftless Natural Division of Illinois, an area of the upper Midwest that escaped the great, continental glaciers of the Pleistocene epoch. During the latter part of this time, vast fingers of ice advanced and retreated but never actually covered the area. The Driftless region (*drift* [also till] refers to materials deposited by glaciers—sand, rock, gravel) was never a true island in a sea of ice; therefore, migration corridors for both plants and animals remained open. The flora of Apple River Canyon reflects this glacial heritage. The area is a unique mix of both northern and southern species. A University of Illinois graduate, Dr. Herman Silas Pepoon (class of 1881) was trained as a medical doctor, but he preferred to teach high school biology and spent much of his life in the Apple River Canyon area exploring its crevices, canyons, and forests. His explorations of the region led to this statement in the 1917 *Transactions of the Illinois Academy of Sciences*: "The 9th day of April 1905 the writer was tramping down the narrow, cliff-confined valley of the west branch of Apple River, spying out the bird life of this sheltered locality, and more than incidentally, keeping

Apple River Canyon from Primrose Trail

both eyes open for the early blossoms of *Hepatica*, *Dicentra*, *Claytonia*, *Sanguinaria* [hepatica, squirrel corn and Dutchman's breeches, spring beauty, and bloodroot, respectively], and other bluff and valley species of plants. His attention was attracted to the peculiar coloration of a high vertical cliff of limestone across and rising directly out of the river. . . . The whole face of the rock for perhaps twenty feet vertically and extending fifty or sixty feet horizontally was a solid hue of pale lavender purple."

Pepoon had discovered a relict species, surviving in this sheltered location since the Pleistocene, the bird's-eye primrose.

The bird's-eye primrose is a northern wildflower that grows on the tundra of Alaska, in the chilly regions of Canada, around the cold Great Lakes, and on the dolomite cliffs above the Apple River. When Dr. Pepoon first found this plant more than one hundred years ago, he excitedly reported the plants "tinting the bare rock a lavender purple with . . . multitudes of blossoms," at a gathering of his peers. He was met with much skepticism and disbelief; after all, this was a plant of the boreal regions. Illinois was too far south for it to grow. He countered the criticism with an invitation for all to come with him the following April on a primrose walk to prove his statement true. His peers came. They drove as far as possible into the canyons and then walked the rest of the way to where the cliffs rose above the river. There, for all to see with their telescopes and binoculars, was the bird's-eye or Canadian primrose. It indeed grew in Illinois!

Bird's-eye primrose is a diminutive plant. Instead of growing upward toward the sun, it shoots out from the cliff at right angles. By the end of April the primrose is in full bloom, and by the beginning of summer the seeds are ripe. Most of its light seeds fall from the cliff and land in the Apple River, but a few are deposited near the parent plant. Bird's-eye primroses are able to survive in less than a teaspoon of soil in the cranny of a rock, exposed to winds, sun, cold, and storms.

Botanists speculate these northern denizens were carried south with the advance of the glacial ice sheets out of Canada. Plants that perished beneath the weight and scouring power of the glacier might survive if their seeds were transported southward on wind or ice and deposited in a similar haunt. As the glaciers missed the Apple River Canyon area, it was here that the tiny seeds of the primrose lodged into the crannies of the dolomite

Apple River Canyon cliff face

Canada Goose nesting on cliff

Bird's-eye primrose in bloom

cliffs. These cliffs, constantly moist, are massive, thick-bedded, and towering. The dripping water, which travels along horizontal layers of impervious chert within the bedrock, is cool, clear, saturated with lime, and keeps the roots constantly cool in the summer. In the winter, it keeps the immediate surface rock layers above freezing, soon forming ice cascades that cover the cliff face and protect the root and crown buried beneath.

The varied terrain and precipitous cliffs here contain much more that just the primroses. Apple River Canyon State Park's namesake, the canyon, is a water-formed gorge cut into the dolomite, with the rocks often forming cliffs 50 to 150 feet high. These vertical surfaces are cloaked with lichens, liverworts, and mosses; cliff swallows find them perfect for nesting. Trails within the park reveal a diverse flora—twinleaf, Canada violet, native white pine, and, growing atop the famous primrose cliffs, expanses of prairie shooting star.

The park's preservation is in part due to Dr. Pepoon's efforts. He began lobbying for the land to be preserved in 1918. During a meeting of the Illinois Academy of Science he spoke about the park and urged its protection. "Springs, seepage areas, and side ravines and miniature canyons are everywhere, and all abounding in a rich and diversified flora. Some sixty species of forest trees and 400 species of smaller plants, many exceedingly rare, add charm to the region and make it a veritable Botanist's paradise." His professional papers and observations leave a wonderful record of the conditions of the area during the early part of the twentieth century.

Visitors who wish to recreate Pepoon's early botanical pilgrimage may do so each spring. Follow the Primrose Trail at Apple River Canyon State Park and wend your way through the woods, past the shooting stars, down into the valley, and across the narrow creek to the base of the limestone bluff. Note the coolness, the vegetation cloaking the moist limestone, and experience a close-up view of bird's-eye primrose, a glacial relict and a piece of Illinois's botanical history.

CHAPTER 2

Ayers Sand Prairie Nature Preserve

Finally!!! An Olympia marble butterfly on sand cress, hanging on as the cress waves back and forth in the cool, spring winds. I can even see the pink overwash on its wings. This is the way to see a life-list butterfly—up close and not moving, and on its host plant!

—Susan Post, May 2007

SAND DEPOSITS in the Illinois landscape are most familiar as the sand and gravel quarries, the geological gift of Illinois's glacial past. Mention sand prairie, though, and most people will think of the relatively large areas of Mason and Iroquois Counties in Illinois that contain these unique, extremely dry habitats. They are the equivalent of the desert landscapes of the southwest, even though we get much more rain here. The porous sand does not hold water, so the landscape is extremely dry. They even have cactus, to solidify their desert-like characteristics.

Ayers Sand Prairie, just south of Savanna in Carroll County, is part of another sand deposit complex along the upper Mississippi River. This area also owes its sandy soils to glaciers. Here, sand lies on top of a terrace, with a random arrangement of small mounds, long ridges, and circular depressions. Wind piles up sand into dunes wherever open sand is available, and though partially vegetated, the dunes remain active.

The sand prairies of this region occupy an expanse between the bluffs on the east and the Mississippi River on the west. This area was once the western edge of the Wisconsin Glacier, where sand was deposited by its meltwaters. As water was shed from the glacier's edge, copious streams and long flows of glacial outwash (water saturated with sand and gravel) poured down the channel ways. Today, all that remains of the glaciers is the sand.

All who visit Ayers Sand Prairie Nature Preserve, and there are relatively few, notice that it is an oasis, situated between fields of corn and potatoes and a regional airport. A short walk into the interior of this preserve of more than a hundred acres provides an easy solitude,

Ayers Sand Prairie Nature Preserve

as the rolling topography blocks the surrounding development, and the ever-present winds rustling the dry grasses mask most twenty-first century sound. In fact, without the sign and small parking area, most would pass it by, perhaps thinking of it as wasteland or fallow agricultural fields. The area, though, is special, with its rolling topography of small dunes and blowouts (areas of open sand caused by wind erosion) and a small grove (called a *copse*) of oaks near its center. During May the edges of the dunes are rimmed with bird's-foot violet—exhibiting all shades of purple—from almost white to a deep violet. Although there are no trails, one can meander about through the short

Olympia Marble on bird's-foot violet

Ornate box turtle in bird's-foot violets

Poppy mallow and flowering spurge

vegetation. But to make sense of this prairie requires some knowledge of various aspects of the landscape, in addition to its geology. Due to the extremely xeric (dry) growing conditions here, both the plant and animal communities are home to species unfamiliar to most Illinois citizens—the Olympia marble butterfly, several unusual reptiles, the striking violet-red wine cup or poppy mallow, and a variety of grasshoppers and tiger beetles. The latter are always a step ahead of your footsteps. Take special note of the tiger beetles, for though small, they have a fierce visage and are formidable predators to all things small that live in this desert environment. Even during cool, blustery September evenings, a visit to the lee side of the copse dominated by black oak may yield a gathering of monarchs, massing for their long trip south. A few dozen, a few hundred, or even several thousand may reward your persistence.

Ayers Sand Prairie is the state's fiftieth nature preserve, dedicated in 1974. The preserve has thirty-nine species of grasses and sedges, sixteen species of woody plants, and nearly one hundred species of wildflowers. All these help stabilize the dunes and blowouts. Beach heather, with its yellow flowers, is the same plant found on the dunes of Cape Cod, with Ayers about as far west as this plant occurs. Three species of blazing star follow one another in quick succession from summer into fall, with rough blazing star blooming last. A visit to Ayers requires nothing more than a curious mind, but a camera, a notebook, and binoculars will allow you to document the unusual things you will see and experience and will allow a portion of this unusual landscape to accompany you on your journey home.

CHAPTER 3

Bluff Spring Fen Nature Preserve

Winding your way down the kame brings you to the marl flat. Here the vegetation appears similar to the runoff channels at Yellowstone's geyser basins. And like Yellowstone, fringed gentians are the dominant fall bloomer.

—Susan Post, September 2007

JUST SOUTHEAST OF ELGIN, embedded in the urban/suburban landscape, exists a topographically varied, lush, isolated valley of greens, browns, blues, and gold. The preserve's ninety-five diverse acres, bordered by two large mining operations, contain a tremendous variety of plants and animals. The topography is courtesy of the relatively recent glaciers that covered this corner of northeastern Illinois. The various hills that dot the preserve are "glacial kames" that formed at the bottom of glacial waterfalls. Here gravel and sand piled up into neat, conical hills, like salt pouring from its distinctive round container onto a flat surface. Over time, many habitats, including a dry, gravel prairie on the kames, interspersed with blacksoil prairie, and marsh in the lowlands, have developed. It's not often that one finds skunk cabbage, marsh marigold, prairie shooting star, and bird's-foot violet all sharing the same preserve and occurring within just a few steps of each other. Uncommon plants like prairie smoke, fringed puccoon, wooly milkweed, and side-oats grama grass grow on the dry, alkaline, gravel soils. Localized butterflies, such as Baltimore checkerspots and meadow fritillaries, ply the airways in the moist regions between the kames, sharing the space with white lady's-slipper orchids and fringed gentians in the fall. The uncommon Baltimore is a wetland butterfly that feeds on turtlehead.

Bluff Spring Fen Nature Preserve is adjacent to the large Bluff City Cemetery and was once slated for gravel mining and other incompatible uses before its preservation. On the west side of the preserve, streams bordered with rare Hill's oaks and giant bur oaks meander through a park-like savanna. The eastern half is perhaps most interesting and

Bluff Spring Fen Nature Preserve

consists of a complex landscape of prairie and wetlands. Possibly the finest fen in Illinois occurs here. Fens have been described as "one of the rarest wetland community types in the entire continental United States." This unusual habitat occurs where cold, highly alkaline groundwater emerges (in nearly thirty spots in Bluff Spring) and maintains odd soil conditions that are not conducive to most plant growth. Even given these potential hostile conditions, much of the plant diversity found here occurs in this unusual habitat. Six species of orchids grow in the fen, including the aforementioned white lady's-slipper, grass pink, ladies' tresses, and snake-mouth orchids.

Evaporation of standing water allows minerals to concentrate in the soil, creating another rare habitat, called marl flat. Plants that can tolerate these conditions—grass of Parnassus, slender bog arrow grass, Kalm's lobelia, beaked spike rush, Ohio goldenrod, and shrubby cinquefoil—thrive here. For its size, the diversity of the fen is staggering, as it supports more than 450 plant species, with thirteen threatened or endangered ones.

Baltimore checkerspot on fleabane

Spring run in alkaline fen

Fringed gentian

More than fifty species of butterflies and skippers occur here from mid-June through July. At least thirty bird species nest here, including red-headed woodpeckers and yellow-breasted chats, while many more pass through. Add the numerous bird species and uncommon invertebrates to the wealth of plant life, and you have a biological adventure that is unparalleled for any similarly sized location in Illinois.

CHAPTER 4

Gensburg–Markham Prairie Nature Preserve

Dense blazing stars—rivers of pink
create colored fingers through the
green prairie herbage.
—Susan Post, August 2004

GIVEN THE ONCE-WIDESPREAD distribution of prairies in central and northern Illinois, and the subsequent agricultural and urban development that has replaced them over the past two hundred years, it is inevitable, yet fortunate, that prairie remnants occur in some very unlikely places. What is truly remarkable is that prairies of the quality of Gensburg-Markham still exist. Located in a triangle formed by interstate highways 57, 80, and 294 in southern Cook County, and owned by The Nature Conservancy of Illinois, this improbable prairie remnant, growing on damp, sandy soil, owes it survival to soils that resisted both farming and suburban development. An old beach ridge that was formed by an ancient glacial lake (Lake Chicago, the precursor to Lake Michigan) runs southeast to northwest through the preserve and is responsible for the difference in relief (however minor) over the preserve. This slight change in elevation allows diverse habitats—wet-to-moist prairie, dry-to-moist sand prairie, and sedge meadow—to occur in the two-hundred-acre National Natural Landmark. Even though the din of I-294 is relatively relentless, a walk through this landscape during any season will transport you back to Illinois's relatively recent past. When the Gensburg family donated the parcel to the Nature Conservancy in 1971, the land was degraded by exotic, invasive plants. Over the decades extensive restoration work, spearheaded by the late Dr. Robert Betz of Northeastern Illinois University (and a host of others), means the original tallgrass prairie flora is once more flourishing.

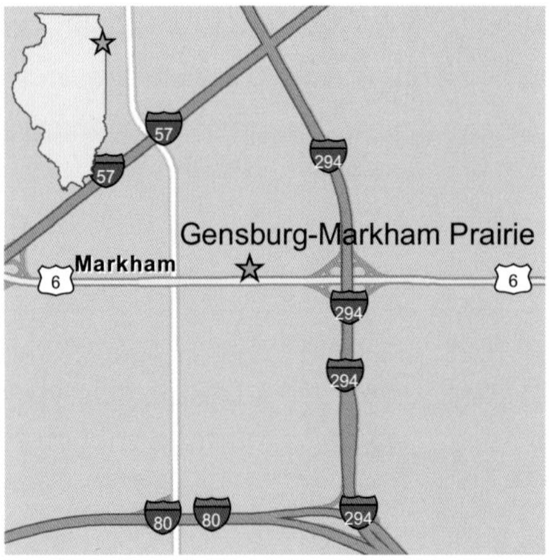

A narrow footpath leads north into the preserve through clumps of shooting star in the spring and nodding wild onion and purple prairie clover in

Blazing star and flowering spurge in summer

Katydid nymph (pink form) on spiderwort

early summer; the display of blazing star in late summer is not to be matched anywhere in Illinois. A look at the extensive plant list (about 250 species) should tell any visitor that a single visit cannot satisfy the need to see this prairie in all its glory. The "classic" prairie succession is abundantly visible here with numerous, low-growing spring forbs (prairie phlox, hoary puccoon, yellow-eyed grass), followed in succession by coreopsis, prairie clovers, leadplant, and Michigan and wood lilies in early summer. Later in the summer season, as heat and humidity build, the blazing stars appear en masse, along with various goldenrods and expanses of flowering spurge. Fall is gentian time, with closed, fringed, and prairie gentians all providing glints of blue mingled among the golden-hued grasses. While such botanical wonder is notable, Gensburg–Markham, much like other significant prairie patches in Illinois, is particularly special for the simple reason that it is extremely diverse. None of the three growing seasons is without its striking plant displays.

A prairie, though, is much more than its plants, and the insect diversity here is, if not staggering, at least enough to maintain the interest of amateur and professional entomologists alike. Spring may yield a bevy of immature katydids, including a rare pink morph that stands out like a pink bow on a wedding dress. Early spring butterflies include spring azures, eastern-tailed blues, and any of the over-wintered commas, question marks, or painted ladies. Summer is the time for birdwing and differential grasshoppers, great spangled and

Crab spider with pearl crescent butterfly

Aphrodite fritillaries, and adults of the katydids that managed to survive being eaten by birds. Look also for goldenrod crab spiders, either yellow or white, as they can change color, and check out butterflies and other insects behaving oddly on a flower head; they likely have fallen prey to one of the cryptic, predatory crab spiders. If you are lucky, unusual insects may appear, such as rabbit bots, large flies that are parasites on small rodents. They are notable because the adults lack mouthparts and do not feed. Check out flowering spikes of white colic root for large, feeding fritillaries, but don't forget the smaller copper, crescent, and checkerspot butterflies, as they also have a taste for nectar. Birds include the rare Henslow's sparrow, and the chatty marsh and sedge wrens. In short, a visit to Gensburg-Markham should include a pack stocked with field guides on prairie flowers, butterflies, birds, and insects. With these helpful books, any visitor can experience a satisfying afternoon exploring the dizzying diversity of this unique landscape.

Wood lily and Indian plantain

CHAPTER 5

Glacial Park Conservation Area

Even though it's mid-summer and the hilly,
hummocky landscape is cloaked with vegetation,
I still feel a "chill" as I survey the various glacial
features so prominently displayed here—kames,
kettle holes, and moraines all speak of a land-
scape formed by these vast, bulldozers of ice.
—Michael Jeffords, July 1997

WHERE IN ILLINOIS does the Ice Age come alive with kames, kettle holes, and glacial erratics? Where can you climb a hundred-foot camelback kame to enjoy a bird's-eye view of the landscape; walk in the ancient bed of glacial Wonder Lake; watch great white egrets fish along the bank of Nippersink Creek, the day-to-day marsh drama in the lives of red-winged blackbirds, and the creek-patrolling behavior of belted kingfishers; or experience the park-like setting of ancient savannas? The answer is simple. Take a journey to McHenry County and spend a day at Glacial Park, just south of Richmond, exploring the remnants of the Pleistocene landscape in Illinois.

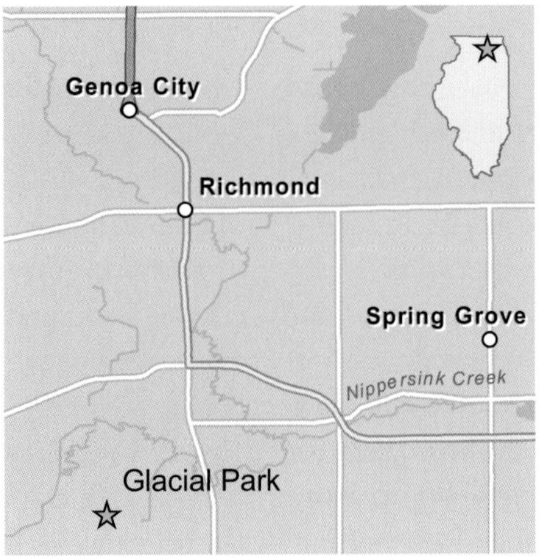

Like the early descriptions of the prairie, the landscape of McHenry County has also been compared to an ocean or sea. A geologist once wrote, "The landscape of McHenry County rises and rolls and falls away with the grandness of an ocean worked with deep swells." Within its northeastern corner lies a county conservation area aptly named Glacial Park. Here, evidence of the last glacier—technically called the Wisconsin Glacial Episode—is everywhere, concentrated into this twenty-eight-hundred-acre preserve. Between twenty-two thousand and fourteen thousand years ago, the Pleistocene glaciers flowed west and south across Illinois. These glaciers and their meltwaters forever changed the area's landscape. As the glaciers scraped and smeared the landforms they overrode, the melting ice carried colossal amounts of rock and earth. When the ice melted, it dumped whatever it was carrying in place.

New landforms—kames, kettle holes, and moraines—were created. When an ice sheet reached its maximum extent and began to stagnate, sand

Camelback kame

and gravel accumulated near its melting edge. Outwash deposits (a mixture of sand, stone, and gravel) collected in large heaps, either along the glacier's margins or in depressions in the ice, and became kames (conical hills). If the meltwater spilled over the edge and deposited the outwash as a ridge, then elongated, camelback kames were created. As large chunks of ice broke off from the main glacier, they were surrounded by—and perhaps even covered with—glacial drift (rocks, sand, gravel) that insulated the giant ice cubes. In time, the ice melted and the outwash fell downward, creating depressions and pockmarks. These low points are called kettles. Kettles usually became self-contained ponds with no surface outlet, and eventually they formed the backbone of several types of wetlands. Glacial Park has two examples of kettles: Kettle Hole Marsh, which is ringed with cattails and is home to geese, wood ducks, and dragonflies, and a unique Leatherleaf Bog, which can be experienced with the aid of a short boardwalk.

Early summer is an excellent time to discover Glacial Park, and the best way to see it is on foot as grasshoppers herald your passage with buzzing, bright-colored hindwings. Begin your journey at Kettle Hole Marsh observation deck. The marsh is alive with mallards and red-winged blackbirds. Competing for the airspace and delectable insects above the marsh are violet-green swallows and dragonflies—green darners, twelve-spotted skimmers, and eastern amberwings. From the marsh, the trail passes through a prairie—pure stands of rosinweed, rattlesnake master, and compass plant—dotted with large boulders. These rocks

Glacial wetland

Leatherleaf Bog

aren't decoration; they are glacial erratics brought in and deposited by the glaciers from far northern lands. The trail continues to Leatherleaf Bog, complete with a boardwalk for intimate views of sphagnum moss, the unusual and dominant leatherleaf, and even poison sumac. Leatherleaf keeps its leaves year round and has an interesting blooming strategy: the number of blossoms depends on the amount of snow cover the previous winter. If the plant is completely covered with snow, almost all of the flowers bloom. Very little snow results in very few blooms.

Exiting the bog leads to an expansive savanna community. These bur, white, black, and Hill's oak groves were once expanses of berry brambles and barnyard grasses (from previous grazing activities), but diligent restoration work has allowed the real beauty of the savanna to emerge. Spiderwort, purple coneflower, and tuberous Indian plantain dot the grove floor, while indigo buntings

Sandhill crane

flit through the trees. Looming ahead is a large mound, the signature glacial feature. Local people call these hundred-foot mounds camelback kames. More than ten thousand years ago, the edge of the glacier rested here. During the summers, meltwaters carried sand and gravel over the edge, resulting in these distinctive landforms. As you climb, look for goldfinches and tiger swallowtail butterflies feeding on nearby thistles, and listen and look for bobolinks. At the top, enjoy a vulture's-eye view of the surrounding savanna and the valley of Nippersink Creek. Today, the creek looks much like it did prior to channelization, thanks to the restoration efforts of conservation staff and volunteers. They broke drainage tiles, restored meanders, marshes, and even mussels, and rebuilt a kame. During fall migration, there can be so many great white egrets that, for a moment, Florida comes to mind.

The ancient Fox River, which flowed in the opposite direction of present-day Nippersink Creek, shaped this broad valley. A shallow lake, known as Wonder Lake, occupied the region after the kames were deposited. As the lake drained, it left the land between the kames flat, dotted with wetlands and wet prairies. Down from the kame, the trail winds through more prairie and savanna. An overlook provides another view of the broad valley and more kames in the distance. You might wonder why there aren't more kames throughout the region. Well, actually there were, but today kames have great value and possess a new name—sand and gravel mines. As you approach Kettle Hole Marsh, check the reed canary grass for small, golden dragonflies perched with geometric precision, perfectly perpendicular to the erect stems. The dragonflies' small golden abdomens, all pointing toward the sun, appear to be mere extensions of the grass. The tips of the grass and the dragonfly abdomens create an ancient sundial.

The next time you need to get away from twenty-first-century life and experience both nature and geology at its finest, spend an afternoon or a day at Glacial Park, Illinois's geological and biological wonderland.

CHAPTER 6

Goose Lake Prairie State Park

What we're talking about is not just some grass and birds, but a whole ecological complex that goes back almost twenty thousand years. We're talking about a very unique thing. If it slips though our hands now, we can never get it back.

—Dr. William Beecher, Director of the Chicago Academy of Sciences, 1969

TO QUOTE EARLY Illinois visitor Ellen Bigelow in 1835, "Nothing can equal the surpassing beauty of the rounded swells and the sunny hollows. The brilliant green of the grass, the numberless varieties and splendid hues of multitudes of flowers, I gazed in admiration too strong for words." It's no mystery that tallgrass prairies in Illinois are vanishingly rare. Finding isolated sites along rail lines or in old cemeteries is a treat, but what was it like to actually experience the tallgrass prairie, so eloquently described by Ellen Bigelow? While few places in Illinois provide this opportunity, fortunately there are options remaining for experiencing a true "prairie landscape"—Nachusa Grasslands (a Nature Conservancy site in Lee County) and Goose Lake Prairie in Grundy County.

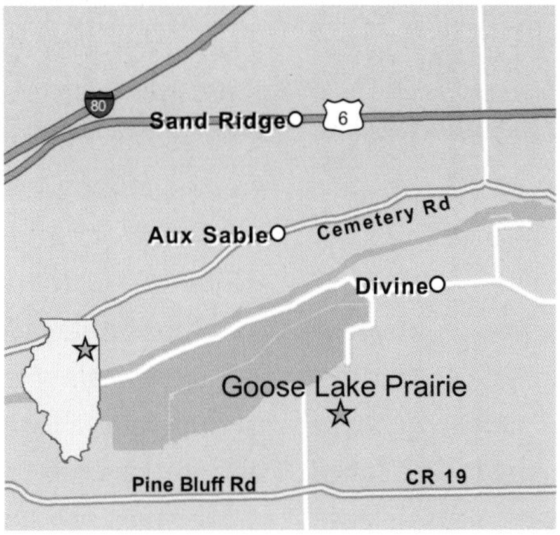

The ancestral fabric of Illinois consisted of a mosaic of forest and prairie. The original prairie was described as a grand sight, made up of grass and flowers, stretching to the horizon over much of Illinois. This prairie was highly suited for agricultural development, and it was soon converted into the Corn Belt, one of the most productive agricultural areas on earth. It is quite remarkable that Grundy County features a jewel of original Illinois prairie of more than twenty-four hundred acres. The preservation of this piece of Illinois history and biological heritage was as important as saving comparable acreage of California redwoods or the Florida Everglades.

Today, Goose Lake Prairie is a habitat of wildflowers, tall grasses, and relentless prairie winds that once supported bison, wolves, greater prairie chickens, and river otters. While those species are now gone (except for the river otter, which is making a comeback), the winds, grasses, and flowers remain, and one can feel the vastness of the prairie

Expanse of goldenrod

landscape and be touched by the past. Waterfowl still use the natural prairie potholes for feeding, and rabbits, muskrats, deer, and small rodents are modern substitutes for the fauna of old. While the original Goose Lake no longer exists—it was drained before the turn of the century for farming and to mine the underlying clay—a series of ponds and marshes still remains. Goose Lake was "discovered" in 1965, and a multiyear struggle ensued whether to preserve this unique part of Illinois's heritage or to convert it into another industrialized "Ruhr Valley" for Illinois. Land purchase began in 1969, and today the landscape is a living laboratory of the Illinois prairie past.

Nowhere else in Illinois can you hike for seven miles through tallgrass prairie without knowing what's around the next bend. Your trip can be one of discovery and surprise as you experience a true prairie pothole—complete with rails and mink cavorting around the edges or juvenile black-crowned night herons fishing in the shallow waters—and see a landscape so dominated by yellow composites in late summer that it boggles the mind. Big bluestem and Indian grass often domi-

Family group of large milkweed bug

Rattlesnake master panorama

nate the scene, but switchgrass (moist), bluejoint grass (wet), and little bluestem (dry) also abundantly occur, each indicating the relative moisture content of the soils below. For those interested in insects and other arthropods, the plethora of blooming plants contains everything from large, bird-winged grasshoppers, to masses of colorful milkweed bugs on developing seedpods, to the very interesting snowy tree crickets that use the various sunflowers as platforms for their courtship displays. A close look will reveal numerous large garden spiders with their classic circular webs, many decorated with late-season milkweed seeds. A butterfly or bumblebee acting oddly on a flower may turn out to be the meal for a diminutive yet powerful yellow or white crab spider. Butterflies abound, especially monarchs and great spangled fritillaries. On trails farther from the expansive visitors' center, one can note an unusual sight in Illinois: white-tailed deer in a prairie landscape. While we usually associate these creatures with woodlands and woods edges, they also occur amid the tall grasses; family groupings, complete with speckled fawns, are frequently encountered.

Garden spider in web "decorated" with milkweed seeds

The plants found here include all the classic species known to occur in Illinois prairies, but the land is most noted for its display of yellow sunflowers each summer and fall. In some areas, prepare to be surprised by masses of a single species, such as rattlesnake master, that seemingly stretch to the far horizon. Goose Lake Prairie is a good location to practice your naturalist skills, so bring along a good plant field guide, an insect guide, and, most certainly, a good pair of binoculars for those ever-present prairie birds. At no time, during any season, will you be disappointed by a visit to the premier prairie preserve in Illinois. It is a marvel of biological diversity and personal solitude, providing a glimpse into the view experienced by Ellen Bigelow.

CHAPTER 7

Green River State Wildlife Area

> I sense a ghost in this place—a shadow of the Great Winnebago Swamp. The killdeers agree, the raccoons agree, the gray, mucky soil agrees. Ruts slash across the bare ground, laid on like the cat o' nine tails on a mutinous back. This offender, however, was not a rebellious sailor, but a tract of 'useless' land converted to something else for the common good. I wonder . . .
>
> —Michael Jeffords, 2005

HEADING NORTH FROM the small town of Ohio, the road soon heads up and tops the massive Bloomington Moraine. To most, this is merely another hill in the rolling topography as the highway crosses into Lee County in north-central Illinois. But to the observant, the land that stretches out, level with the horizon, is markedly different. If it's an early morning in midsummer, the flat tableland, although populated with the ubiquitous corn and soybeans, is covered with a ground-hugging haze—the ghost or shadow of what was once here: the Great Winnebago Swamp. Early settlers who built cabins near here were beset with swarms of mosquitoes that could only be alleviated by standing near the heat and smoke of a massive campfire. The settlers knew where the hordes originated, and dubbed the nearby swamp as the "place of despondency."

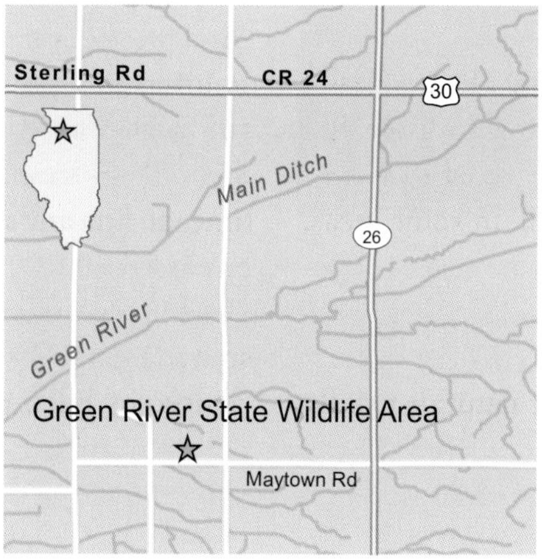

Officially named the Green River Lowland section of the Grand Prairie Division, the area encompasses more than seven hundred thousand acres and was originally a complex mosaic of wetlands, prairies, and scattered savannas. During the fall, millions of ducks would darken the sky while hundreds of acres of ground would be covered with sandhill cranes. Not only did market hunters exploit the bounty, pioneers were able to supplement their diet with the plentiful game. Drainage activities began in the 1870s, and by 1900 more than five hundred thousand acres had been drained by massive steam dredges and converted into farmland. After the drainage was complete, a citizen commented, "A land that once overflowed, land that was a riot of rushes and gigantic grass, now produces corn with ears like stovewood." The slow-flowing Green River was also channelized

Expanse of rough blazing star

along much of its length to facilitate drainage. Although most of the natural habitats from the vast tract of "useless land" are gone, a twenty-six-hundred-acre remnant—the Green River State Wildlife Area—still exists and provides visitors with a sense of what the landscape used to contain. Habitats here include swampy slough areas, various prairie restorations, open field, cultivated areas planted for wildlife, and woodland. For many, the area is best known for its field trials for dogs and horses, and for hunting. To the nature enthusiast, though, Green River can be a spectacular location for birding, butterflying, or just having the pleasure of visiting a vast, open landscape dotted with large oaks that create a pastoral, savanna setting.

Driving the back roads adjacent to Green River (actually out of the conservation area) also has its moments. A spot visited along the shore of the Green River where the stream had cut across the crest of an old sand dune, leaving a bank sixty feet high, revealed several ancient spruce logs eroding from the soil. Spruce has not grown naturally in this area for millennia. Yet, here they were, a not-so-subtle clue to the area's heritage—forest relics covered and preserved by the departing Wisconsin Glacier some twenty thousand years ago.

Exploring the area by car or by foot is interesting and can occupy many days. A favorite location is a restored prairie along the southeast edge of the conservation area, bordered by the Maytown Blacktop and Pump Factory Road. Just north on the latter, a small parking area provides access to a trail that heads into and traverses a landscape of sand prairie and sand savanna, and even provides an overlook of a rare sand pond. During spring, the sand prairie is a riot of puccoon and spiderwort. These sand prairie specialists dominate the season. The stocky plants of yellow puccoons take the low road while spindly spiderworts send their sky-blue blooms above the surrounding vegetation, each flower lasting only a single day. If the spring and summer have been relatively moist, a visit around Labor Day will yield a spectacular show. First, the hordes of mosquitoes that bedeviled the early pioneers may do the same to you, so wear repellent. But, most important, the moisture will trigger one of the best wildflower displays in Illinois, the annual blooming of masses of pink, rough blazing stars. The flower spikes spread from the trail, following the undulating landscape in a spectacle not seen elsewhere. Ruby-throated hum-

American birdwing grasshopper

Monarch on rough blazing star

mingbirds feed at the tall spikes, often competing with monarch butterflies for nectar. On the isolated oaks, later in the season, one may find masses of monarchs as they gather for their yearly trek to the Sierra Madre of central Mexico.

Other species to note are the milkweed flowers, often attracting numerous butterflies—swallowtails, fritillaries, buckeyes, and common wood nymphs—and interesting insects such as a large, black-and-orange mydas fly. The area also has its own cadre of grassland birds, so keep a lookout for the occasional and rare upland sandpiper, as well as bobwhites, wild turkeys, grasshopper sparrows, sedge wrens, and even yellow-headed blackbirds and sandhill cranes. Farther along, the trail passes through a savanna, complete with large black oaks growing among the ever-present blazing star. The scene can be magical and presents a unique glimpse into this grand ecosystem from the not-so-distant past.

CHAPTER 8

Harlem Hills Nature Preserve

Periodically, the grass-covered gravel terraces are invaded by pink-and-purple-clothed armies. Early spring brings the fuzzy lavender of pasque-flowers, low to the ground and protected from the cold. By early summer, hundreds of pale purple coneflowers erupt and flow down the terraces like pinkish-purple lava. Summer's end is signaled by the bright pink of blazing stars, each concealing brilliant yellow spiders in their tall, pink spikes.

—Susan Post, June 2007

THE CITY OF ROCKFORD is located in a region of rolling topography, drained by the Rock River. Within the confines of the second-largest city in Illinois, an explorer is able to experience the illusion of nothing but rounded hill following rounded hill, each covered with prairie grasses and forbs. As poet William Cullen Bryant wrote in *Prairies* in 1832, "These are the gardens of the desert, these the unshorn fields, boundless and beautiful, for which the speech of England has no name—The Prairies." This is an apt description of Harlem Hills.

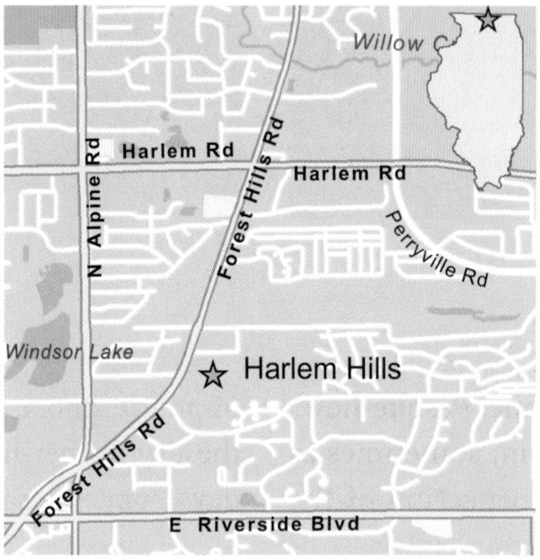

A look at the soil of the area will reveal not the deep, fine-particle soils of areas to the east and south, but rather coarse glacial till and outwash—a mixture of sand, gravel, and dolomite bedrock, covered by only a thin layer of soil. On a topographical map, the city looks as if it resides on a lion's paw. These knuckles were left by the retreating Wisconsin Glacier and were originally cloaked with vegetation more commonly noted from the high plains of the American West. Called gravel terrace prairies, all but one of them—Harlem Hills—have succumbed to the ever-growing city.

Harlem Hills Nature Preserve is situated on gravelly soils deposited by Pleistocene glaciers. The soils are calcareous, with a high pH; conditions are often bone-dry due to the well-drained soil and the slope of the land that usually faces south or west, allowing maximum exposure to the sun. Harlem Hills is not only the state's best example of a gravel terrace prairie, but it is also the largest, containing two-thirds of the state's remaining gravel prairie habitat.

This dry, seemingly harsh habitat is dominated by grasses—little bluestem, northern dropseed, and side-oats grama. But it is the spring forbs, the

Prairie smoke seed heads

Pale purple coneflowers on gravel terrace

small spots of color poking through the dry, brown grass that make a visit worthwhile. Pasque-flowers are the first flowers to bloom, sometimes as early as mid-March. A close inspection of the plant reveals a kitten-like covering of soft hairs to help protect it from the wind and cold. Prairie smoke's rose-colored spheres appear about two weeks later. The closed flowers can only be pollinated by insects strong enough to force their way into the interior of the blooms. Bumblebees can often be seen muscling their way into the interior for a meal of pollen and nectar. The real pleasure of prairie smoke is not its diminutive flowers but the airy, feather-like seed heads that, even on calm days, appear to move and wave, resembling nothing so much as a wispy, old man's beard. After the pasque-flower and prairie smoke have set fruit, a procession of color follows. Striking displays of cream wild indigo, blazing stars, and pale purple coneflowers often tumble over the terraces. A final search in early fall will reveal prairie gentians with their sky-blue flowers hidden among the drying

Pasque flowers in early spring

herbage, a fitting bookend to the Easter egg blooms of spring pasque-flowers.

Whether it is a large, fat, yellow-and-black bumblebee trying to pollinate the maroon spheres of prairie smoke, a goldfinch riding the summer winds on a compass plant, great spangled fritillaries nectaring on blazing star, a yellow or white crab spider enjoying a meal of a hapless pollinator, or a common wood nymph butterfly always staying just ahead of you in the grass, never allowing a close-enough approach for pictures, a short stroll through Harlem Hills Nature Preserve is a once-in-a-lifetime experience, one that can be had during any season and by anyone with the desire to see an all-but-vanished segment of the Illinois landscape.

Crab spider on pale purple coneflower

CHAPTER 9

Illinois Beach State Park

It's fifty-five degrees with a sharp wind off the lake, and yet a dozen hoary elfins flit close to the blooming bearberry, all buffeted by the wind. They land and lean into the wind. Their wing color resembles dried bearberry leaves, but when they land you can see glints of green off their wings. I try to follow one but soon lose it in the dry, bearberry detritus.

—Susan Post, May 2011

FINDING SOLITUDE and a diverse set of habitats in the bustling region of northeast Illinois can be a challenge. In Illinois's most northeastern county (Lake), though, a short drive eastward from the city of Zion will yield an abundance of opportunities to experience the unique landscapes that make up the Illinois dunelands. Extending from near the Wisconsin border to just north of Waukegan, Illinois Beach State Park follows the sandy shore of Lake Michigan and has a mixture of rare plants and interesting insects, backed by a park-like forest of black and blackjack oak. This area is the most recently glaciated region of the state, and evidence, in the form of numerous old beach ridges and wet swales (low areas between beach ridges), parallel the shoreline and march inland. Dry sand prairies occupy the high points, while wet sand prairies and marshes follow the swales (old lakeshores). This swell-and-swale topography developed as the Wisconsin Glacier was melting some ten thousand to twelve thousand years ago. The newly formed Lake Michigan was larger than it is today. As the climate changed and the lake dwindled in size, it left behind the ridges and lowlands we see today. An aerial view of Illinois Beach shows the glacially derived topography as a series of parallel lines, resembling wrinkled corduroy.

During the blooming season, a walk along the Dead River Trail yields an ever-changing artist's palette of color—a profusion of pinks, purples, yellows, and reds. Northern orchids, wood lilies, Indian paintbrushes, lupines, and the occasional carnivorous sundew can be seen. In 1964, due to its unique plant diversity, the area became the state's first nature preserve.

Occupying one of the larger swales is a permanent body of water called the Dead River, so

Starry false Solomon's seal in North Unit savanna

Hoary elfin butterfly on bearberry

named because it follows a swale to the current lakeshore. During periods of low water, its connection to Lake Michigan is lost, thus, the Dead River then becomes a long, sinuous lake. At other times, the water flows into Lake Michigan. The edges of the Dead River are surrounded by marsh and wet sand prairie. A walk from the lakeshore inland yields a diversity of habitats, from bare sand to small dunes covered with early-stage, dune-binding vegetation. Here you find plants more common to the far north: upright and creeping juniper, marram grass, and bearberry. The latter supports the only population of the uncommon hoary elfin found in Illinois. This diminutive, brown butterfly, no larger than a thumbnail, can be found flitting about on the bearberry, even on the coolest, windiest days of spring. In summer, the dunes can be tinted pink with the open flowers of prairie rose. Behind the dunes, prickly pear cactus forms horizontal clumps that bloom with bright yellow flowers in early summer. Ephemeral ponds behind the dunes contain large displays of yellow bladderpod,

Delphacid leafhopper on fringed gentian

Lake Michigan from the shoreline

Black oak savanna on old beach ridge with adjacent swale

a carnivorous aquatic plant. Crossing yet another old dune leads to a broad marsh with wild blue iris, arrowhead, cattails, rushes, and purple gerardia. Soon, the climax community for this area appears, a savanna of black oak and blackjack oak. The trees have a windswept, gnarly appearance—the climate here, especially in winter, is extremely harsh. Many understory plants are unique to the dunesland. Of particular note is fringed gentian, perhaps one of the latest-blooming species in Illinois; in late September these glorious, sky-blue flowers open on sunny days. When it's cloudy, the flowers tightly coil to save their nectar for the various pollinators that are not usually about when the sun is not shining. This biennial species moves about the oak savanna from year to year, and it's difficult to predict how large the population will be and where to find it. A diligent search, even during down years, will yield a few of these botanical treasures. Earlier in the season, the savanna supports a wealth of spiderwort, hoary puccoon, starry false Solomon's-seal, and a host of other species, including wild lupine. Known to occur here at one time, a rare butterfly, the Karner blue, feeds exclusively on wild lupine. In certain areas of the wet swales, populations of wood lily, a spectacular, orange-red species from the north, and grass pink orchids bloom around the Fourth of July. Close inspection of the wet sands may even yield isolated populations of glistening, carnivorous sundews.

Illinois Beach is divided into two regions—the North Unit and the South Unit. The South Unit is reflected largely in the description above, while the North Unit has expanses of sand prairies and several small ponds of open water. From the end of August to the end of November, the North Unit is a great place for hawk watching, as raptors migrate through Illinois. During this time, the North Unit becomes an official Hawk Migration Association of North America viewing site. Illinois Beach is a good site due to its location along Lake Michigan. The wind pushes thermals to the lakefront, which helps the hawks gain altitude. When there are westerly winds, the birds move closer to the lakefront. Both hawks and thermals hit the lakeshore, resulting in large numbers of birds funneling down

Beachfront panorama with black oak

the shoreline. In Illinois, the hawks follow a progression. Beginning from mid- to late September, it's mostly broadwing hawks; during October it's falcons and accipiters; and from the end of October to the end of November it's large flights of red-tailed hawks and others.

In mid- to late summer, the sand prairies are also in full bloom, with tracts of various sunflowers and pink blazing stars forming a startling contrast under the brilliant, blue sky. Early spring, around mid-June here, will yield expanses of shooting star, Indian paintbrush, and starry false Solomon's-seal. Bullfrogs, green frogs, and northern leopard frogs inhabit and breed in the ponds, while shorebirds and gulls frequent the ever-changing lakeshore.

Exploring the various areas of Illinois Beach for wildlife is a naturalist's dream—that is, if your idea of wildlife tends toward the small. The area supports a diverse orthopteran (grasshoppers and katydids) community, as well as various species of leafhoppers and planthoppers. Various butterflies patrol the many wildflowers, accompanied by native bees and wasps, and the abundant milkweeds always have their cadre of milkweed beetles, bugs, and, of course, the ubiquitous monarch butterfly. A trek across the sandy dunes, through the marshes on several boardwalks, or through the open forest to experience all the nature that the dunesland can offer, can take a day, a week, or a lifetime. The journey is never really complete.

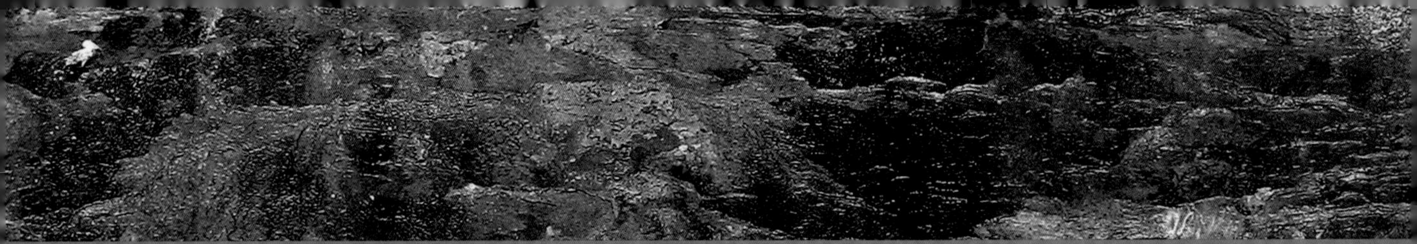

CHAPTER 10

Matthiessen State Park

During my last winter visit to Matthiessen, I was intrigued by a small creature the color of the sandstone walls, running along the icy stream edge. My first thought was a mouse, as all I could see was something brown scurrying in the snow. It was no rodent, however, but a winter wren, bouncing, hopping, and bopping, a small, compact bundle of energy, drinking at a hole broken in the ice, then poking and probing, looking for a tasty, invertebrate tidbit.

—Susan Post, January 2007

IF A NEW YEAR'S resolution includes more exercise, then winter hiking is a must. The hike should be a treat for the feet, a little test of that resolution, and also a feast for the eyes. One park comes to mind that fills the bill—Matthiessen State Park, located in LaSalle County near Oglesby. With a January thaw, the air smells of spring, yet snow still covers the decaying autumn leaves and masks any problems a park might have. The question is, can an area be interesting in winter without its cloak of greenery or cadre of wildflowers? For a winter challenge, in and out of a deep canyon, up and down hundreds of steps, navigating various streambeds, and marching along a ridge top fit for mountain sheep, the trails of Matthiessen are enough to test the nimbleness and balance of any hiker. Snow adds not only beauty to the surroundings but also an extremely slick dimension to the trails. Waterfalls that have become icefalls are statuesque, sculpted blocks of ice; but here, the water has not given up and is still trying to flow. As a result, huge chunks of ice break off, leading the imagination to places far away where pieces of glaciers break off and tumble into the sea.

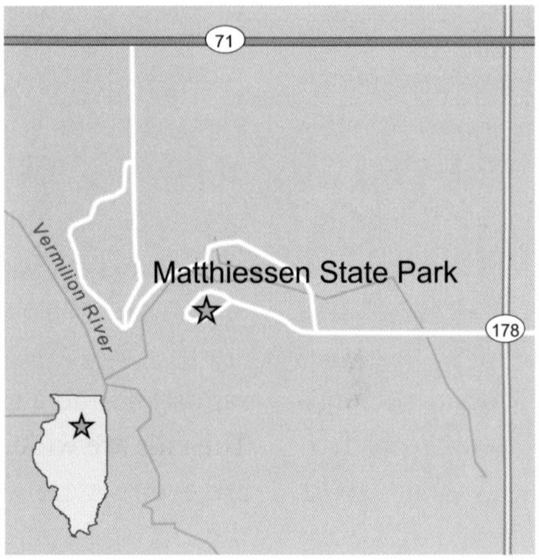

The geological structures of the park, its rocky dells, have been sculpted from St. Peter sandstone, their color warming the winter-weary body. Seeping groundwater evaporates and deposits its mineral load to produce vividly colored canyon walls. The LaSalle Anticline, a massive, convex fold in the underlying layers of rock that has its oldest rocks at its core, runs through the middle of Matthiessen State Park.

Matthiessen State Park was originally purchased by Frederick Matthiessen, an industrialist and philanthropist from nearby LaSalle in the late nineteenth century for use as a private park. His

Matthiessen Canyon

original holdings consisted of 176 acres and contained a long, narrow canyon with a small stream flowing through it (the Upper and Lower Dells). Matthiessen named the area Deer Park, due to the large number of white-tailed deer in the area. With a large work crew, he oversaw the construction of the park's first bridges, trails, and stairways; some of these are still in use today. When Matthiessen passed away, the park was given to the people of Illinois. It opened as a state park in 1943, and the name was changed to honor Mr. Matthiessen. Today, the park consists of more than nineteen hundred acres.

Water is evident everywhere in Matthiessen, especially in winter. From the obvious stream that crisscrosses the valley floor—flowing through both the Lower and Upper Dells to create frozen cascades that tinkle, drip, and crackle—to its subtle appearance in unexpected places—layer upon layer of ice mysteriously wrapped around logs, covering crevices, and emerging from dark holes in the rock walls—water is a prime force here. The canyons of Matthiessen State Park were formed by water erosion. If you begin your journey at the bridge that crosses Cascade Falls, to the right are the Upper Dells and to the left, the Lower Dells. The Upper Dells offer the opportunity to discover the Giant's Bathtub—a pothole formed when strong stream currents swirled cobbles and pebbles in eddies and ground a depression in the sandstone—and Lake Falls, which during the winter is usually spectacularly frozen.

To the left are the Lower Dells. By descending the steps from the rim, you enter the canyon of Matthiessen. Your eyes will be drawn to the icefall—a cirque (round depression in the rock) whose frozen waterfall is so thick it is a glacial, blue-green color. Named Cascade Falls, it was created when water encountered a resistant layer of St. Peter sandstone and a terrace formed in the sandstone. The falls are wide, tall, and quite dramatic. Icicles are everywhere; water continuously flows down the sandstone and freezes, leaving a clear, glasslike surface. Three or four frozen cascades may form a shell over the ever-running water, and massive icicles litter the base of the icy tower. In a short box canyon (a canyon with no outlet) downstream from the falls, you'll find Devil's Paint Box. Here, a seep has allowed dissolved minerals to precipitate

Lake Falls in winter

Giant swallowtail butterfly caterpillars

Winter wren on canyon floor

on the canyon walls and floor, leaving a palette of light-colored powders.

In the cool of spring, enjoy the wildflowers (hepatica and spring beauty) or water striders that create patterns as they walk on the still water. Hot summer days are moderated by quiet walks in the deep canyons, and a faint trail leads down the canyon to its confluence with the Vermilion River. In late summer, seek giant swallowtail caterpillars on the wafer ash trees that line the trails. The large caterpillars resemble a cross between an alligator and a bird dropping. Whatever the season, though, the final trek out of the canyon, up the many steps, and along the narrow ridges back to the parking lot leaves one exhilarated, tired, yet eagerly anticipating a future visit.

CHAPTER 11

Mississippi Palisades State Park

> During spring, my wildflower field guide is a constant companion as I hike the Sentinel Trail, attempting to identify every colorful bloom. By late summer, the flowers have been replaced by three-foot stinging nettle, and my botany book with a bird guide. I try not to linger in the nettle as I gaze upward at flitting fall warblers.
>
> —Susan Post, September 2010

WHILE WE CALL ATTENTION to how glaciers shaped the Illinois landscape, the question occasionally surfaces, "What was Illinois like before glaciers?" Even though this question might be answered with visits to far western Illinois, near the confluences of the Illinois, Mississippi, and Missouri Rivers and to the south, in the Shawnee Hills, perhaps the most dramatic and scenic area to experience "ancient Illinois" is in Mississippi Palisades State Park. Located just north of Savanna, the rugged sandstone outcrops and hilly, ravine-laced topography make hiking here somewhat challenging, at least for Illinois. The hikes, though, are well-worth the effort as they afford imposing views of the Mississippi River that include long-range panoramas of backwater lakes strewn with American lotus in summer; populations of bald eagles and waterfowl in winter; and white pelicans in spring and fall.

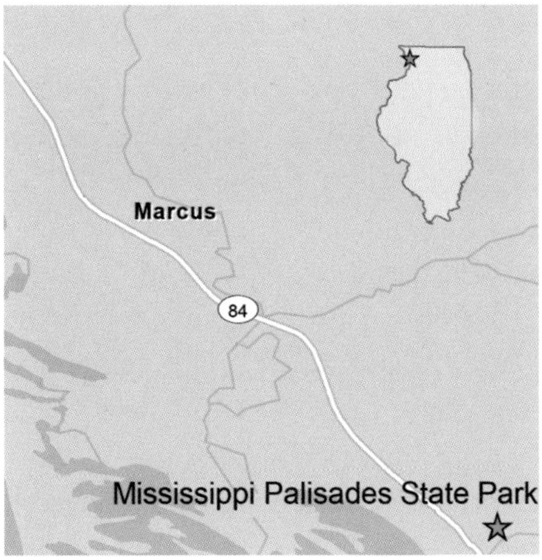

The real wonders, though, occur within the park proper. The term "palisades" refers to the high, steep cliffs that border the Mississippi River. A hike along the bluffs reveals startling sandstone features with evocative names like Indian Head and Twin Sisters. In 1973, the U.S. Department of the Interior designated Mississippi Palisades as a natural landmark. While all trails throughout the park are interesting and will get the attention of flatland legs, perhaps the best spot to see nature is on the Sentinel Trail. Here, most likely, is the finest and most diverse spring wildflower display in Illinois.

It's worth noting that anyone desiring to symbolically "present" flowers to a deserving mother for Mother's Day should consider a trip to the Sentinel Trail. Historically, around the middle of May, the Sentinel Trail has a carpet of trilliums, bluebells, shooting stars, and a host of other species. Over the

View of Mississippi River from Sentinel Trail

past thirty years, however, the blooming dates have been steadily migrating earlier into spring. Now, you must visit around late April to May 1 to see the magnificent floral show. Since the flowers bloom based on degree-day accumulation, this may be an early indicator of global warming. The timing notwithstanding, this area is a true botanical paradise. The mile-long trail through Sentinel Nature Preserve leads upward through a north-facing slope that begins with various ferns, interlaced with early meadow rue, bloodroot, wild ginger, Virginia bluebells, and even the occasional yellow lady's-slipper orchid. Finding these beauties is not easy and requires a sharp eye. A mere hundred yards into the hike, the real show begins with expanses of great white trilliums flowing down into the adjacent stream and up toward the ridge above. Displays of trilliums equal to this are usually associated with the Great Smoky Mountains and Cumberland Uplift of east Tennessee. Seeing them in this abundance is a rare sight in Illinois. Even more notable are the isolated clumps of erect trillium (also known as stinking Willy, for its odd odor). These bright, maroon-red denizens of eastern forests are found here in a decidedly isolated or disjunct population—in other words, one far away from the species' normal range. Botanists disagree on how these gems came to be in the park. Farther up the bluff, after a series of slippery wooden steps, the trail narrows and follows the bluff edge. For those familiar with prairie, a glance down might elicit the comment, "Look, bright pink prairie shooting stars! What are they doing here?" While the typical prairie shooting star comes in a range of colors

Expanse of jeweled shooting stars

Showy orchis

(from white to light pink) and is often found in open woods as well as prairies, a closer inspection of these beauties reveals subtle differences. They are more diminutive than their prairie cousins, exhibit a much brighter amethyst color, and grow in deep woods. Botanically, these jewels are actually a different species. Appropriately named the jeweled or amethyst shooting star, they grow on loess-covered bluffs along major rivers in Illinois. (Loess is finely ground rock with the texture of flour. It was created by glaciers and, when dry, was picked up by the wind and deposited in layers of varying thickness across Illinois.) While once relatively common, the shooting stars are now confined to isolated patches, but here they are easily seen in all their spectacular, spring attire. In fact, the trail courses directly through the fifty-yard-long patch, so tread carefully. The trail leads to an observation point that provides a stunning view of the upper Mississippi River and its backwater lakes.

Following the trail along the ridge, the flowers decline somewhat, but here you experience the difference that *aspect* makes to the forest community. Aspect is the direction the land faces with regard

Great white trilliums with Virginia bluebells

to the sun, and also the slope of the land. This area is markedly drier (it faces to the south and southwest) and has different species of trees and understory plants. Soon the trail heads down a relatively steep incline, and the north-facing slope becomes carpeted with maidenhair ferns, their flat-topped whirls of tiny green leaves on wiry, black stems resemble miniature umbrellas. Look for several different types of ferns along here, and if you're lucky, you may find an isolated plant of showy orchis. After a night of rain, large millipedes—long, maroon tubes with dozens of paired legs moving in perfect synchrony—may be seen moving over the moist rock faces. The trail soon reconnects with the steps leading down, and a repeat experience with the trilliums is a fitting finish to this walk through a true wildflower haven.

The many other trails throughout the park are definitely longer and also support populations of wildflowers, including colonies of large-flowered bellwort, and even additional small colonies of jeweled shooting star on the high ridges. Here you are likely to see small flocks of wild turkeys, the inevitable white-tailed deer, and on the ridge tops overlooking the Mississippi River far below, you may come eye to eye with a turkey vulture using the thermals that rise along the steep palisades, seeking its evening meal.

CHAPTER 12

Midewin National Tallgrass Prairie

We begin to walk the aptly named Henslow Trail, and soon all man-made interruptions are replaced by buzzing, tinkling, or an electric rasping—greetings by the resident grassland birds—grasshopper sparrow, bobolink, and eastern kingbird.

—Susan Post, June 2012

IN 1830, CHARLES REED, the first white settler in the area south of Joliet, purchased 162 acres from the U.S. government and began to farm. One hundred years later that same federal government bought his land and the land of 149 other area settlers to build a munitions plant—the Joliet Arsenal, later renamed the Joliet Army Ammunition Plant. The arsenal, one of sixty-two such plants in the United States, was located in the rolling hills of Will County, just east of the confluence of the Illinois, Des Plaines, and Kankakee Rivers. The rivers and prairie that encouraged Charles Reed to settle in the area offered the army a safe haven to produce its wartime wares and easy transportation to move them about the country and the world.

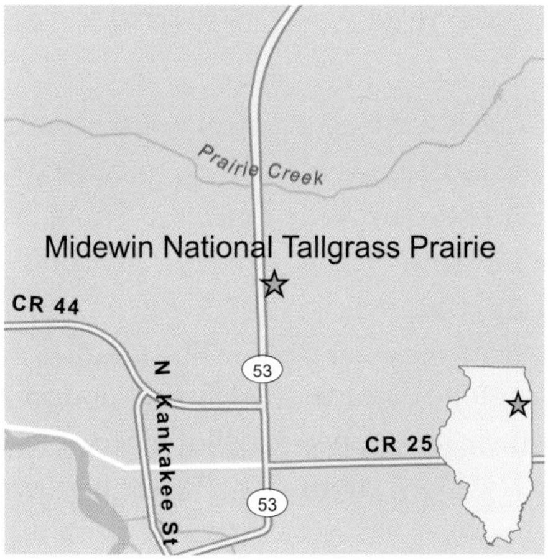

The arsenal was created in 1939 to supply the Allied forces in Europe and the Pacific with munitions. At its peak, during World War II, fourteen thousand people were employed at the forty-thousand-acre arsenal; they made TNT in fifty-pound blocks for use in shells, hand grenades, and land mines. The plant was one of the world's leading producers, turning out tons of TNT each week. After the war, the plant was placed on standby and was later reactivated for both the Korean War and Vietnam War.

By 1993, the federal government decided the plant was no longer useful and began to look for civilian uses. In 1996, congress approved a bipartisan plan that earmarked nineteen thousand acres of the arsenal as a national tallgrass prairie. The Midewin National Tallgrass Prairie, named after the Ojibwe word for "healing," became the first national tallgrass prairie and the largest prairie preserve east of the Mississippi River.

Among the bunkers, railroad tracks, miles of chain-link security fences, and fallow fields is a

Midewin grassland

landscape of small prairie remnants, but the area contains mostly old agricultural fields, abandoned pastures, and woodlands that support one hundred species of breeding birds. Perhaps most important, sixteen of the state's threatened and endangered animals may be found here. Four of those species—the red-winged leafhopper, Blanding's turtle, loggerhead shrike, and the cerulean warbler are also on the federal threatened or endangered species list. Amid the major landscapes at Midewin are the relics the army left behind: hundreds of sod-covered concrete bunkers, reminders of the area's violent past. These bunkers, used for the safe storage of TNT, now dot the recovering landscape like so many regularly spaced, pocket gopher mounds, a mammal that also calls Midewin home. The arsenal's railroads and roads have been converted into thirty-three miles of trails, and the public has access to over nine thousand acres of the preserve.

While most of Midewin is a long-term ecological restoration project (in other words, prairie is being planted), the vastness of its grassland pastures means that species of birds like grasshopper sparrow, dickcissel, and bobolink find the area to their liking; you can easily view them by walking one of the grassland trails. The roadside hedgerows support Bell's vireo. The area also has one of the largest populations of upland sandpipers in Illinois. It's not all just old fields and pastures, though, as significant natural features are embedded in the thousands of acres that constitute Midewin.

Bobolink in grassland

Calling dickcissel

The Drummond Dolomite Prairie, located in the northwestern corner of Midewin, is an important natural area. The very thin soils over the magnesium-rich dolomite bedrock support wet, moist, and dry prairie that house a wide range of plant and animals requiring the unique conditions that exist here. The wet dolomite prairies support bluejoint grass, cord grass, and the charismatic swamp milkweed. The dry dolomite prairies support populations of prickly pear cactus, which come into bloom each June. Red foxes sometimes dot the surrounding open grasslands, and due to their curious nature, they allow views by quiet hikers.

For anyone seeking solitude, the feel of the ever-present prairie winds rippling the various grasses that stretch to the far horizon, or the chance to see and photograph some of Illinois's more charismatic grassland birds, make Midewin a great hiking, biking, and even horseback-riding destination. The new visitors' center features a replica of the journal from early Illinois traveler Eliza Steele. A quote from her as she traversed Illinois in 1840 sums up a visit to Midewin. "I was in the midst of a prairie! A world of grass and flowers stretched around me, rising and falling in gentle undulations. . . . We passed whole acres of blossoms all bearing one hue, as purple, perhaps, or masses of yellow or rose; and again a carpet of every color intermixed, or narrow bands, as if a rainbow had fallen upon the verdant slopes."

CHAPTER 13

Moraine Hills State Park

The Leatherleaf Bog Trail is a symphony of sound—with cricketing frogs, honking geese, the *"skreeee"* of red-winged blackbirds, a low chattering and chiding of chipmunks, and the distant, off-key rattle of sandhill cranes.

—Susan Post, May 1996

LOCATED IN THE northeast corner of Illinois, just three miles south of McHenry and east of the Fox River, lies a legacy of the Pleistocene glaciers. These massive, slow-moving, icy bulldozers left northeastern Illinois with a mosaic of many wetland habitats—bogs, fens, marshes, and glacial lakes. Moraine Hills State Park is an excellent place to view many of these features, modified by ten thousand years of vegetative activity. Nearly half the park's acreage is composed of glacially derived wetlands and lakes. The park's name is from the geologic feature known as a moraine. Moraines were formed where the ice margin of a glacier temporarily stood in one place. The leading edge of the glacier, melting back the same amount as it moved forward acted like a giant conveyor belt, leaving ridges of boulders, gravel, and other rock debris. These eroded moraines are evidenced by the slight hills that one encounters on the trails that traverse the park.

Lake Defiance, near the center of Moraine Hills, is a kettle hole lake formed after a glacier melted. The depression filled with water, as it was below the water table. Unlike manmade lakes, the edges of glacial lakes are much less evident. The shore of Lake Defiance is unstable, due to an accumulation of peat (partially decayed plant material), and the lake itself is fed by the park's wetlands. It is ringed with a riot of vegetation—cattails, rushes, and sedges—that slowly give way to deeper water. Here, white water lilies take hold, providing a pleasing, pastoral landscape before the open water at the lake's center. Leatherleaf Bog was also formed from a kettle hole, but unlike Lake Defiance, the bog is poorly drained and has no inlet or outlet. The depression gradually filled with ever-thickening layers of peat

Black Tern Marsh at Moraine Hills State Park

Calling yellow-headed blackbird

to form the unstable mat that you see today. The bog gets its name from the evergreen leatherleaf shrub found there. The common name refers to its tough leaves. It is the first shrub to enter a bog after the sphagnum moss is established, and it is shade intolerant. During the spring, the plant produces white flowers that dangle from the branches like little bells. During spring and fall, sandhill cranes can often be seen flying over or feeding around the edges of the bog. Red patches on the forehead highlight the birds' gray countenance.

Another area formed from a shallow kettle hole is Pike Marsh; but unlike Leatherleaf Bog, it receives groundwater. The bedrock gravel found near Pike Marsh is also high in minerals. Thus, the surrounding marsh is a fen, a wetland where many plants are adapted to the highly alkaline conditions. Ohio goldenrod, turtlehead, and grass of Parnassus grow well here. Its thick layer of peat is formed from decaying grasses and sedges, not the typical, acid-loving sphagnum moss.

The park is relatively large and spans River Road, but access to both sides is provided by a hiking underpass that leads to both Black Tern and Yellow-head Marshes, and to the shore of the Fox River. While sightings of black terns can be sporadic, it is usually possible to see several yellow-headed blackbirds, the occasional green heron, and large numbers of great white egrets and great blue herons. The small oak copses that occur along the trail can be havens for spring wildflowers and for migrating warblers. Look for both common and unusual dragonflies along the wetland edges—green and swamp darners, Carolina and black saddlebags, as well as a multitude of amberwings, tenspots, and other species.

With its variety of plant communities, interesting glacial terrain, and numerous encounters with wildlife, especially wetland birds, Moraine Hills State Park is a great site for a long or short leisurely hike that provides great nature viewing.

Glacial lake panorama with white water lily

CHAPTER 14

Nachusa Grasslands

> I am a steward because Nachusa is one
> of the most beautiful places on earth.
> I will never live to see the land restored
> to its former majesty, but at least I can
> be a small part of the restoration effort.
>
> —Anonymous, taken from
> *Prairie Smoke,* March 2010

WHEN THE NATURE CONSERVANCY (TNC) first purchased Nachusa, starting in 1986 with 250 acres, the land was classified as a degraded remnant prairie complex that contained threatened and endangered species. In short, Nachusa was going to need some work. Shortly after his arrival at the site, preserve manager Bill Kleiman stood on Doug's Knob and looked out, thinking, "This is a great place to do great things." A visit today showcases the result of more than twenty-five years of dedication by TNC staff and an army of volunteers. The process was often arduous but always systematic, with a view toward the future. Workers planted old fields with locally collected seeds, battled invasive brush, conducted periodic burns, removed old fences, and offered protection to endangered plants. Kleiman encouraged volunteers to adopt sections of the vast preserve for management activities. The process succeeded and continues to work.

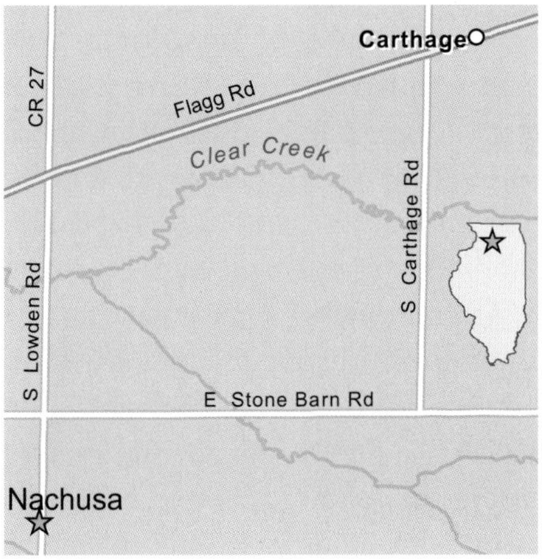

Nachusa Grasslands, still owned by The Nature Conservancy of Illinois, consists of thirty-five hundred acres nestled on the county line between Ogle and Lee Counties. To the south of Nachusa is Franklin Creek Natural Area; to the north is Castle Rock State Park and Lowden-Miller State Forest, all owned by the Illinois Department of Natural Resources. These four areas form a corridor along the Rock River. Biologically, Nachusa is defined by a series of unique, sandstone knobs, and the area supports nearly twenty-five state threatened and endangered species and eleven different plant communities. A quick look at Nachusa reveals how big the place actually is, and that it isn't all prairie. The landscape gives a good impression of what Illinois was like during pre-European settle-

Great spangled fritillary on pale purple coneflower

ment, a complex mosaic of differing yet interconnecting landscapes. Nachusa imparts clues to its past, with remnants of rolling prairies, oak woodlands, and wetlands. These habitats are being reconnected through landscape restoration of areas that were once agricultural fields. As time passes, the evidence of former disturbance becomes less visible. Restoration has proceeded outward from these natural pieces (prairie, woodland, and wetland), referred to as *pearls*. "There are quite a few pearls here," Bill says. "And our job is to string these pearls together."

Anyone looking at Nachusa in the early 1960s could only find scattered remnants of prairie in the midst of corn and soybeans. These prairie islands occurred on knobs that were either too hilly or troublesome to farm. Conservationists Douglas and Dorothy Wade drove across the countryside in Lee and Ogle counties during the summer of 1964. They spotted a hillside (knob) covered with the rare downy yellow painted cup. The plants were growing on a nearly pristine, dry gravel hill prairie. The knob, later named after the landowner, Schafer, was the catalyst needed to start preservation efforts of the area. The Nature Conservancy's 1986 purchase included a section of Schafer's Knob as part of the deal. Schafer's Knob is considered one of the pearls of the area and is one of the most diverse of any of the dry hill prairies found in the state.

What are knobs? Above ground, Nachusa is a checkerboard of prairie, woodland, and wetlands. Below ground it is one of the most geologically complicated areas in northern Illinois. Nachusa is located on the southwest flank of both the Ashton Arch (an arch causes a buckling of underlying rocks) and the Sandwich Fault Zone (a fault is a break in the rocks). Running northwest to southeast (near Manhattan in Will County to Oregon in Ogle County) is the axis of the Sandwich Fault Zone. At Nachusa, bedrock outcrops (knobs) are found. These knobs are rounded, erosional remnants of St. Peter sandstone, brought close to the surface due to the fault. These sandstone knobs are covered with a thin, gravelly soil and support prairie plants adapted to these dry conditions. The knobs of Nachusa support the best prairie of the area, as most were not farmable, and their dry conditions and gravelly soil slowed the invasion of weeds.

Nachusa Grasslands contains 60 percent grassland, 30 percent woodland, and 10 percent wetland and stream habitat. These habitats support the plants and animals—whether threatened, endangered, or common—that represent the pearls of Nachusa. Threatened and endangered organisms have played their role in the preservation of Nachusa, from the hillside of downy yellow painted cup that attracted the Wades, to the upland sandpipers and prairie bush clover that attracted The

Diverse flowers at Nachusa Grasslands

Big bluestem grass in early fall

Nature Conservancy. The knobs, capped in the more common pale purple coneflowers, however, delight and inspire everyone from near and far.

Nachusa supports nearly 550 native species of plants, from skunk cabbage mingling with gray, weathered, beaver-cut tree stumps in a sand seep, to hundreds of bird's-foot violets heralding spring on the dry prairie, to the goldenrods and asters of autumn. The federally threatened prairie bush clover, called the "rarest of rare," has a foothold in Nachusa and occurs in the driest of prairies. The species is an endemic (occurring nowhere else) Midwestern tallgrass prairie species. It is known from only forty sites throughout Iowa, Wisconsin, Minnesota, and Illinois, with the population at Nachusa the largest known from any site in Illinois.

The creation of this large, unfragmented grassland has provided premier habitat for grassland birds. Four notable species—upland sandpipers, northern harriers, Cooper's hawks, and Henslow's sparrows—nest at Nachusa. More common species include bobolinks, grasshopper sparrows, dickcissels, and the secretive Bell's vireo.

The once tattered remnants are now part of a large preserve, and more and more organisms are calling Nachusa home. Badgers, which need fairly large territories, have taken up residence. The gorgone checkerspot butterfly has been successfully relocated here. When the preserve was first introduced to members of The Nature Conservancy, the desire for a preserve large enough to support bison seemed only a dream. Each year, that dream gets a little closer to reality, and bison are slated for the preserve starting in 2014.

Finding Nachusa requires a bit of searching, but once there, park in the roadside parking lot and follow one of the many trails that lead through the preserve. Note the rolling, windswept topography, marvel at the amazing displays of single species, or just enjoy a landscape that continues to evolve and surprise with every visit.

CHAPTER 15

Rollins Savanna Forest Preserve

Soon after leaving the village, we came onto a
beautiful and very rich prairie, covered with grass
and flowers, and surrounded by oak openings.
—Colbee Benton, *Traveling on Horseback
from Chicago to Northern Illinois,* 1833

THE EARLY SETTLERS to northeastern Illinois were beset with a great diversity of natural communities as they made their way west and north around the immensity of Lake Michigan. One can imagine that wagons, as they headed inland from the lake, were alternately slowed by the dry, sandy soils near the lakeshore or forced to climb densely wooded hills (old glacial moraines), obstacles that ran roughly parallel to the lakeshore. Between each hill were swales, replete with wet, boggy soils that clamped onto wagon wheels and the boots of slogging settlers with equal ferocity. Many times a day decisions had to be made whether to traverse (or go around) the marshy ground so prominent in this, the most recently glaciated area of Illinois. As late as twelve thousand years ago, this area was still covered with a sheet of glacial ice that likely reached a thickness equal to that of the tallest skyscrapers that now grace downtown Chicago. It was hard, exhausting travel.

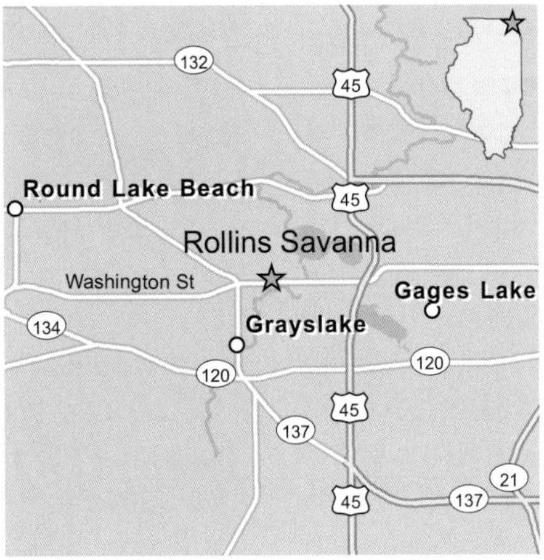

After a long day of slowly making their way west, alternating between marsh, forest, dune, and even bogs, perhaps the settlers marveled as they approached a seemingly endless, park-like vista of widely spaced oaks, a pristine stream insinuating itself through the rolling topography, and even waterfowl-laden wetlands that could provide that much needed protein for a hearty dinner. This would be the place to stop, perhaps for an evening encampment, maybe for a day or two to rest up before moving on, or perhaps for a lifetime, as this area provided wood for shelter and fuel, deep, black soils for farming, and abundant water. Such is the pleasant landscape that presents itself today to visitors to Lake County's largest forest preserve, the twelve-hundred-plus acres of Rollins Savanna.

Sandhill Crane flock at sunset

What makes Rollins Savanna exceptional is that the preserve is unbroken by roads and other man-made structures. It is a place to roam freely on the nearly six-mile loop trail and experience a part of Illinois that largely ceased to exist as the great urban centers of northeastern Illinois grew. The mosaic of expansive oak savannas, tallgrass prairie, a winding loop of Mill Creek, and interior wetlands provides myriad opportunities for wildlife and nature viewing. The walk is easy, along a paved trail, with bridges, boardwalks, and an elevated viewing platform that allows visitors to concentrate on observing without worrying about where to place their next step.

The extensive prairie restoration has resulted in something that has become vanishingly rare in Illinois: a large acreage of tallgrass prairie, much the same landscape a few earlier settlers so eloquently described in their journals. Colbee Benton

Ancient bur oak toppled in wind storm

Pond at Rollins Savanna

traveled in this area more than 180 years ago. While the villages are now larger than those he traveled through, the scenery will still impress when you reach Rollins Savanna. The savannas and oak openings beckon to be explored, and who knows what discoveries await.

The area has experienced many permutations of development and disturbance since Benton's visit, yet the landscape is recovering. The birding has become compelling enough that the National Audubon Society declared Rollins Savanna an Important Bird Area in 2005. Birdwatchers simply call Rollins a "birder's field of dreams." Look for grassland specialists like dickcissels, bobolinks, and grasshopper sparrows; search the numerous wetlands for ruddy ducks, blue-winged teal, northern pintails, great blue herons, great white egrets, and sandhill cranes. The latter always provide a spectacular surprise when their eerie calls echo high above from a V-shaped assemblage against the sky, or as they appear as gray wraiths, stalking their way through the tall mash vegetation. Perhaps you will be lucky enough to experience the guttural croak and spectacular appearance of male yellow-headed blackbirds among the cattails. Common out west, they are at the edge of their range in northern Illinois. A winter visit may yield northern harriers, rough-legged hawks, short-eared owls, and American tree sparrows. A day spent birding at Rollins can yield upwards of fifty species.

Even though tallgrass prairie and wetlands form a large part of Rollins Savanna, the real habitat prize of a visit is the chance to experience the namesake oak savannas, located on the rolling hills in the northern part of the preserve. The magnificent, spreading canopies of the bur and white oaks speak to a time from our distant past. Eminent Harvard biologist E. O. Wilson postulates

Short-eared owl perched and seeking prey

that because humans developed in the savannas of East Africa, we have an innate, inborn response to open, tree-dotted landscapes. Perhaps this is because our early ancestors, walking upright, could view the horizon in search of potential predators and climb the trees for safety, something not necessary today. But for whatever reason, Rollins Savanna provides an uplifting experience for any visitor—birding, searching for elusive butterflies, enjoying the brilliant prairie flowers, or simply savoring a long walk through part of the ecological history of Illinois.

CHAPTER 16

Spring Lake Wildlife Conservation Area

Today, at least a dozen dogface sulfur butterflies flitted along the levee trail, always just out of reach of my camera. Not what I would expect for northern Illinois, as seeing just one of these anywhere in Illinois is the norm. I'm accompanied by the rattle of sandhill cranes and the scolding of catbirds.

—Susan Post, September 2012

ANYONE DRIVING ON Illinois Route 84, heading north from the Quad Cities and paralleling the upper Mississippi River, is usually intent on visiting Galena, one of Illinois's signature tourist destinations. While glimpses of nature along the river can be had, especially in winter when numerous bald eagles roost in trees along the shore or sit on the partially frozen river, it takes a little detective work and a spirit of exploration to enter a world the Army Corps of Engineers designates as Pool 13, between river miles 532.5 and 536, hardly a description to excite the senses. While numerous opportunities appear as brown road signs, one of the best places to visit, and one with an easy access, is Spring Lake. This 3,300-acre lake and backwater complex is bounded on the west by the natural riverbank of the Mississippi River, and on the other sides by a levee that runs around the perimeter. Located about two miles south of Savanna, the area boasts diverse wildlife and nature-viewing opportunities. Anyone may walk along the levee system and enjoy an intimate view of backwater lakes, with their massive complement of American lotuses (in full bloom during midsummer), small pools and ponds during the dry summer that often support many species of waterfowl, numerous egrets and herons, and even large flotillas of the grand American white pelican.

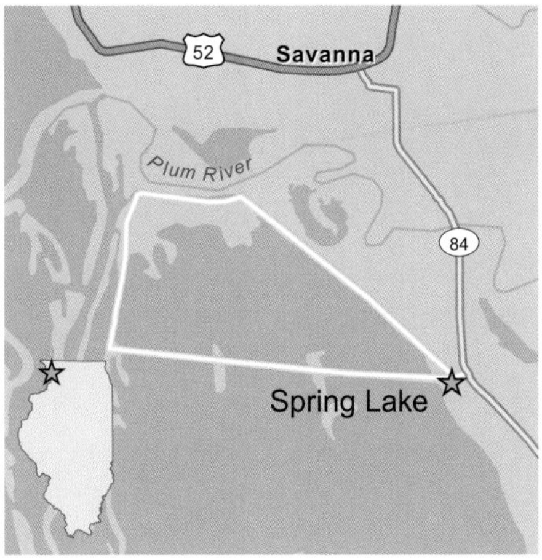

The history of the area follows a predictable scenario. After World War I, the region known as Spring Lake was drained, diked, and ditched for farming. In 1938 and 1939, however, the U.S. Army Corps of Engineers acquired the area as part of an upper Mississippi River channel project. Later, responsibility for managing the area fell to the U.S. Fish and Wildlife Service, and it is

Spring Lake panorama

Bronze copper butterfly

Mating green darner dragonflies

Sneezeweed blooming in late summer

now managed as a unit of the Savanna District of the Upper Mississippi River National Wildlife and Fish Refuge.

Both Upper and Lower Spring Lakes were once highly productive sources of aquatic vegetation, a heavily used resource by migratory waterfowl on the Mid-American Flyway. After these human alterations, various consequences (sedimentation from river flooding and encroachment by woody vegetation) caused the area's value to waterfowl to decline sharply. In fact, peak waterfowl use days (a way to measure how productive a wetland system is) decreased from 113,000 to less than 30,000. Anyone who visits the area will note that numerous dikes and water control structures now dot the area. These devices control water levels to increase wetland plant production, much to the delight of migratory waterfowl, especially dabbling ducks. A visit to Spring Lake can include a short walk along the levee or a four-mile hike around the entire lake that includes views of a backwater lake complex, nice views of Plum Creek, and a covered wildlife viewing platform, a great place for a quiet few minutes rest and possible close-up views of wood ducks and great white egrets. The ethereal, lonely call of a sora rail may even interrupt your reverie.

Don't limit yourself to avian viewing, though, as the area has a diversity of dragonflies (upward of a dozen species may be identified on a short walk), and several species of grasshoppers that keep your eyes busy noting their various antics and wing colors. Even several species of butterflies that can be difficult to see in most parts of Illinois fly along the levees. In early September, look for patches of blooming asters, as these will likely have small populations of the uncommon bronze copper but-

Mass emergence of mayflies from the nearby Mississippi River

terfly. Small by wildlife standards (about the size of a quarter), but a giant among its relatives (the family Lycaenidae), this striking little butterfly will often pose for photos as it nectars on the white asters. In addition, those familiar bright yellow butterflies one "sees" everywhere in Illinois may just turn out to be the uniquely patterned dogface sulphur, with an upperwing pattern that resembles either a poodle or a beagle. Photographing these may be a bit more challenging, but a good pair of butterfly binoculars should provide nice views.

The levees also are lined with a variety of prairie grasses, including Indian grass, side-oats grama, big bluestem, and switchgrass. In spring and fall, the days are mostly warm and sunny, the sky a brilliant blue dotted with puffy white clouds, and you may even be treated to a close-up view of the brightly patterned northern leopard frog. Seeing any or all of the creatures that call Spring Lake home is a treat and a welcome respite. So take your time, have a leisurely hike, and enjoy nature to its fullest at Spring Lake.

CHAPTER 17

Starved Rock State Park

For those attuned to John Wayne westerns,
being trapped in a blind canyon usually meant
a fight to the death with outlaws or Indians.
Here, though, the many blind canyons yield
waterfalls, icefalls, or just a cool, quiet, solitude,
difficult to find in the twenty-first century.
—Michael Jeffords, April 2010

HIKING IN NATURE should be a rewarding experience. Simply trekking through miles of forest, a green, verdant sameness, or walking through any relatively uninteresting terrain, can leave one jaded. This is not the case for hiking in Starved Rock State Park, as each trail has a significant destination, and each walk is rewarded with hydrological, geological, and biological splendor!

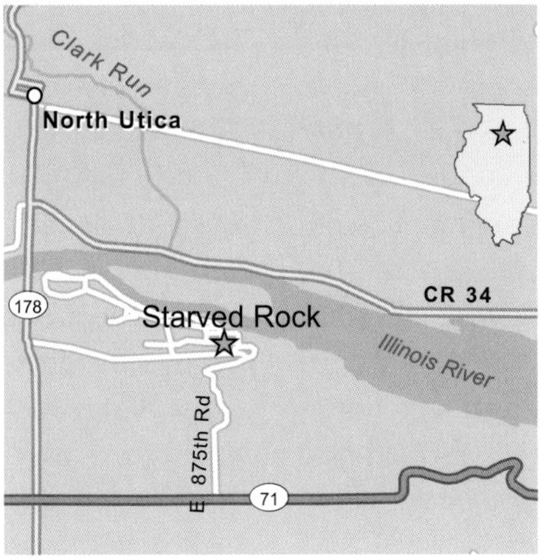

To one sated with the wide, horizontal vistas of the Illinois landscape, the bare-rock cliffs that form the canyons and towering walls of Starved Rock State Park afford relief. Starved Rock and the adjacent canyons are formed from porous St. Peter Sandstone, deposited millions of years ago by a shallow inland sea. The sandstone was brought to the surface as a result of a huge upfold, known as the LaSalle Anticline. Water from melting glaciers cut across the anticline, leaving behind the deep canyons and high bluffs. At the beginning of the early glacial meltwater torrents, the Illinois River flowed at the same height as the top of the signature feature of the park, "starved rock." Located between Ottawa and LaSalle, and stretching seven miles along the Illinois River, Starved Rock State Park encompasses many features that can be enjoyed during any season.

Spring is cool, with the rock formations masked by an ephemeral, gauzy green haze of developing leaves. Rainfall and water from the winter thaw create waterfalls at the canyon heads. The waterfalls, in combination with the moss-covered vertical walls, leave a memorable impression. Summer is dense, often hot, but the canyons remain cool and moist. By summer, most falls have slowed to a mere trickle or completely dried up. Autumn is spectacular as the leaves change and carpet the rocks with the summer's deciduous pro-

A rock shelf with small falls

duction. Winter is special: falling water becomes ice columns, ice bridges, and frozen cascades. The falls in St. Louis Canyon are the only continuous waterfalls in the park, flowing even in midsummer. Fed by springs, this canyon stream never dries up, and in winter the falls are transformed into columns of ice, enhanced by continuous trickling and freezing.

The plant communities in Starved Rock are diverse. Water falling on the porous sandstone rock quickly soaks through, and the sandy surface remains essentially dry. The plants found in the canyons are restricted to those species able to gain a foothold on the steep rock walls—usually lower forms of plant life. At least one third of all Illinois fern species are part of Starved Rock's flora. Liverworts grasp the canyon walls like moist fingers. An unusual aspect of the area is the presence of survivor or relict species. When the glaciers receded, they left behind representatives of a colder climate. Such survivors as harebells, reindeer lichen, yew, and mountain holly are hidden in the coolness, amid the craggy surfaces of the canyons.

A short trek to the top of "starved rock" will afford a view of the middle Illinois River Valley. Looking upstream reveals Starved Rock Lock and

St. Louis Canyon icefall

Green frog rests in a quiet pond

Dam. Open water near the dam becomes a haven for various gulls during winter. Downstream find Plum Island, an Illinois Audubon Preserve that is a refuge for overwintering bald eagles. The fifty-two-acre island has been cleared of years of debris and planted with thousands of trees by local volunteers. Although closed to the public, eagles are often in plain view as they perch and fish along this stretch of the Illinois River.

While Starved Rock can be crowded in peak season, especially around the visitors' center and lodge, the population soon thins as your feet put in distance on the many miles of trails. In most of

Gulls rest on mudflats along the Illinois River

the cool, dark, blind canyons, you can find solitude and have the waterfalls—whether a trickle, a torrent, or an ice cascade—all to yourself. Large, green frogs often sit quietly in the slow-flowing streams during summer, surrounded by black-winged damselflies and serenaded by the drone of dog-day cicadas.

Whether you come to hike the many trails to observe the waterfalls and unique flora, or you just want to be entertained by the chipmunks cavorting among the crevices and fallen trees, Starved Rock State Park offers the opportunity to explore a unique area of Illinois.

CHAPTER 18

Upper Mississippi River National Wildlife and Fish Refuge

In the distance tree stumps poke through the frozen, snow-covered backwater lakes. As we get closer, they are not stumps, but bald eagles standing on the ice—resting, watching, waiting . . .
—Susan Post, March 2007

ANYONE WHO ENJOYS trips on cruise ships has likely toured the unique Inside Passage from the Pacific Northwest of the United States to Alaska. The network of forested, steep-sided islands that make up the Alexander Archipelago support an abundance of wildlife, from humpback whales to sea otters; yet most people cruising the passage remember the eagles, seemingly countless numbers of bald eagles. In fact, at least one bald eagle nest occurs for every mile of this watery paradise's shoreline, and from twenty thousand to twenty-five thousand eagles call the area home.

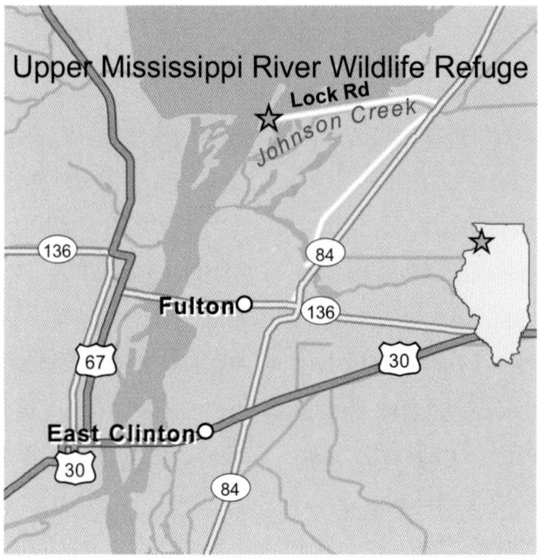

So, must any Illinoisan who needs an eagle fix book a cruise and tour the Inside Passage? Not so, as Illinois's major rivers—the Mississippi and the Illinois—and even some of the smaller streams—the Sangamon, the Spoon, and the Cache—support the second-largest aggregation (Alaska is first) of bald eagles in North America. Each winter, large numbers of eagles fish the partially frozen rivers and streams, and during the warmer parts of the year, some even nest. In midwinter, when the soul begins to crave the out-of-doors after being cooped up in the house, where does one go for an eagle-viewing adventure? A suggestion is Illinois's version of the Inside Passage, a corridor along the upper Mississippi River that stretches from Moline/Rock Island to Savanna. Unlike the watery corridor of the "true" Inside Passage, in Illinois the "cruise" is by automobile, up US 84 that heads north from Interstate 80 just before it crosses the Mississippi River into Iowa. This winding road passes through many small towns, including Rapids City, Cordova, Port Byron, Albany, and Fulton. Along the highway and in each town (all have access roads that lead down to the Mississippi) the river is constantly in view,

Backwater lake in early winter

and when partially frozen, with areas of open water, the river is a haven for overwintering bald eagles. Many sit on the edge of the ice, while others fly up and down the river corridor fishing. In some areas, large numbers gather in the tall trees along the shoreline, creating an eagle spectacle—black and white against the stark, leafless trees along the shoreline. Both adults and juveniles spend most of the winter here, and a daylong excursion can yield hundreds of eagle sightings. A few may even be seen feeding on road-killed deer! Perhaps the prime location most accessible to the public is the region around Fulton, where Lock and Dam 13 creates Pool 13 on the upper Mississippi River. On special days, the spillway below the dam supports dozens of eagles and hundreds of gulls, all feeding, resting, and seemingly enjoying the optimum fishing created by the turbulent waters of the river as it passes through the dam.

The Upper Mississippi River National Fish and Wildlife Refuge, which begins near Cordova and runs for 261 river miles and ends at the mouth of the Chippewa River in Wisconsin, covers an immense area (more than 240,000 acres), and is an unmatched expanse of wildlife and fish habitat in the central United States. The area has been designated a wetland of international importance and a globally significant bird area. The land is a maze of small, forested islands, backwater lakes, sluggish river channels, and floodplain forests. Visit here in the winter to see America's symbol of freedom, the bald eagle, the only eagle that is unique to North America (golden eagles also occur in Europe and Asia). The bald eagle sits atop the food chain, which

Bald eagle resting on icy river channel

Mass of eagles roosting along the Mississippi River

Aerial view of Upper Mississippi River basin in summer

makes them vulnerable to whatever toxic chemicals have accumulated in their fishy prey. The near demise of the species in the mid-to-late part of the last century was due to the widespread use of DDT and its breakdown compounds that accumulated in worldwide food chains. The ban on the use of DDT in the early 1970s led to a slow recovery for the species, and today the bald eagle is doing well enough to be removed from the endangered species list (since 2007). With a body length approaching three feet and a wingspan of more than seven feet, the eagle is an impressive bird, and you can obtain good views without having to approach too closely: all you need is a good pair of binoculars.

For those interested in a more intimate view of this majestic creature, stop along Route 84, just north of Fulton, at Spring Lake (see chapter 16). A small parking area is the access point for nearly nine miles of levee trails that lead into the refuge. A quiet walk in midwinter will definitely provide solitude and maybe a close-up view of eagles as they go about their winter routine.

Canada geese fly-in

Cruising to Alaska on the Inside Passage means you are on the water while viewing the passing land. Wending your way north on Illinois's inside passage entails viewing the icy, watery landscape that passes before you from the comfort of your car. So bring your binoculars and your camera (preferably with a long lens), and enjoy exploring the second-best eagle-viewing location in North America. In this case, second best is not bad, as the hundreds of eagles along the way will certainly attest, making your visit a memorable excursion.

CHAPTER 19

Volo Bog State Natural Area

Don't make us leave, Dad, there's
no better place than this!
—As overheard by Susan Post
while exiting the bog boardwalk,
September 2000

TO FULLY APPRECIATE a bog one must delve into Illinois's distant human past or into its recent geological past—the Late Pleistocene (twelve thousand years ago). Volo Bog is a true relic of the Pleistocene glaciers that carved and shaped much of the Illinois landscape of today. Located in the extreme northeastern corner of Illinois, Volo Bog is the only remaining open-water bog in Illinois. Formed when a large chunk of glacial ice was left behind by the receding glacier and buried by glacial till (rocks, sand, and gravel), the massive ice chunk eventually melted, leaving a large, circular depression filled with water. Because no streams flowed into or out of the basin, the water became anaerobic (lacking in oxygen) and acidic. Over time dead plant material accumulated, partially decayed, and formed peat. This layer of peat consists of the organic remains of trees, grasses, shrubs, fungi, and even animals. The peat floats on the water in ever-thickening layers until it can support plant life. Eventually the peat thickens to the point where the basin is full and transitions to other habitats, such as lowland forests. At Volo Bog, while much of the basin is full of peat, a central "eye" of open water several feet deep still exists. What makes this area special is that peatlands, while common farther north, are rare in Illinois.

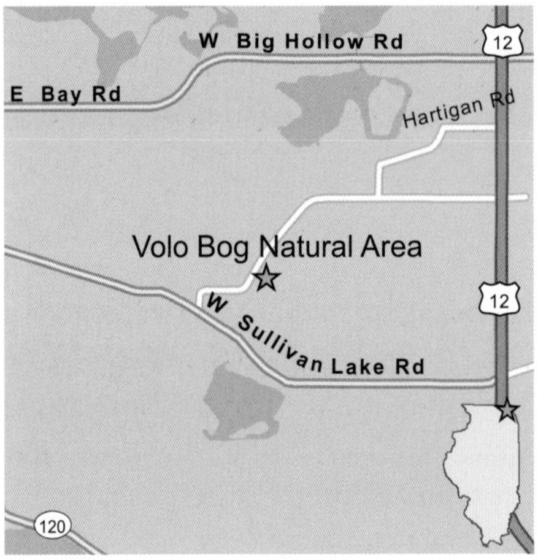

All this may seem of little interest to the normal citizen, but a visit to a bog is a novel and enlightening experience. As you might expect, exploring a bog appears to be a wet, dirty, even dangerous endeavor—and it could be. The spongy layer of peat may not be solid or thick enough to support a human body, and a plunge to knee, waist, or shoulder level is not improbable. The basin of Volo Bog is at least fifty feet deep, so a misstep here

“Eye” of Volo Bog in summer

American larch in fall color

Snake-mouth orchid blooms

could be extremely hazardous. What makes a bog trip so special and worth the effort? The floating, acidic, peat mat that is saturated with water and low in nutrients supports a unique plant community. Species that are rare or found nowhere else in Illinois thrive here. American larch (tamarack), cinnamon fern, royal fern, winterberry, sphagnum moss, snake-mouth and grass pink orchids, poison sumac, and pitcher plants flourish because they have found ways to cope with the excess water, acidity, and lack of nutrients.

Hummocks form around the bases of the larch trees, and early visitors to Volo Bog actually leapt from hummock to hummock to explore the area, causing the surrounding trees to swing like pendulums. Fortunately, today the exploration of Volo Bog is greatly aided by a boardwalk that traverses the marshy moat, the winterberry fringe, the larch forest, the edge of the open water eye of the bog, and then heads out and up to an informative visitors' center (a converted dairy barn). Here you can learn much about the bog landscape, its formation, and its plants and animals. Interestingly, the boardwalk of today is the latest version, as several (four or five) have sunk into the peat over the years. While a visit any time during the year is special, late spring and fall are favorite times, as the orchids and pitcher plants are in bloom (late spring) and the larch are in full, golden color (fall).

Descending from the visitors' center, you enter the marshy moat surrounding the true bog. The plants here are marsh species with cattails, rushes (grass-like plants with round stems), tickseed, and the occasional blue iris present. Look for various species of dragonflies basking in the warm sun, or butterflies and bumblebees visiting the yellow coreopsis. Several yards farther on is the winterberry zone. This head-high and taller shrub forms a green façade around the bog in spring and summer but reaches its dramatic conclusion in fall. The leafless stems then support an incredible display of bright red berries, the envy of any horticulturalist, and a seemingly impenetrable red wall protecting the bog proper. The boardwalk, however, provides a narrow access point, and soon you encounter American larch, a deciduous conifer tree with thick, inch-long, soft needles that turn a striking golden hue in fall before dropping off. The only other deciduous conifer found in Illinois is the bald cypress, from far southern Illinois. Interlaced within the larch you'll find red-stemmed, poison sumac, adorned with white berries in the fall. Do

Bog fringe of winterberry

not touch, as this plant has potent sap that will produce a serious rash on the unwary. Growing on the hummocks and between the larch are various species of ferns, and, if the season is right, wild orchids. The occasional pitcher plant is also present. There used to be many more of each species, but collection by local students and others before the area was protected decimated the populations. The species are slowly recovering, so enjoy the brilliant plants, but photograph only! Shortly, the open water "eye" of the bog comes into view with a dock that leads a short way from the main boardwalk. Sit quietly here and note the concentric rings of vegetation around the slowly closing eye. Bogs have no mud, only peat (plant material in varying stages of decay). Note the large bullfrog tadpoles swimming about the dock. They normally wouldn't survive here, but over the years the water has become less acidic, and frogs have colonized the open water. If you visit in fall, this spot is particularly scenic, especially when an incredible blue sky and golden-hued tamaracks are reflected in the quiet waters of Volo Bog.

You may also hear the primordial "rattle" call of sandhill cranes. These large wetland birds are seldom visible, except for flyovers, but they regularly occur in the marshy fringes of the bog. A short trek through dense shrubs will lead out and up, and your bog experience is ended. For the more adventurous, a three-mile trail circles the entire glacial depression and provides views from above of the bog community. Here you might glimpse various waterfowl and other wetland birds that use this most unusual of Illinois habitats. One could travel to the far northern United States, even into Canada to experience bog communities, but Illinois offers a great opportunity for exploration only a short drive northwest of Chicago.

CENTRAL

CHAPTER 20

Emiquon Preserve

For an hour we wait and watch an ever-growing "oil slick" of white and gray birds—gathering, gathering, gathering. . . . We are not the only ones waiting—at least a half dozen juvenile bald eagles are watching, standing on the ice just outside the expanding slick of birds. An adult eagle flies in, and chaos ensues—twisting, turning, and swirling—a living snow globe of snow geese.

—Susan Post, January 2012

ALONG THE WESTERN EDGE of the Illinois River near Havana is an area called Emiquon—a name used by the Native Americans who once lived here. It translates roughly to *squash*, a reference to the plant that grew along the area. As you cross the Illinois River from Havana, you may note a hint of wildness; a bald eagle roosts in the trees overlooking the many barges waiting to be loaded with Illinois corn. Flooded ditches and ponds occur along Route 78/97. Before long, glimmering like a mirage, a huge body of water appears—the heart of Emiquon. Known as Thompson Lake in the nineteenth and early twentieth centuries, it was an immense cornfield not so long ago.

Dickson Mounds Museum lies perched on a hill at the western edge of Emiquon. A century of archeological studies here have documented Native American activity in the area. For more than twelve thousand years Native Americans took advantage of the biological productivity of the river. By the late seventeenth century, French explorers, the first Europeans to travel up the Illinois River, were awed by the fertility of the river valley and the abundance and diversity of wildlife. One catfish caught in the river served as supper for twenty-two men! As late as the early twentieth century, this area was one of the premier fishing and waterfowl hunting areas in the Midwest.

The source of the river's phenomenal productivity was its large floodplain. At Emiquon, just upriver from its confluence with the Spoon River, the Illinois flows through the former valley of the ancient Mississippi and Mahomet (ancestor to the Ohio) Rivers. These relatively large rivers, and the meltwaters from retreating glaciers, eroded an especially broad floodplain—as wide as seven miles—that

Snow and blue geese "darkening the sky"

Emiquon waterfowl panorama

Coupled green darners with female laying eggs

the present Illinois River occupies from here to its confluence with the Mississippi near Grafton.

Over time, channel meanderings between the bluffs created a mosaic of different landforms on the floodplain, including side channels, sloughs, lakes, and seasonally dry land. This multitude of landforms supported abundant, diverse plant and animal communities, such as wet prairies, marshes, and bottomland hardwood forests.

In the *Sportsman's and General Guide of 1877,* the area was described as "'bottom lands,' and generally heavily timbered, but in some places open, except brush, flags [wild iris], weeds, etc. On each side, back a convenient distance for hunting, lie about twenty lakes, sloughs and ponds, varying from three miles and half down to the ordinary pond. . . . The most prominent are Thompson's." Thompson Lake was considered among the Illinois River's most beautiful backwater lakes. Its shallow waters produced three hundred pounds of fish per acre per year; the lake was known as the "Inland Fishing Capital of the World." Thompson Lake was also feeding grounds for migrating ducks. In 1893, one hunter described the scene: "We were surprised at the great numbers of water fowl. There were simply square acres of the lake's surface covered with Ducks, Geese and Brant . . . thousands of Ducks and Geese to take to wing; the air was black in every direction with great circling flocks." In 1894, President Benjamin Harrison hunted waterfowl here.

Unfortunately, during the first half of the twentieth century hopes for economic gain dramatically changed the Illinois River Valley. The city of Chicago diverted Lake Michigan waters down the Illinois as a relatively cheap method of transporting waste materials (in other words, sewage) away from the city's Lake Michigan water supply. In addition to polluting the water far downriver, the diversion raised water levels and decimated much of the native flora. Also, by the 1930s about one-half (nearly two hundred thousand acres) of the Illinois River's floodplain had also been isolated from the river by levees, used mostly to create and protect agricultural lands.

Simultaneously, agricultural and urban development along the river basin destroyed wetlands in the uplands, and by the 1960s the native plant

Nesting pied-billed grebe

and animal communities that had helped sustain both Native American and the contemporary river communities had been severely degraded.

Such was the case at Emiquon; between 1917 and 1922, the Thompson Lake Drainage and Levee District built levees and ditches that separated the river from its floodplain. Bottomland forests were cleared and the land planted to crops. Thompson Lake was converted to agriculture and intensively farmed for the remainder of the century.

In May 2000, The Nature Conservancy's Illinois chapter purchased 7,527 acres in the Emiquon area. The property included nearly six thousand acres of floodplain and the bed of the former Thompson Lake, today isolated from the river by more than twelve miles of levee. The primary purpose was to restore natural ecological processes and habitats to promote and sustain the native species and natural communities once found in this region of the Illinois River and to use this restoration as a model that could be replicated up and down the Illinois River. This would become one of the country's largest wetland restoration efforts.

During the fall of 2004, the last harvest of grain from the old Thompson Lake bed was a cause for celebration, as the machinery created a dusty ballet of pick, shell, and pour. The observant noticed a great blue heron flying low over the fresh stubble, while a tan mayfly with extra long cerci (tails) rested on a broken corn stalk. The flat, unending cornfield was gone; left in its place was nothing but infinite possibilities. The restoration of Emiquon had begun. By 2008, three hundred thousand native trees had been replanted and eight thousand pounds of grass seed spread about. When the pumps were turned off that helped to drain water and keep the area farmable, a natural lake sprang to life as the old lakebed filled with water. Native plants slowly reemerged naturally, but fish could not. As a result, nearly two million native fish were restocked. Within a few months the birds returned, not just thousands of ducks, but eagles,

Greater yellowlegs

ospreys, and avocets. Something most people don't need to consider during a restoration is what to do with large quantities of concrete and asphalt. About twenty acres of concrete remained on the property—a legacy of livestock operations—and most of the material was recycled and reused in concrete walls, riprap, and as road top. Due to the success of the restoration efforts, Emiquon has recently been designated as a Wetland of International Significance under the Ramsar Convention.

Today, a visit to Emiquon provides a remarkable wildlife viewing experience. Indeed, waterfowl once again darken the sky with their massive numbers. Shorebirds haunt the water's edge in search of aquatic life that has recolonized this former cornfield. Dragonflies patrol the wetland vegetation lining the various marshes that help make up Emiquon—green darners, Carolina saddlebags, various species of clubtails, and any number of species of the ubiquitous pond skimmers. American white pelicans form vast rafts in the distance, but often they are more easily observed as they soar overhead in black-and-white-on-blue-sky, V-shaped formations. Herons and egrets have returned in numbers and provide white, blue, and black contrasts against the rippling, shallow water. Red-winged blackbirds patrol American lotus colonies, and the list goes on, seemingly endless and boundless. A viewing platform and interpretive signs help visitors understand both the current state of Emiquon and its history. The Emiquon National Fish and Wildlife Refuge (adjacent), Chautauqua National Wildlife Refuge, and Spring Lake Wildlife Conservation Area (across the river), are nearby, and together they form a large area of diverse wetland habitats.

A visit to the neighboring Dixon Mounds Museum and a trip to its upper-floor viewing platform provides a panoramic view of Emiquon. With a little imagination it can be a solemn experience, one that early explorers likely had as they stood atop the nearby Native American mounds and surveyed this vast, watery, wildlife paradise.

CHAPTER 21

Forest Park Nature Preserve

Taking advantage of the "listening points," not only did I enjoy silence, but I heard distant turkey gobbling, an exuberant Carolina wren, and the high-pitched squeaks of an eastern chipmunk.

—Susan Post, March 2009

THE EARLY EUROPEAN explorers of the Illinois River valley would have taken a water route—a maze of interconnected waterways, backwater lakes, and dead-end sloughs. Near the area that was to become Peoria, massive, forested bluffs were surely noted on both the east and west flanks of the large river floodplain. Mysterious, difficult to access, and wondrously diverse, these high bluffs, interspersed with deep, cool ravines, were the site of the first permanent European settlement in Illinois—Fort Pimiteoui (1691). Later, a town established around the fort, today known as Peoria, incorporated in 1845.

The river has changed, the landscape has been forever altered, and graceful homes now abound on the bluffs overlooking the current permutation of the Illinois River—large, lake-sized pools maintained by navigation dams that keep the channel's depths appropriate for one of the busiest waterways in North America. One might think that experiencing the region's natural habitats is a thing of the past, relegated to perusing the memoirs of French explorers René-Robert Cavelier and Henri de Tonti. But such is not the case, for a visit to Forest Park Nature Preserve, located along the bluffs and surrounded by the city of Peoria, provides access to one of the more interesting landscapes found in the Illinois River valley. The Forest Park Nature Center provides a good introduction to the area.

After hiking any of the numerous, hilly, thigh-burning trails in the preserve, it should become evident why explorers chose the water route through this area. The bluffs and ravines are cloaked with oak-hickory forests that have persisted here for more than eight thousand years. After the Wisconsin Glacier receded, the forest that developed was open and somewhat

Wild ginger expanse in fall woods

Mating acorn weevils

Female polyphemus moth laying eggs

park-like, maintained and shaped by periodic fires. These fires opened up most of the central Illinois landscape and facilitated the formation of tallgrass prairie. Here, the rugged topography prevented the fires from burning hot enough to kill the thick-barked oaks and hickories. Instead, they burned slowly through the leaf litter and promoted the growth of native wildflowers and grasses.

Forest Park is a fine example of the original vegetation that once cloaked the Illinois River bluffs. The rich woods, topping the relatively parallel ridges, are dominated by white oak and shagbark hickory, with an understory of hop hornbeam, gray dogwood, and black cherry. A sparse, herbaceous layer, growing in open areas in the forest, consists of pussytoes (a host plant for the American painted lady butterfly), the aptly named bottlebrush grass, and golden Alexanders. Along moister slopes—many of which are relatively steep—red oak replaces white oak, and sugar maple adds its exuberant color to the otherwise burnished bronze and rust of fall hues. Deer and many small mammals typical of central Illinois woodlands inhabit the area, and more than one hundred species of birds have been observed here. A short hike across the highway from the nature center on the Pimiteoui

Eastern chipmunk gathering nuts

Trail leads upward through the woods to a series of curious openings that face west and southwest and are devoid of trees. These habitats are called hill prairies, and they typify the landscapes found on the rough topography occurring in western Illinois along the state's major rivers. The Mississippi, the Illinois, and even the Sangamon have extensive hill prairie systems. Hill prairies are islands of prairie vegetation maintained by their hot, dry aspects (exposed to the sun for most or all of the day) and by fire. In today's world, unfortunately, these habitats are changing with the encroachment of woody vegetation from the surrounding forest. The main culprit has been the cessation of natural and human-created fires (by Native Americans) over the last several hundred years. These periodic burns kept the area open and promoted the combination of prairie species found here. The hill prairies found in Forest Park are the result of stewardship activities that include removal of woody vegetation by staff and volunteers, and prescribed fire.

Unlike some areas in Illinois, where unique species draw visitors to the nature contained there, this area is worth visiting and exploring because of its history. It's also an island of natural landscape in an otherwise heavily urban and industrialized landscape that continually offers surprise encounters with spring wildflowers (large expanses of wild ginger along the ravine bottoms) and native wildlife (a family of red foxes along the edge of a hill prairie). Finally, a visit here provides the opportunity to view a quiet panorama of rugged, forested land that grades into an expansive river valley ending at the distant bluffs on the eastern edge of the floodplain.

CHAPTER 22

Funks Grove

For a few days, blue-eyed Marys and Virginia bluebells surround and lap at the bases of the large maples, engulfing large, fallen limbs like the waves of the sea. When the "water" recedes, it leaves in its wake only withered stems and wood nettle.

—Susan Post, April 2012

MANY PEOPLE WHO VISIT Funks Grove do so at maple sugaring time—late winter into early spring—for the sweet treat much more indicative of New England than Illinois. Even though New England has the seeming monopoly on creating maple syrup, the tradition at Funks Grove, named after the Funk Family, has been around since 1824. Located south of Bloomington and just north of the small town of McLean, Funks Grove owes its existence to the same factors that allowed for the development of tallgrass prairie in Illinois. After the Wisconsin Glaciers left Illinois, a series of habitats emerged, beginning with tundra and proceeding through spruce/fir forests to mixed hardwood forests, and eventually tallgrass prairie. This sequence occurred over about seven thousand to eight thousand years, with prairie formation taking place when the weather patterns changed to hotter and drier during the Hypsithermal Interval (a period of global warming that occurred between seven thousand and five thousand years ago). As massive fires swept across the Illinois landscape during and after this period, they tilted the balance from forest to prairie and savanna. In areas where the forests received a measure of protection from fires (on the lee side of streams, on slopes, or in areas too wet to burn), the trees persisted, often in isolated prairie groves. Here the tree and understory diversity remained intact, and when the first Europeans settled in central Illinois, they noted these unique groves and often settled in them. The 1879 history of McLean County described the grove: "Unlike most timber along the little creeks, which is usually small, stunted growth of oak and basswood, the timber along Sugar Creek at this point is of a heavy growth of walnut, maple, and oak."

Expanse of prairie trillium and ramp

A "sea" of Virginia bluebells

Today, Funks Grove is one of the largest expanses of old growth forest in Illinois. Once extending more than three thousand acres, over the years the forest has been reduced, but it still contains more than one thousand acres of land that retains much of its ancestral character. Some tracts of forest in Funks Grove are of nature-preserve quality (for example the Thaddeus Stubblefield Grove Nature Preserve), supporting large, old trees, a healthy shrub layer, and, most notably, what is perhaps the best spring wildflower show in central Illinois.

The forest consists of thirty-three species of trees, dominated by sugar maple but closely followed by white oak. Several dozen trees are very large, with canopies towering 120 feet, and trunks ranging from four to five feet across. They vary in age from 250 to 400 years. Other than for the maple sugar, Funks Grove devotees come for the spring flower show. The most commonly encountered species, often blooming in remarkable numbers, include white trout lily, mayapple, impressive displays of Virginia bluebell that tint the forest floor a pastel blue, bloodroot, Dutchman's breeches, hepatica, blue phlox, and bellwort. Less commonly encountered species that require more searching include snow trillium, squirrel corn, blue-eyed Mary, Jack-in-the-pulpit, and the seep-inhabiting skunk cabbage and marsh marigold. The seep, located along Timber Creek, is easily accessible by

Sugaring the "old fashioned" way

a short trail that originates in the parking area for Sugar Grove Nature Center, which is a great place to begin your exploration as it features exhibits, materials about the area, and trail maps.

Spring bird watching at Funks is excellent, as many migrants stop here to rest or to breed. The bird list includes such notables as woodcock, various thrushes, the wet-forest-nesting wood duck, numerous hawks and owls, the brilliant scarlet tanager, indigo buntings, and house wrens. Summer is a time to explore the prairie restorations that surround the nature center and to enjoy displays of typical tallgrass prairie plants, an appropriate counterpoint to the surrounding prairie grove. The prairie supports populations of various interesting insects and butterflies. Summer flowers lure swallowtails, red-spotted purples, and red admiral butterflies from the forest to nectar on bee balm and various sunflowers. Pollinators feast on the nectar and pollen in flowers while trying to avoid the sometimes numerous yellow crab spiders that await unsuspecting prey. Numbers of large, showy garden spiders lace together the plant stems with intricately woven orb webs. These are best viewed in early morning when outlined with crystal-like droplets of dew. Late summer brings milkweed pods, often supporting family aggregations of large milkweed bugs, their black and orange color warning away potential predators. They, like the milkweed-feeding monarch caterpillars, are toxic. Fall speaks for itself, as the preponderance of sugar maples can only lead to a spectacle of yellows that turn Funks Grove into a veritable fairyland. Visit on a warm, overcast, rainy day when color is at its most dramatic, and experience one of the best fall color displays in the state.

So, turn that weekend or weekday visit into more than just a quest to satisfy a sweet tooth, and explore a grand, relict landscape. Funks Grove is likely the best remaining example of a prairie grove left in Illinois, and perhaps the Midwest; a visit during any season will be a rewarding and surprising glimpse of wild Illinois.

CHAPTER 23

Kankakee Sands

Pembroke Savanna Nature Preserve & Iroquois County Conservation Area

Our car lunges and lurches on the sandy road. I'm thinking we're going to get stuck. We make it to a pull-in and begin to climb the highest point in the county—a giant sand dune. The view is amazing: widely spaced oaks, pink blazing stars with numerous butterflies floating on the breeze—monarchs, cloudless sulfurs, and red-spotted purples. The landscape appears to be untouched by civilization. We explore, yet all too soon we must go back, taking with us the sand in our shoes, a few sand burs clinging to socks, and images of Illinois as it once was.

—Susan Post, Pembroke Savanna Nature Preserve, August 2004

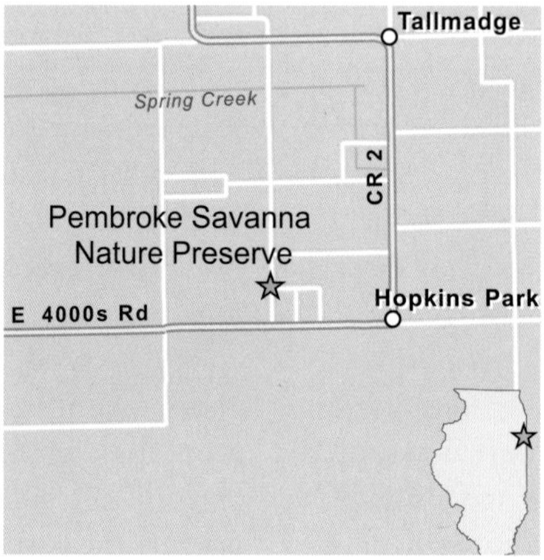

LIKE A TENTACLE stretching across the sea of grass, the sands of the Kankakee basin jut into the prairie to form the Greater Kankakee Sands ecosystem, a region encompassed by Kankakee and Iroquois Counties. The Kankakee Torrent, a flood produced by the receding Wisconsin Glacier, shaped this landscape and created its deep sand deposits. While most of the area's swamps and marshes have disappeared, the sand load of the torrent is still evident in Kankakee and Iroquois Counties. This region is one of the principal sand areas in Illinois. Here lies the ancient bed of a large glacial lake. Dunes, some reaching almost seven hundred feet above sea level, and swales (interdunal low spots) characterize the area. Sand savannas and sand and shrub prairies are some of the interesting communities found here, while the sandy-bottomed streams support fish species that are rare or found nowhere else in Illinois. The Kankakee River, the artery coursing through this sandy tentacle, has one of the most diverse and abundant mussel populations in the state.

The Kankakee River valley is relatively flat with low, sandy ridges of glacial outwash. Before the land was drained and cultivated, sand prairies and marshes were common along its banks. The Kankakee River valley is divided into two basins: the upper basin in Indiana, and the lower basin in Illinois. The upper basin was

Pembroke Savanna in spring

Eastern hognose snake

Great spangled fritillaries on colic root

Iroquois County Conservation Area sand forest with butterfly weed

Iroquois County Conservation Area shrub prairie panorama

more-or-less level land and consisted of wetlands (swamps and marshes); it was called the Grand Kankakee Marsh. The lower basin was also flat, but no swamps of any magnitude occurred here, and the banks of the river were high enough to prevent overflow. The Kankakee River is unusual in Illinois as it flows on or near limestone bedrock. Thin sand, gravel, and small areas of silt overlie this bedrock. In Illinois, the Kankakee flows as a naturally meandering stream. In Indiana, it was straightened and channelized to drain the great marsh.

As forest trees slowly encroached upon the sand, a transition community between forest and prairie eventually developed—a sand savanna. Sand savannas were maintained by fire in presettlement times, but they were not overly burned due to their special topography—undulating dunes interspersed with low, marshy areas. The seedlings of only a few tree species were able to withstand the extreme conditions of the shifting sand—the hot surface layer and the almost total lack of protection against winter winds. Oaks—black, white, and pin—dominate the Kankakee Sands. Understory plants include cream wild indigo, wild lupine, and starry false Solomon's-seal. Pembroke Savanna Nature Preserve is one of the state's best examples of a sand savanna.

In addition to sand savannas and sand prairies, shrub prairies occur here. Shrub prairies are a mix of shrubs and wildflowers, with mosses usually forming a continuous ground cover. These prairies occur on acidic, sandy soil and are limited to areas of both northern and north-central Illinois. Look for the shrubs black chokecherry, low-bush blueberry, and black huckleberry, interspersed with big and little bluestem, lance-leaved violet, colic root, cinnamon fern, common milkweed, and dayflower.

Much of this region was once covered with colorful prairies and the shifting sand stabilized by

Mating net-winged beetles

the grasses—porcupine, June, and big and little bluestem. Forbs, however, provided the color and interest. Each spring, mounds of lavender bird's-foot violet painted the hillsides blue, while in late summer the hillsides blushed, tinted pink with blazing star. At Pembroke Savanna, this is still true. Although the sand prairies receive the same amounts of heat, light, rainfall, and wind as the rest of the state, they experience larger variations in temperature from day to night and from surface to subsoil; the water-holding capacity of the sandy soil is also very low. In open areas, the surface sand is constantly shifting, sometimes forming dunes or blowouts (areas where the sand and vegetation are scooped out and blown away by the wind). To survive the sand, plants have evolved several strategies. The leaves of many of the plants are narrow and small, thereby reducing the amount of surface exposed to the sun. Leaves may have a protective covering of silvery hairs or scales, giving them a grayish-green color. Perennials possess deep roots that develop in response to the limited supply of water and frequently grow in tufts or bunches to reduce exposure to the wind. Plants such as the prickly-pear cactus—with thick, succulent stems—form mats that grow close to the sand and tend to spread over a larger area each year.

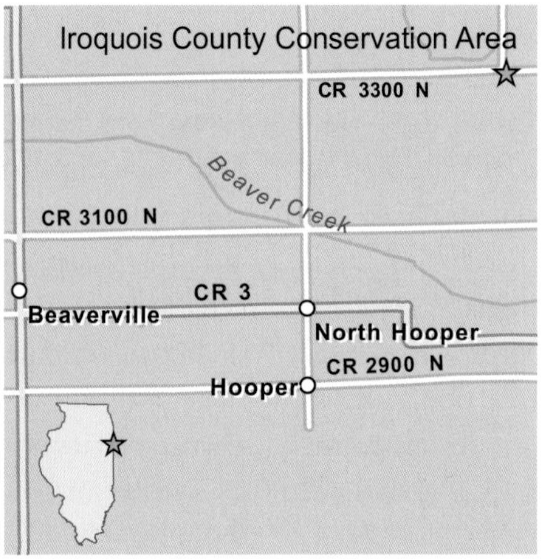

At Iroquois County Conservation Area, interesting remnants of a northern bog habitat still exist. A diligent search through the tall grasses can yield a low, wet area carpeted with sphagnum moss and drying peat. Viewed from ground level, the rounded, sticky-leaved, carnivorous sundews glisten in the sun, each clear drop of liquid on the leaves a lethal trap for some small, unsuspecting insect. Scanning across the adjacent wet sand prairie, one sees fairy rings of cinnamon fern interspersed with masses of colic root, false wild indigo, and marsh phlox in early summer. Blazing star and goldenrod prevail in late summer and fall. Here, also, note that about 10 percent of the blazing stars are sparkling white, not pink. During most

Soldier beetles on white morph of blazing star

years, the wet, shrubby prairie is alive with butterflies—Aphrodite, great spangled, silver-bordered, meadow, variegated, and regal fritillaries—and most can be seen in a single day! For those more botanically inclined, spring yields six species of violet: common blue, arrow-leaved, lance-leaved, bird's-foot, sand, and primrose. Again, all can be discovered in a single visit. Across the road from the parking area stands Hooper Branch Savanna, an example of a sand savanna. A mile loop trail leads through a dramatic landscape of large oaks interspersed with shrubs and prairie vegetation.

To a biologist, a trip through this area is like walking into a smorgasbord of biodiversity. Exploration reveals a landscape with very little human disturbance—only rolling, sandy hills punctuated with black oaks and the occasional pin and Hill's oak. Ornate box turtles corkscrew themselves into the sand to regulate their body temperature, regal fritillary males flit low through the vegetation, awaiting the later emerging females, and a blur across the sand materializes into a slender glass lizard. Everywhere the mounds of pocket gophers appear like tiny, ancient volcanoes, long dormant with their vents sealed over. One encounters the familiar, but scattered about are the unusual, the unfamiliar, and even organisms that elicit the response, "What is this doing here?" This area of Illinois is unique, having a relatively large number of species of plants and animals (more than thirty) with unusual distribution patterns that are either separated from the main population or that extend away from the main population. These species include pumpkin ash, swamp cottonwood, summer tanager, and orange-fringed orchid.

All things considered, this area of Illinois can be described by a single word—unique! The mix of odd species, unusual habitats, and a landscape still shaped by its not-so-distant glacial heritage makes for a region of the state that is, and should continue to be, the focus of nature lovers everywhere.

CHAPTER 24

Ballard Nature Center

Today, Ballard Nature Center gave me the blues. A Baltimore oriole chasing a blue jay, bluebirds flitting above yellow, brown-eyed Susans, and blue, narrow-bodied damselflies lined up on emergent grasses, bodies pointed toward the sun.

—Susan Post, July 2011

MENTION "LEGACY" and many different scenarios come to mind—perhaps long-term help for the less fortunate, a children's hospital wing, or even a long history of political activism. The gift of Ernie Ballard and family, however, left a legacy of nature—210 acres of land for habitat restoration and ample funds for the construction of a nature center. Here, future generations (adults and children) could learn about and benefit from the conservation practices implemented by Ernie during his lifetime. The site, located between Altamont and Effingham, just off old Route 40, represents a landscape formed during the Illinoian Glacial Age (125,000 to 25,000 years ago), the glacial epoch that preceded the Wisconsin. The landscape is more rolling, and the streams have had time to entrench (in other words, develop valleys, some relatively steep-sided) cloaked in a diverse forest. Plants grow on a hard, gray clay soil (materials deposited by the glaciers) that tends to hold moisture. Most of the prairies found here are called "gray prairies," due to these soil characteristics. Many of the forests are oak flatwoods, and because of the dense, clay soils, the trees only live around 150 to 200 years before they blow down.

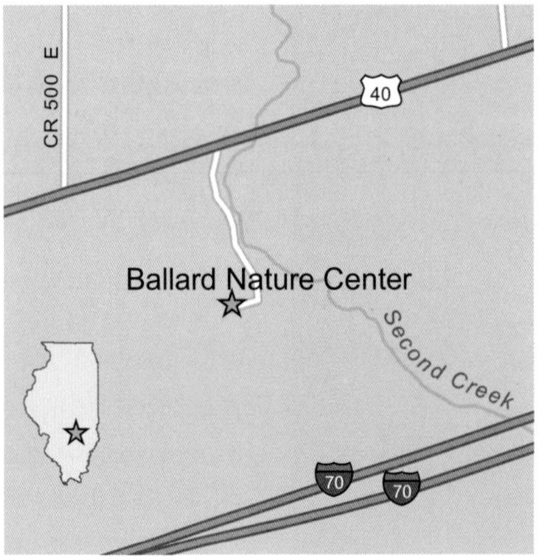

Their root systems are shallow, as they cannot penetrate the dense clay and tend to spread out. The trees inevitably tip over when they reach a certain size. But visitors do not come to Ballard to be entranced with this remote history; they come for the immediate—the chance to walk through a remarkable prairie restoration with its diverse flowers, stroll by a series of large, created ponds that are patrolled by a diversity of dragonflies, or hike along the cool, sometimes rugged trails through deep forest. When originally purchased by Ballard,

Wetland panorama

Resting green darner dragonfly

much of this landscape was farmland, interspersed with forest. He soon contacted various state and federal agencies for advice on erosion control and practices to improve the quality of the forest. Over time, Ernie's vision for the land grew.

Today, Ballard is an outdoor laboratory for habitat creation and restoration. The activities have included formation of a nine-acre, shallow-water wetland—a haven for frogs and several species of dragonflies: green darners, both black and Carolina saddlebags, white-tails, and even the rare comet darner shows up on occasion. Additional wetlands were soon built to imitate the potholes of pre-European settlement of Illinois. A board member com-

Mating long-horned milkweed beetles

mented, "The response by waterfowl, marsh birds, insects, reptiles, and amphibians to these newly constructed wetlands has been tremendous." As you walk the wetlands, be alert for dive-bombing red-winged blackbirds, a female wood duck herding her young across the water, or various sized turtle heads peering out of the water like periscopes. The restoration of prairies and savannas involved planting grasses and wildflowers in late winter, and later adding fire-tolerant trees (oaks and hickories) to create a savanna. A walk through the prairies in summer is a gratifying experience as the diversity of plants—purple and yellow coneflowers, blazing star, rattlesnake master, prairie clovers, bee balm, and even cardinal flowers—attracts hummingbirds, numerous butterflies, and various other insects. The prairie, in essence, is a naturalist's dreamscape. If the prairie becomes too warm on a summer's day, or if you visit in spring, head into the maze of woodland trails. Each spring provides a nice showing of typical spring flora, including wild ginger, spring beauty, Dutchman's breeches,

Expanse of Ballard prairie restoration

and dwarf larkspur. In summer, the up-and-down, shaded trails through the woods provide a cool respite from the wide-open expanses of the prairies and wetlands. Unnoticed by most, the woods must be doing well, as several years ago a nighttime black-lighting excursion into the forest (using ultraviolet lights to attract insects) yielded large numbers of mantisflies (unique insects that look like a cross between a preying mantis and a wasp and that are parasites of spiders), luna moths, and a magnificent royal walnut moth!

While Ballard's original goal was to provide viable habitats for common species, with little emphasis on rare or declining species, rarities have shown up and provide exclamation points that only add to the bounty of *nature experiences* available at Ballard. Nowhere else in Illinois can you have more viewing opportunities in such a short time. The location is a delight and a treat for all lovers of the outdoors and for those who desire intimate encounters with the plants and animals of Illinois.

CHAPTER 25

Along the Vermilion and Wabash Rivers

This is on the borders of the "Grand Prairie," and here is a most delightful country. This township is well watered by the Vermilion River and its tributary streams, and is rolling and uneven for this country.

—Chester Loomis, *A Journey on Horseback through the Great West in 1825*

AN OLD ADAGE proclaimed that in pioneer times a squirrel could travel from the east coast of the United States to Illinois without ever touching the ground. While the great deciduous forest that once blanketed the eastern United States is now mostly a patchwork of fragmented woodlots, remnants of this once vast, forested landscape still exist. The western edge of this great forest, now stretching from Vermilion County in east-central Illinois, south along the Wabash River to its junction with the Ohio River, barely reached into Illinois. It can still be experienced, however, with visits to Kickapoo State Park, Forest Glen Preserve, Robeson Hills Nature Preserve, and Beall Woods State Park. These areas provide intact forest ecosystems that are high quality. Kickapoo State Park also contains the Middle Fork of the Vermilion River, Illinois's only Wild and Scenic River, while Forest Glen offers Forest Glen Seep Nature Preserve, a unique wetland with plants reminiscent of the far north. These locations are all strung like precious beads along the eastern border of Illinois. Historically, this area contained the Forest of the Wabash, the trailing edge of the eastern deciduous forest. In this relatively narrow corridor in Illinois grew some of the largest deciduous trees in the United States. Botanists characterize this habitat as a mixed, mesophytic hardwood forest (many deciduous tree species growing on moist soils). In fact, some of the best tree-growing conditions in the United States occurred here, and giant examples of sycamore, Shumard oak, pecan, and others were documented in the 1870s by Smithsonian biologist Robert Ridgway. While he authored the first *Birds of Illinois*, he also commented extensively on the trees of the area, and old photographs show Ridgway and crew standing in front of trees that were at least seventeen feet across. Ridgway wrote, "If viewed from a high bluff the forest presented the appearance of a compact, level sea of green, almost endless; tree tops swaying in the passing breeze and the general level broken by occasional giant trees which rear their massive heads to overlook the surrounding miles of forest." The only trees larger than these were the redwoods of the West Coast. Tree diversity, at least for the temperate zone, is immense, with between eighty and ninety species occurring here. Perhaps the most distinct of these

Middlefork Woods Nature Preserve fall color

species is the American beech, a tree that can grow very large and one whose smooth, gray bark is as irresistible as wet concrete: the bark is often disfigured by carved initials that remain for the life of the tree.

Kickapoo State Park—Middle Fork Woods Nature Preserve

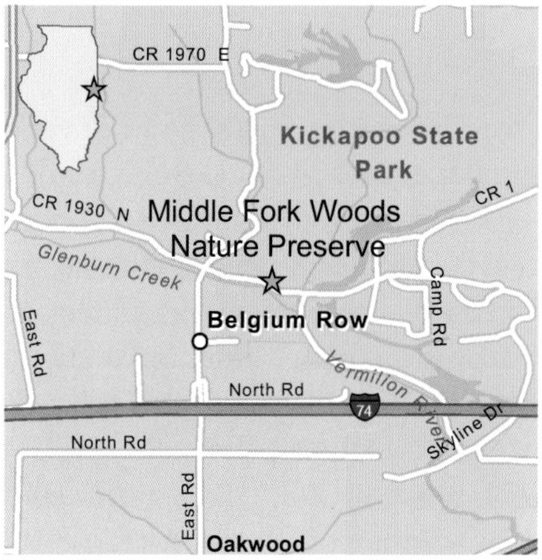

Kickapoo State Park, the first state park in the United States created on scarred, turn-of-the-century strip-mined lands, has somewhat recovered over the last half-century. Most visitors to the area enjoy the many clear, deep-water ponds (fishing, canoeing, even scuba-diving), hike, bike, or run the many miles of trails through the hilly forest, or canoe the Middle Fork of the Vermilion River. Out-of-the-way places, though, allow visitors to experience the forest solitude that once blanketed most of the Wabash Border Division, a region that reaches its northernmost extent in Vermilion County. Middle Fork Woods Nature Preserve, on the western edge of Kickapoo, is easily accessible by a hike up the bluff on an old roadbed. The area is upland forest with ephemeral pools that become raucous breeding grounds for various amphibians each spring. Tiny spring peepers compete with chorus frogs for calling perches in the debris-filled pools, while the din of larger wood frogs provides an ear-splitting concert in early spring. Numerous other amphibians call this area home, as well as more than forty species of mammals. The forest is a mix of black and

Calling spring peeper frog in ephemeral pond

Shooting stars in open woodland

white oaks on the uplands, basswood and sugar maple on the slopes. This is what the land looked like before coal mining. Occasional examples of American beech dot the preserve, and each spring the understory is filmy yellow from the blooms of thousands of spicebush, a shrub that is the food plant of the spicebush swallowtail butterfly. If the adult is beautiful, the caterpillar is downright dramatic, resembling the head of a rough green snake. Spring is also the season for wildflowers, and Middle Fork Preserve has an impressive population of prairie shooting stars, growing along the tops of the ravines and extending into the valleys. Although thought of as a prairie plant, this species also inhabits open woods. Each autumn, the contrast between yellow sugar maples, golden oaks, and ochre-leaved beech make this area a fall spectacle. A glimpse of a gray fox or the sight of large tadpoles ruffling the surface of the ponds makes this an unforgettable yet easy getaway from the cornfields of central Illinois.

Middle Fork of the Vermilion River

Just a short walk from the Middle Fork Woods Nature Preserve parking area, and across the bridge, leads to Illinois's wild and scenic Middle Fork of the Vermilion River. Well known for its canoeing opportunities and forest-lined bluffs, the river is also home to a bevy of creatures less familiar but nevertheless significant as they inhabit streams

Mating wood frogs in ephemeral pond

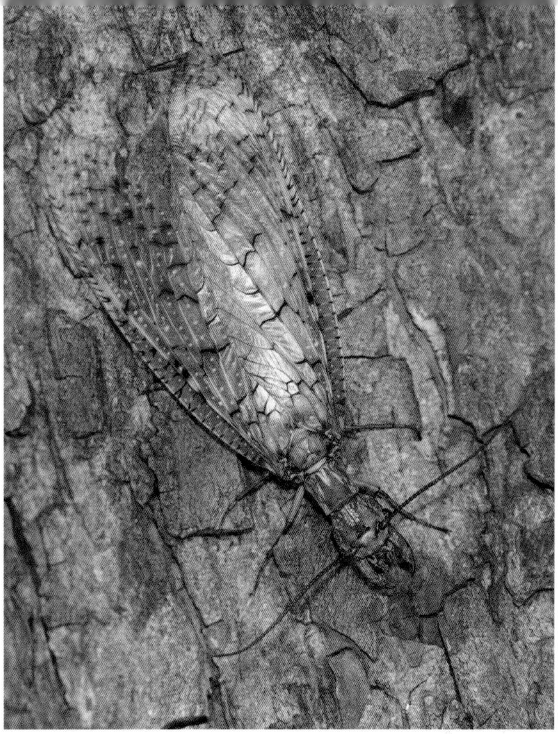

Female dobsonfly

Cruiser dragonfly larva in
Middlefork of Vermilion River

Winter stonefly adult on bridge

Middlefork of the Vermilion River (upstream)

that are clear, free flowing, and gravel or rock-bottomed—a rarity in Illinois. Turning over rocks in the streambed may yield weird, otherworldly insect larvae—dragonflies, dobsonflies, water tiger beetles—or perhaps a cerulean flash of a blue-breasted darter. Large dragonflies patrol the banks, including green darners and emerald-eyed river cruisers. An uncommon damselfly, the ruby-spot, also is a familiar encounter. If you visit in winter, stop and look for winter stoneflies as you cross the concrete bridge. They are the exception to the rule that insect activity ceases with cold weather. They appear as dark, tiny tubes with six legs, scurrying along the sides of the bridge. Against the cement, they look like defects in the concrete.

Forest Glen Preserve—Forest Glen Seep and Russell M. Duffin Nature Preserves

A drive south from Kickapoo State Park, with some wending through country roads, leads to Forest Glen Preserve. The site is well known by locals who use it extensively for picnicking and camping, but the real draw of Forest Glen is the nature preserves contained within its boundaries. One of the most distinctive and certainly least visited is Forest Glen Seep, a mile walk from the nearest parking area—the trek is well worth the effort. Seeps are wetlands characterized by saturated soil. They are usually found at the base of a hill where groundwater that has percolated downward through the soil reaches an impervious layer (either clay or bedrock) and flows outward, creating an area that is always wet. Seeps may be basic or acidic, depending upon the materials through which the groundwater flows. The seep here tends toward the basic side of the pH scale. As early as late winter, the partially frozen or snow-covered wetland comes alive with the unusual skunk cabbage, a plant that is restricted to seep habitats and is the first to bloom during an Illinois calendar year. Skunk cabbage sends up a succulent, maroon and yellow structure that resembles a hood (called a spathe), which actually generates its own heat to melt its way into the late winter landscape. Each spathe contains the flowering parts (called spadix) that attract flesh flies for pollination. The fact that they smell (and resemble) rotting meat just increases the plant's odd lifestyle. As spring advances, the shriveling spathes and spadices disappear and are replaced by knee-high, bright green, caladium-like leaves, some of the largest leaves of any Illinois plant. But the show is not over; a short time later in the spring the seep becomes a golden carpet of marsh marigold, a buttercup whose petals seem to have a special, metallic glint that catches the sunlight and causes them to sparkle. This plant is often associated with the north woods of the United States and Canada. By late summer, Joe-Pye weed, several yellow sunflowers, and the uncommon swamp thistle are blooming. The area may even be dry enough to walk through. Why visit a seep in the heat of summer? Because here,

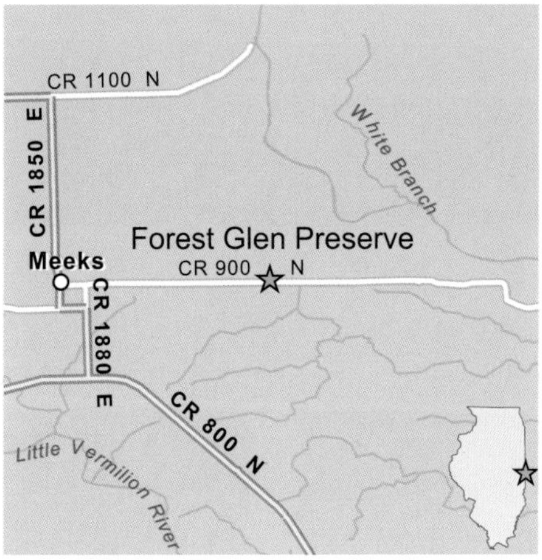

Marsh marigold in early spring

Forest Glen Seep Nature Preserve summer panorama

Skunk cabbage in late winter

Female black swallowtail

Russell M. Duffin Nature Preserve

Mayapple in American beech buttresses

Pair of cedar waxwings

Male and female polyphemus moths

on any given day, you may encounter twenty to thirty species of butterflies, ruby-throated hummingbirds, and, if you're lucky, all six species of Illinois's swallowtails!

A short distance after entering Forest Glen, note the signs for the Russell M. Duffin Nature Preserve, complete with a small parking area. If the term "steeply dissected terrain" is foreign to you, a hike through this preserve will certainly be educational. The area is part of the watershed of the Vermilion River, and the rich, beech-maple forest is a climax community growing on a series of ridges and steep-sided valleys. The forest is a fragment of one that once extended all the way to the East Coast but is found in Illinois only in its extreme eastern and southern parts. Most Illinoisans are unfamiliar with a *climax forest*—one that has escaped disturbance by outside forces long enough to have settled into a condition of relative stability, where composition and structure don't change much over long periods. Most woodlands in Illinois have been cut-over many times, and the "typical forest" has relatively small trees, all about the same size, with a thick, impenetrable understory of shrubs (mostly maples or perhaps exotic and invasive honeysuckles). It doesn't take long, however, to fully appreciate a climax forest. Walking through Duffin Nature Preserve, you can see more than forty species of trees—many large examples towering overhead—a park-like, diverse shrub layer and a verdant layer of spring wildflowers. More than 150 species of birds have been recorded from the area, along with at least a dozen amphibians, and the forest even supports small colonies of celandine poppy, a bright yellow flower far north and west of its normal range. A walk may reveal a diminutive, red-backed salamander surveying it surroundings from a decaying log, but the signature "beasts" of the area are the numerous, smooth, gray-barked American beeches that give this forest its characteristic look. Although many species of trees call this place home, a fall walk will leave you spellbound by the golden-hued beech leaves that seem to dominate every aspect of this diverse woodland. Stop on any ridge top and survey the surrounding terrain, as it is a rare sight in today's Illinois.

Robeson Hills Nature Preserve

Heading due east from Lawrenceville on Route 50—through typical, flat, Illinois agricultural lands—soon reveals something unusual on the horizon—an isolated uplift of rounded hills directly on the Wabash River, across from Vincennes, Indiana. These two square miles of hills are the last rise of the Cumberland Mountain Range of eastern Kentucky and Tennessee before it fades into the prairies. A little routine map work and a steep drive up an obscure dirt road leads to an old-growth remnant of the great, eastern deciduous forest. Robeson Hills, perched almost one hundred feet above the Wabash River, is a 120-acre forest tract (divided in half by Route 50) of moist, upland forest in the Wabash Border Division. Named after William Robeson, who purchased the land in 1875, the preserve is actually part of an outdoor laboratory and environmental education site of more than five hundred acres, managed by nearby Vincennes University. Robeson Hills is the most prominent topographic feature of the Wabash River bottomlands. The rugged, dissected terrain has narrow, flat-topped ridges, steep slopes, and deep ravines that provide for diverse habitats. The very ruggedness that characterized the area also protected it from exploitation. The most significant feature of the preserve is a stately, beech-maple forest growing on deep loess (wind-blown sediment) deposits overlooking the Wabash River. The massive maples and American beeches offer a trip back in time and reveal a landscape that John James Audubon visited (he actually painted birds here). Beech trees, large and small with pearl-gray bark, dominate the rolling terrain. Their bark creates a stark contrast to the wildflowers clustered at the base of the trees. These woodland wildflowers are abundant and exist in unusual combinations, such as a spring show of Virginia bluebells interspersed with purple larkspur. The unusual sessile trillium

also grows on the steep hillsides. Sessile trillium looks superficially identical to the more familiar prairie trillium, yet a closer look reveals that its flower lacks a stalk and appears to rise directly from the three leaves. Other large trees that reach the distant canopy include ash, tulip tree, oaks, basswood, and various hickories. If you visit in the fall look for beechnuts—small, triangular morsels that are half fat—the preferred food of the extinct passenger pigeon. A single adult pigeon could down a cup of nuts at a single feeding. A short trail system leads one through this fairyland forest of a bygone era.

Robeson Hills Nature Preserve forest

Curious red fox cubs

Sessile trillium

Coffee Creek in Beall Woods Nature Preserve

Beall Woods State Park and Nature Preserve

The lower Wabash River, south of Mt. Carmel, by virtue of its mild climate and deep, fertile soils, contained one of the greatest hardwood forests the world had ever seen. Trees twenty to thirty feet in circumference and 175 feet high were common. A remnant of this early Forest of the Wabash miraculously escaped destruction by logging, and it has been preserved today as Beall Woods State Park and Nature Preserve. Some considered this forest to be one of the wonders of the world. Today, the woods are both diverse and impressive for the size of the trees. Sixty-four tree species have been identified, and nearly three hundred have diameters greater than thirty inches. Several state champion trees—black gum, green ash, shagbark hickory, shellbark hickory, mockernut hickory, and sugarberry—grow here. Among the giants were sycamores, bottomland trees characterized by light-gray outer bark that scales away to reveal a white inner bark. In moonlight, these white branches and trunks stood out like lighthouses and marked the river's edge for early navigators. One of the largest trees to exist between the Allegheny and Rocky Mountains was a sycamore that stood on the banks of Coffee Creek, south of Mt. Carmel. Unfortunately, it succumbed to the saw in 1897.

The woods resonate with the call of the pileated woodpecker, a denizen of ancient forests. To appreciate this region of Illinois requires a sense of the past and an appreciation for trees. Tulip poplars and oaks grow too large for your arms to reach around, while massive, wild grapevines dangle like suspension cables from their limbs. Sycamores shoulder great, white branches that tower overhead—stark, pale ghosts of even larger specimens before them. Here was the last citadel of the eastern forest, a home to giant trees, lush vegetation, and meandering streams—an incredible display of photosynthetic prowess.

Ancient Shumard's oak

Old-growth forest in Beall Woods

Pileated woodpecker in late winter

CHAPTER 26

Lodge County Park

Yellow trout lilies in full bloom—what a surprise! Bright yellow bits of spring sunshine have landed on the hillside among the vivid green leaves of ramp and the foliage and flower buds of Virginia bluebells.

—Susan Post, April 2010

NESTLED IN A QUIET CORNER of Piatt County, just north of Monticello and residing along the scenic Sangamon River, is a small, unobtrusive area rife with nature and natural history: Lodge County Park, Piatt County's largest forest preserve. The park is named after William F. Lodge, the previous owner of the 470-acre preserve. While a conservationist and an authority of wildflowers and trees, Lodge was also a lawyer interested in "forest preserve law." He thought "it would be a fine thing if we could preserve some of these natural forests for the benefit of posterity." Known mostly to area residents, Lodge Park is a nice place to walk your dog, view a Fourth of July fireworks display, spend a leisurely afternoon bank fishing in the small, created lake, or have a summer picnic under the spreading oaks. Few see or are aware of the real treasures of the area: a spring floral display that is unmatched in Illinois for diversity, the opportunity to easily observe and photograph winter birds, including the increasingly uncommon red-headed woodpecker, or to view the dynamic nature of the Sangamon River as it interacts with its ever-changing floodplain.

Spring in Lodge Park begins early (mid- to late March), when a few plants of the elusive skunk cabbage emerge from the muck and bloom in a small seep, located across the road from the lake's spillway. Seeing the skunk cabbage, though, is merely the entrance into a botanical world that starts with the blooming of snow trilliums and only ends as the dry days of early summer cause all the spring wildflowers to fade. The area in question is the slope that follows the loop road just past the dam. Biologists might call this half-mile stretch a *river slope*, the transition zone between the upland and the Sangamon River floodplain. Although the

River terrace and Virginia bluebells

park is heavily used, and the early road construction and adjacent pine plantation have had an effect on much of the park, this sinuous stretch of steep slope is of "nature preserve quality." Its plant diversity speaks to its pristine nature. Where else in Illinois, within an area only a few yards wide and less than half a mile long, can one see: four species of trillium—snow (the first to bloom in spring and the smallest), drooping, prairie, and great white; both species of the distinctive trout lily (yellow and white); sharp-lobed hepatica with flowers that range from pure white to deep blue; expanses of spring beauty that literally carpet the adjacent floodplain; Dutchman's breeches so numerous the feathery foliage forms a blue-green canopy a mere six inches above the ground; and bluebells, growing on a slope that follows the floodplain for a quarter mile? The flowers, forming a continuous, narrow band, end abruptly where the highly active floodplain meets the river slope. Because of the more than periodic flood pulses of the Sangamon, the floodplain may be bereft of flowers during wet years or produce expanses of buttercups and blue-eyed Mary during dry periods.

There is no need to head to the Smoky Mountains for the yearly ramp festival, as the display of this brilliant green, onion-scented lily covers large expanses of the upland forest adjacent to the slope. A walk through here in early spring satisfies the craving for any hint of green after a long, gray, dreary Illinois winter. Other species present include bloodroot, early meadow rue, starry false Solomon's seal, and wild geranium. Anyone who wishes to study and learn spring wildflowers should frequent Lodge Park from late March through early May. It's a spring wildflower textbook.

Farther down the loop road, the wildflower show is replaced by overlooks of the scenic river

Dutchman's breeches in spring

Early blooming clump of snow trillium

valley. The Sangamon flows freely here, winding back and forth, doing what rivers do: eroding from cut banks, depositing silt on lengthy river bars, and then repeating the process. A bench overlooking the river has been moved back several times over the past few years, highlighting the dynamism and capricious nature of the Sangamon. Mid-spring, viewed from here, is a lattice of pink redbuds and ephemeral greens of newly emerged leaves, interlaced with the stark, white branches of large, riverside sycamores. Spring migrants show up here with regularity and include most of the warblers and even the occasional scarlet tanager. Barred owls frequent the area, as do numbers of downy woodpeckers.

While the park is closed in winter (officially opens on April 1), a small parking area just past the entrance allows all-season walking access, and winter is a great time to appreciate the majestic stand of giant, open-grown oaks near the park's entrance. A slow walk through here on a snowy day will inevitably yield close up views of red-headed woodpeckers diligently working the trees for insect larvae and largely oblivious to any human

Red-headed woodpecker in winter

presence. Down the slope, just past the dam and at the edge of the woods, is a feeding station for birds, kept stocked by some nearby, mystery bird enthusiast, that provides innumerable opportunities to see and photograph winter residents—tufted titmice, cardinals, red-bellied and downy woodpeckers, blue jays, white-breasted nuthatches, and chickadees. Sitting quietly near the feeding station will yield a plethora of photographic chances, challenging the eye-finger-shutter coordination of even the most experienced photographer.

Lodge Park, a fitting memorial to Mr. Lodge, is a definite all-season destination for individuals who think "interesting nature" only resides somewhere else. During any season, Lodge Park will prove them wrong; every visit yields a new observation or perhaps a new insight into the natural landscape of east-central Illinois.

CHAPTER 27

Pere Marquette State Park and the Lower Illinois River Valley

American white pelicans gliding overhead
in a formation of five, framed by a blue sky,
disappear into the distance like fading clouds.
—Susan Post, May 2008

NO OTHER REGION in Illinois offers the variety of landscapes and wildlife viewing opportunities found at Pere Marquette State Park and the lower Illinois River valley. The eight-thousand-acre park, perched on the bluffs above the lower Illinois River, offers hiking in deep, forested ravines, trekking along dry, loess-covered bluffs to distant hill prairies that overlook the river valley, and a meandering trail that passes moist rock outcrops of ancient bedrock. The Illinois River offers bald eagle viewing in winter and an American white pelican migration spectacle each spring.

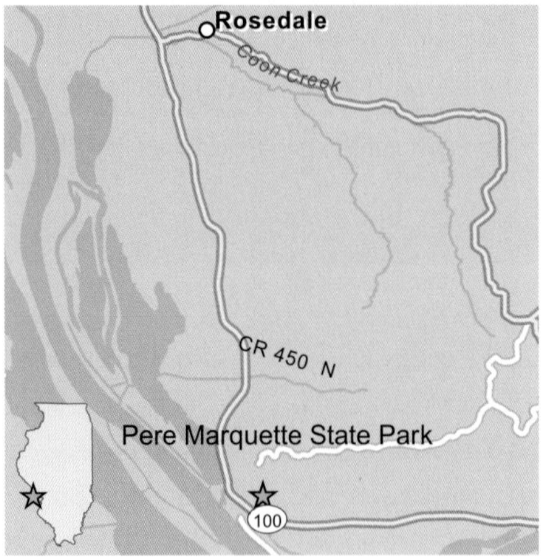

To talk about Pere Marquette without discussing glaciers and the products of their actions would be equivalent to studying the Civil War without mentioning Abraham Lincoln. In both instances, the two are inextricably tied together. During the Pleistocene, as the glaciers covered much of the Illinois landscape, their erosion of rocks and other materials were equivalent to the grinding stones of ancient native Americans. Fine powder resulted that was carried from the glaciers in a network of streams and meltwater channels and deposited along the edges of the melting ice. As the pulverized rock dried, winds carried the fine material (called loess) and deposited it downwind, especially against slopes and hillsides. The many layers of ancient soil deposition, often several feet thick, are evident along the roadsides and trails that interlace Pere Marquette. Loess is a unique material: extremely soft and friable, you can push your finger into a loess bank, yet it holds its shape when your finger is removed. This characteristic makes loess banks prime nesting locations for swallows and other cavity-nesting birds and also for native bees. Loess is also important to Illinoisans, as it is the parent

Doll's-eye seeds in late summer

Common garter snake

material from which most of the state's remarkably fertile soil developed. Just add organic material to the ground-up rock flour that is loess, wait a few millennia, and you have deep, dark, rich topsoil.

Few people visit parks, though, to view the soils, so what else brings visitors to Pere Marquette? Hiking through the oak-hickory forests on the north side of the main park road yields a plethora of woodland experiences. In spring, note the diverse wildflowers, including the familiar spring beauty, wild geranium, and Jack-in-the-pulpit; but you can also find relatively large numbers of the less common doll's-eye—bright green, tall (up to two feet), and may be three feet wide. Its flowers are bright white, produced on a stalk in a dense cluster that thrusts above the leaves. Doll's-eye is most noted, though, for its strikingly colored fruit, which ripens over the summer and displays its characteristic white spheres with black dots (the doll's eye), all clustered together on bright red stems. Look but don't touch, and certainly don't eat them, as they are poisonous to humans and

Loess bank along woodland trail

ingestion can lead to cardiac arrest and even death. The berries, however, are harmless to birds and pass through a bird's gut to be dispersed in the forest. Also along the trail one may encounter garter snakes. While small, they can be pugnacious, coiling and striking, and even emitting a foul-smelling musk when disturbed. These snakes, like the doll's eyes, should be viewed and enjoyed from a discreet distance, but both make for wonderful photographic opportunities.

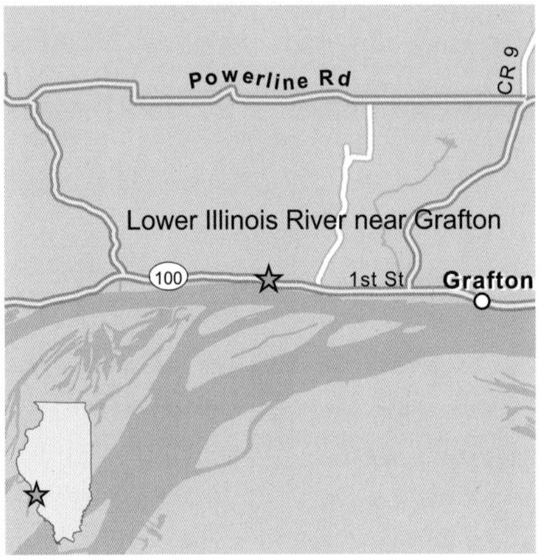

Hiking along the bluff tops to McAdams Peak, nearly four hundred feet above the lower Illinois River valley, may yield other pleasant surprises, including larkspur (both purple and white forms), small numbers of dwarf-crested iris, and the showy yellow of hoary puccoon. Side trails lead to small hill prairies, dry sites that, because of their aspect (orientation to the sun) and slope, support prairie rather than woodland vegetation. They were originally called goat prairies because of the steepness of the slopes, as only a goat was nimble enough to graze them. To continue your wildlife excursion, it's only necessary to exit the park and travel north or south a short distance on Route 100, for here the yearly spectacle includes both American white pelicans in spring and bald eagles each winter.

You might think that to see large numbers of pelicans, a trip to the Gulf Coast is in order. That species, however, is the brown pelican, an icon of the U.S. coastlines and a poster child for the demise of DDT. It was the thinning of the eggshells of the brown pelican (and other

American white pelicans along the Illinois River

species, including bald eagles) that led to their endangered species status and exposed the environmental problems associated with the widespread use of DDT. American white pelicans, although similar in size and shape to their brown cousins, are associated with the upper Midwest, the Great Plains, and even the mountain West. While they may spend part of the winter along the coasts, they only breed inland, and over the past few decades their populations have been growing. This population increase is especially notable in Illinois, as the species is now frequently seen along the major rivers and lakes of our state. From deep southern Illinois to the far north, large rafts of American white pelicans now grace Illinois waterscapes. Views of them, however, are often limited to white specks or blurs in the hazy distance, or their signature V-formation flights overhead. While sometimes mistaken for snow geese, their distinctive bills and large, black-tipped wings usually give them away. Close-up views of these magnificent birds, one of the largest species in North America, can be difficult and frustrating for the photographer and/or nature lover, except in this area of Illinois. Heading north from Alton along Route 100, called the Great River Road because it parallels the Mississippi River until it heads inland along the Illinois River, is prime territory for viewing the American white pelican. From the small town of Grafton, and points north, during any season but especially during spring and fall, large numbers of white pelicans dot the shoreline, form large rafts on the quiet backwater lakes and sloughs, and can even fill the sky with their distinctive shape. View them from the road itself and along various pull-offs. Perhaps the most intimate experiences, however, are along the numerous access roads that lead to places with evocative names like Upper and Lower Stump Lakes, the Mark Twain National Wildlife Refuge, and Flat Lake. Finding a good parking spot is usually not a problem, and a quiet walk along the numerous levees and trails should yield plenty of opportunities to see large numbers of pelicans, flying, feeding, and interacting with each other.

An American white pelican panorama

Early morning is often best, as the soft, early light lends an eerie, foggy, ethereal quality to the landscape that can transport anyone from the mundane to the miraculous.

An added bonus is the large number of other water birds likely to be encountered—bald eagles in winter (around two thousand spend the winter here), herons and egrets during most any season, various dabbling and diving ducks, and large numbers of double-crested cormorants traversing the river corridor each morning and evening. These large, black, emerald-eyed fish-eaters use the river as a highway, flying from roosts upstream to their various feeding sites along the river valley. The show can be a cacophony of black and white—pelicans, egrets, and cormorants, all vying for the seemingly limitless fish resources associated with the Illinois River.

While the Grafton area and Pere Marquette can serve as the focal point for pelican viewing, spend time on a leisurely drive north, enjoying the river views on the left and the bluffs on the right. In spring, these bluffs are dotted with innumerable blooming redbuds and dogwoods that make a trip up the Great River Road, perhaps Illinois's most scenic byway, a memorable excursion.

While the days of the early explorers are long past, today anyone can explore and discover this unique corner of Illinois. The area provides a window into what was once one of the most productive flyways and waterfowl areas on earth. Over the years, this has changed somewhat, but due to extensive restoration and preservation activities all along the river valley, the landscape is healing, and it provides increasingly relevant, even spectacular, glimpses into what was once here.

CHAPTER 28

Loda Cemetery Prairie Nature Preserve

> While I came to Loda to look for butterflies, I've left with so much more. My top three observations of the day: one of the largest mydas flies I've ever seen, prairie cicadas exploding like quail in front of my footsteps, and an unexpected encounter with a worn, gray copper butterfly.
>
> —Susan Post, July 2012

FLYING OVER CENTRAL ILLINOIS in a small plane is like staring down at a chessboard placed at your feet. This chessboard, however, stretches in all directions, horizon to horizon, green on green, green on brown, unbroken, and unchanging. Occasionally, though, the straight-sided monotony is interrupted by squared-off tufts of forest, remnants of prairie groves that still dot the agricultural vastness, or the gridded patterns of small towns, each lorded over by massive, cylindrical towers—the local grain elevators. Many of these small communities have park-like cemeteries, often named for features that no longer exist.

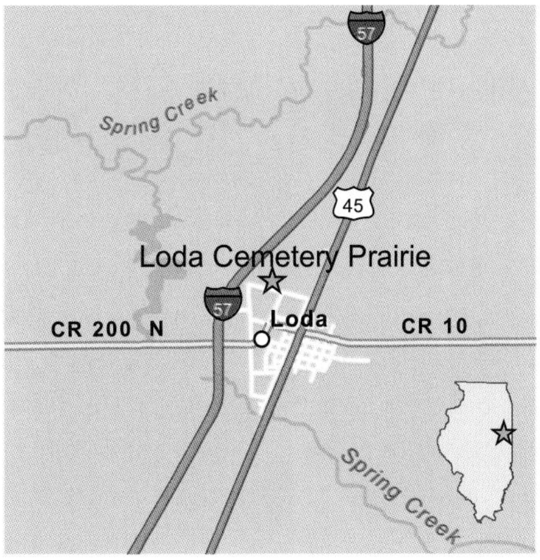

Such is not the case, however, for the small cemetery north and west of Loda in Iroquois County. Its name, Pine Ridge Cemetery, bespeaks the dark-green conifers that preside over the final resting place of local residents. When viewed from above, a curious green and brown smudge of nonagricultural vegetation appears on the north and east sides of the manicured, pine-strewn cemetery sward. Most would pass off this observation as merely wasteland, waiting its turn for development as more burial plots are needed, but this is not true. Here resides, in a mere 3.4 acres, one of the finest examples of tallgrass prairie left in central Illinois, and perhaps in the entire state.

In 1981, the above scenario of the "wasteland waiting to be developed" nearly came to fruition as the local cemetery association was running out of burial space and had made plans to expand into the prairie. Even though this area had been regularly mowed to "keep the weeds down," it had never been cultivated or pastured—both anathema to a prairie's survival. To make a long story short, a deal was brokered between The Nature Conser-

Diverse expanse of prairie wildflowers

Mydas fly on rattlesnake master

Prairie cicada

vancy (TNC) and the cemetery board, whereby the TNC acquired five acres of farmland that was then available for cemetery expansion. In trade, the cemetery association agreed to dedicate the "wasteland" as an Illinois Nature Preserve. Officially named Loda Cemetery Prairie Nature Preserve, the area is one of the few outstanding examples left of the original moist, black soil prairie of the Grand Prairie Division. Grand Prairie Friends, a local conservation organization, is the current owner and manager of the preserve.

The best word to describe the tiny prairie remnant is diverse, as more than 130 native plant species call this living botanical library home. While the grasses, like Indian grass, prairie dropseed, and big bluestem, are dominant, it's the forbs that take center stage during growing-season visits. Spring flowers, common here but vanishingly rare across the Illinois landscape of today, include prairie shooting star, downy phlox, and yellow star grass. Rattlesnake master, compass plant, prairie dock, and wild quinine are typical during the summer. Goldenrods, asters, and gentians complete the blooming spectacle each fall. A small population of eastern white-fringed orchids may also be found here. This orchid, listed as endangered in Illinois and as threatened on the federal list, is one of the few orchids of the central U.S. prairies. Although once described as "a blanket of white on the moist low prairie," at present there are fewer than sixty populations in the United States.

While the small size of Loda Prairie limits its value as a "typical" *wildlife refuge* (fortunately, this term applies only to birds and mammals that require more extensive habitat), the insects here can be spectacular. A visitor is likely to experience many common butterflies—black swallowtails, clover and alfalfa butterflies, pearl crescents—but also uncommon species that either are restricted to prairie or visit regularly to find a wealth of nectar-producing flowers—common wood nymphs, the very local gray copper, the migrant checkered

Prairie white-fringed orchid and prairie phlox

white, and giant swallowtails. Perhaps the showpiece organism for the site, however, is one of the largest and most charismatic insects in Illinois: the prairie cicada. Few places are left in the state where this large cicada can be heard singing and seen flying about in July and August. On most any midsummer's day, a walk though the thick vegetation of Loda will yield a plethora of encounters with prairie cicadas. Males perch high on the blooming stalks of prairie dock and compass plant, singing in the midday heat, and if you are observant and lucky, an amorous pair may just put on a courtship show for your viewing pleasure, with males buzzing and trilling in front of indifferent females. Other insects, too, call Loda home, and everywhere you look produces a new entomological discovery. Giant mydas flies (black, wasp-like, with bright orange legs and antennae) love to sip nectar from rattlesnake master flowers; giant garden spiders spread their lacy yet lethal nets to trap unwary fliers. In fact, the first close-up view of a prairie cicada is likely to be an unwary male trapped and neatly trussed up, dangling in a garden spider web. Other small, but no less potent predators include the bright yellow crab spider, adorned with red lightning bolts and often seen feasting on one of those uncommon butterflies. Praying mantises regularly perch on the emergent vegetation, and a search of the stem of gaura may yield the unusual caterpillars of the gaura moth, thought to be mimics of toxic monarch caterpillars. For those interested in ecology and how the natural world functions, Loda is a classroom, as everywhere you look, the "food chain" is alive and well and functioning properly.

Visitors to Loda Prairie Nature Preserve must park along the county road south of the preserve. The short hike was once bordered by cemetery on the left and cornfield on the right, but not anymore: in 2007, Grand Prairie Friends took a bold step to further protect this incredible remnant of tallgrass prairie by purchasing nearly nine acres of adjacent farmland to restore prairie and create a buffer. This agricultural land was planted to the same prairie plants that occur in the preserve and during the last few years has literally "blossomed" into a "prairie in development." While not as diverse as the millennia-old remnant it protects, if you ignore the small area of corn stubble still visible on the surface of the soil, the display of prairie flowers, often laden with colorful butterflies, is remarkable. The former dull walk into the preserve is now something special and adds to the experience of visiting this postage-stamp-sized, yet truly important, piece of Illinois prairie heritage.

CHAPTER 29

Revis Hill Prairie Nature Preserve

I stand atop Revis Hill Prairie with a group of intrepid butterfly aficionados. We are with *Illinois Natural History Survey Skipper Field Manual* authors James Sternburg and James Wiker, seeking the elusive Ottoe skipper. Revis is the only site in Illinois where this diminutive yet delightful skipper may still be found. Purple prairie clover and leadplant are in full bloom—the latter laden with its purple blossoms and orange pollen. The visiting bees look as if they are wearing puffy, orange leggings. A second instar prairie walking stick, a dogface sulphur butterfly, an adult ant lion, and a Horace's dusky wing next appear. As we watch the tops of the fading pale purple coneflowers, we get lucky—an Ottoe skipper—a real treasure at Revis and one James Sternburg had not witnessed in his eighty-plus years of butterfly studies.

—Susan Post, June 2006

REVIS HILL PRAIRIE, located in southern Mason County, is named after James A. Revis, an early pioneer in the region. The area is part of the north valley wall of the Sangamon River and rises 250 feet above the mile-and-quarter-wide floodplain of the river. The predominant soil is loess (windblown silt) over glacial till, but there are also some fine-sand deposits and gravel outcroppings. Hill prairie is the dominant plant community found on the rolling land and steep slopes. Forests, dominated by oaks, are present in the ravines between the bluffs. Revis is the largest hill prairie complex in Illinois.

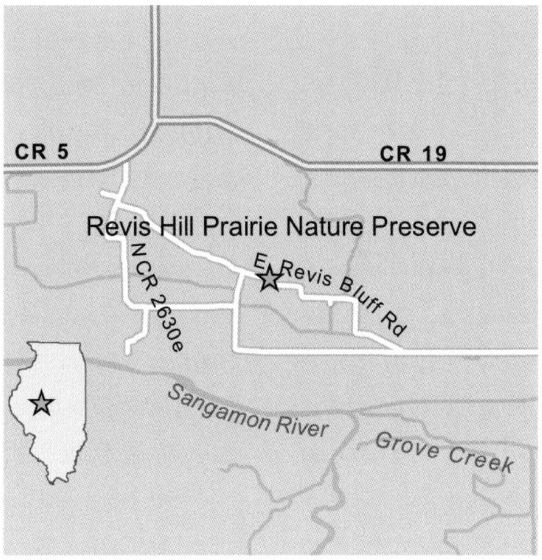

To visit Revis requires a bit of bushwhacking. Although the area has an official parking lot, continue on for about a mile, and park along the road just past the large house on the north side of Revis Springs Road. For those who persevere in the uphill struggle along the faint path through thickets and brambles, the view of the river valley alone is worth the trip; but hill prairies have other rewards. During May, the hilltop can be alive with expanses of the yellow flowers from the partially parasitic wood betony, emerging from the dry remnants of last year's grasses. Later, the pale purple coneflowers come into bloom, followed by perhaps the best display of leadplant in Illinois. In late summer and early autumn, forbs such as blazing star, goldenrods, asters, and gerardia mingle with the orange-brown stems of the dominant grasses—little bluestem and prairie dropseed.

Revis Hill Prairie Nature Preserve

The jewel of the fall, however, is the scented ladies' tresses orchid, which casts its heady scent on the wind, detected long before the plant is seen nestled in the grasses. This orchid belongs to the genus *Spiranthes*, the name being derived from the Greek and meaning coiled flowers, alluding to the spiral arrangement of the blossoms. Although we associate orchids with spring and with wet areas, this group has taken advantage of hill prairies and occupies the most severe habitat of any of our native orchids. It also blooms later than any other Illinois orchid, beginning in mid-September and continuing sometimes until early November.

In addition to more than 160 plant species, some unusual animals found here are the western hognose snake, western slender glass lizard, Ottoe skipper, arogos skipper, and gorgone checkerspot butterfly. While orange and clouded sulfur butterflies may be abundant, look closely at any yellow or orange example, as both sleepy orange sulfur and dogface sulfur butterflies are here as well. The prairie walking stick was rediscovered at Revis in 1990, seventy years after the last one was seen anywhere in Illinois.

Don't confine your explorations to the uplands, however, as a walk along the road that follows the base of the bluff will often yield a plethora of butterflies, including the impressive (larger and longer-tailed) summer form of the zebra swallowtail. Hill prairies continue to exist in Illinois, largely

Zebra swallowtail on blue vervain in summer

Prairie walking stick on leadplant bloom

Fall-blooming ladies' tresses orchid

because of their inaccessibility. Threats to these unique habitats include encroachment of the surrounding forest (historically kept at bay by fire), pasturing of livestock, and nearby home-site development. Despite this, hill prairies still exist and can provide anyone with an afternoon of heart-racing exercise followed by absolute solitude—your reverie broken only by the soft, ever-present winds and the high-fives as you and your companions celebrate discovering a true hill prairie gem.

CHAPTER 30

Prairie Ridge State Natural Area and Illinois Audubon Sanctuaries

Prairie Promise—the color of the inflated sac pouch of a male greater prairie chicken as it emits its soulful love song.

—Susan Post, paint-chip color described after viewing the greater prairie chicken booming, Prairie Ridge State Natural Area, April 2007

WHILE WE THINK NOTHING of making a dinner reservation or calling ahead to book a motel for the evening, the prospect of needing to make a reservation to "see nature" may seem a bit strange to most. But that's what is necessary to observe one of the most primeval, ancestral, and unique wildlife events in Illinois—the spring mating rituals of the greater prairie chicken. Their mating has been described as "complex, flamboyant, and theatrical—Broadway meets the prairie." To visit the "booming grounds" of this highly endangered bird requires a bit of planning—call ahead to reserve a spot in a specially constructed blind (from late March to mid-April) and arrive at least an hour before sunrise to this remote location south of Newton in Jasper County. The Prairie Ridge State Natural Area is owned and managed by the Illinois Department of Natural Resources. As the sun rises and features of the booming grounds begin to appear, an eerie, otherworldly sound insinuates itself upon your consciousness. Described as "the sound of someone blowing into a large, empty bottle" or the "noise of a distant foghorn on a misty morning," the low frequency boom allows the sound to travel up to a mile and seems to come from everywhere, and nowhere. Forms materialize on the short-grass stage before you: chicken-sized birds, their neck pouches inflated a brilliant yellow-orange, pace back and forth in an indefatigable display to attract females. When two males approach, they raise their feathers, dance on feathered feet, and leap up with a distinctive "quoik!" noise as they seek to impress an observant female and intimidate a rival male. This show lasts for an hour or two, with the much-less-colorful females finally making an appearance later as the sun rises, selec-

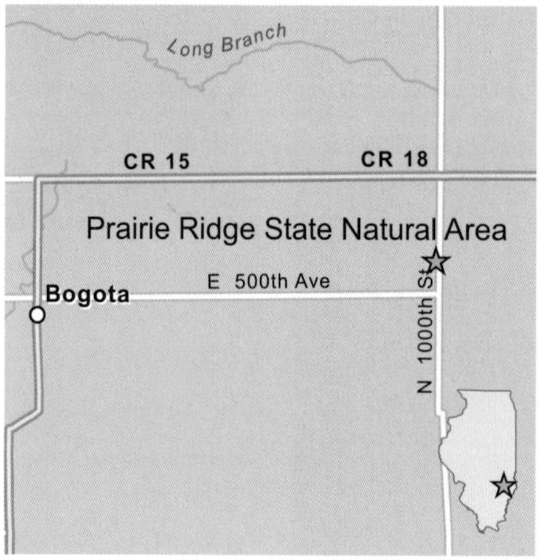

Booming male prairie chickens

Mating Halloween pennant dragonflies

tive, choosy, aloof, and according to the reactions of the males, "Oh so desirable." As the sun rises, the show diminishes, and visitors can backtrack to the nearest breakfast bar or stay and enjoy the rest of the preserve, dedicated to the preservation of habitat for some of Illinois's most endangered and rare grassland birds.

Prairie Ridge was established in the early 1960s as a greater prairie chicken refuge. From millions of birds in the mid-1800s to around two hundred at present, Prairie Ridge has prevented the extirpation of the species from Illinois. The flock at Prairie Ridge is one of the few that remain east of the Mississippi River. The area is not one place, but more than twenty separate sanctuaries, all surrounded by farmland. The forty-one hundred acres are clustered into two groups in Marion and Jasper Counties. This scattering allows for a mosaic of habitats, interspersed with agricultural land. Areas of restored tallgrass prairie, cool-season grasses, and wetlands provide a variety of habitats that increase wildlife diversity.

Male crayfish frog

The preserve is not just for the greater prairie chicken. A number of endangered, threatened, or species-of-concern regularly found at Prairie Ridge includes the upland sandpiper, short-eared owl, northern harrier, loggerhead shrike, dickcissel, grasshopper sparrow, Henslow's sparrow, and eastern meadowlark. Other species that call this place home, a landscape indicative of the Southern Till Plain Division, include the crayfish frog, prairie cicada, and numerous species of butterflies. Unique plants also find a home here, as populations of prairie rose gentian and royal catchfly have been reestablished. While early spring is certainly the signature time to experience the greater prairie chicken *on parade*, other seasons can be rewarding, especially winter, when unseen populations of southern bog lemmings and prairie and meadow voles attract various raptors. In late afternoon and around sunset, on a clear winter's day, the sky can be alive with northern harriers, flying low and quiet across the rolling, brown sward. The stunning gray males and tan-brown females and juveniles are easily distinguished by their flight pattern and the white spot near their tail feathers. The harriers are soon followed by the eerie, bat-like flight of short-eared owls. They rise up, silent, seemingly from nowhere—dark, ominous silhouettes (at least to small rodents) patrolling the cold, darkening sky. The land around you is totally quiet, peaceful, and you are alone with the colorful, fading horizon, the increasing chill in the air, and a wildlife experience few will ever have in Illinois.

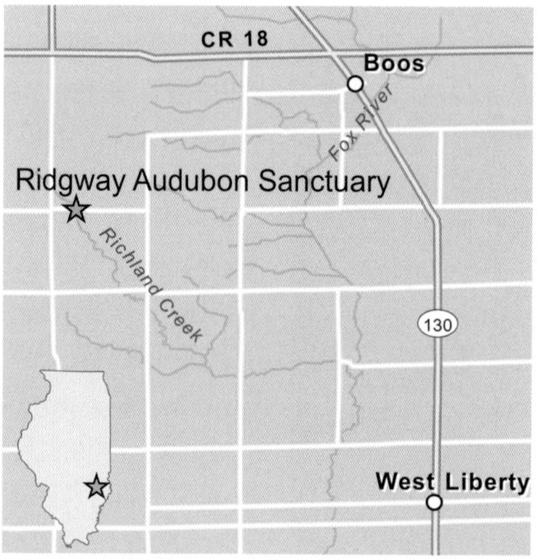

Within Prairie Ridge are three Illinois Audubon sanctuaries—Ridgway, Bartel, and Graber. The forty-acre Robert Ridgway Sanctuary is not far from the headquarters of Prairie Ridge. Named after Robert Ridgway, a Smithsonian naturalist from the 1870s and author of Illinois's first *Birds of Illinois*, the preserve provides habitat for the same grassland-dependent birds mentioned above, but it also features a prairie wetland to enhance the value of this site. From the raised platform, one can note the presence (via calls or by a chance sighting) of bitterns, rails, and other wetland species such as killdeer, and red-winged blackbirds, which nest in the adjacent restored prairie. Visitors in spring are likely to have very close encounters with the red-wings, especially in the vicinity of the viewing platform, as the colorful males are likely to dive-bomb unsuspecting spectators in their zeal to establish breeding territories. So put on a hat,

Territorial male red-winged blackbird

be wary, and enjoy the show. A loop trail traverses the preserve and provides views of the wetland; in summer, enjoy a restored, blooming prairie, alive with insects, tallgrass prairie plants, song sparrows, exploding northern bobwhite quail, and the ceaseless winds that characterize the vast prairie landscape of Illinois. Graber Grasslands is north of Ridgway. Bartel Land and Water Reserve is in Marion County, and both grassland and wetland restorations are underway. The process is already successful, as greater prairie chickens are even now "booming" on the sanctuary, and the wetlands have attracted migrating yellow rails.

The goal of all these preserves is simple: to develop a grassland/wetland ecosystem capable of maintaining viable populations of various avian species, both migratory and residential. From our numerous visits to the sites, the process appears to be imminently successful and available for all to experience and enjoy.

Female northern harrier at Ridgway Sanctuary

CHAPTER 31

Robert Allerton Park

Sunny silence at the restored prairie, no house wren, no indigo bunting, no yellow-breasted chat calling . . . The highlight is a pair of giant swallowtail butterflies courting on the blooming ironweed, their slow, languid flight, yellow and black against a blue sky . . . twirling, swirling, higher and higher, until out of sight . . .

—Susan Post, August 2009

WHEN THE ILLINOIS Bureau of Tourism announced the results of its "Seven Wonders of Illinois" promotion—sites nominated by and voted on by the public in 2007—the press bemoaned the fact that nothing on the list had anything to do with our sixteenth president. After all, this is the "Land of Lincoln." In addition, with one or two notable exceptions, all the sites were human-created. As biologists, we were also less than happy with these results, but our perspective on the world likely is different from that of most folks. Ironically, one of those *exceptions*—Robert Allerton Park and Retreat Center—chosen for its iconic, historic mansion, music barn, retreat center, thirteen formal gardens with sculptures from around the world, and, as an afterthought, its wooded trails, was deemed the perfect tranquil escape. Most visitors to Allerton, located just southwest of Monticello, come to stroll the paths through the Garden of the Fu Dogs, visit the massive Georgian mansion (called by some the finest example of its kind in the country), marvel at the formal gardens with European hedge mazes, or visit the uplifting Sun Singer at the far western edge of the park. The "afterthought" wooded trails mentioned in the press release, though, are actually a complex network of fourteen miles of trails that traverse and crisscross this unique, fifteen-hundred-acre corner of Piatt County. They showcase the real marvels of Allerton, its natural wonders. The park is a sanctuary for over 1,090 species of plants, sixty species of breeding birds, thirty species of mammals, and twenty-eight species of reptiles and amphibians. The landscape features the Sangamon River and its floodplain, both lowland and upland forests that are in good to very good condition, small oak openings (drier sites that have

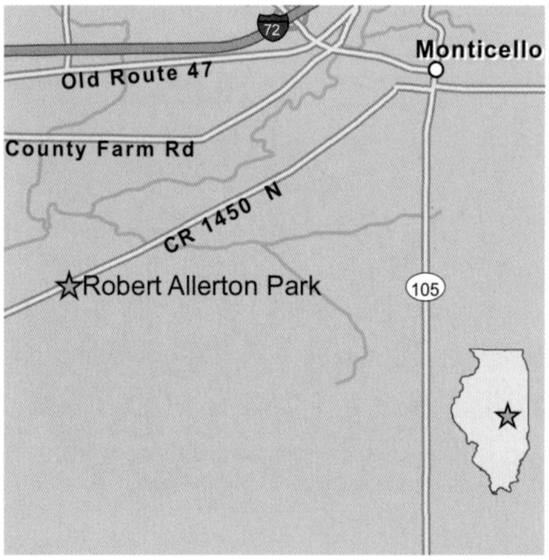

Winter at Allerton House pond

a more sunny understory) on the ridges, wildflower-carpeted ravines, and two prairie restorations.

To really enjoy Allerton requires exploration and a sense of adventure. Each winter, particularly after a midwinter snowstorm, brave the slick roads and enjoy the tranquility and quiet of dark tree trunks rising from a blanket of unbroken snow; break a trail down to the river and note that it's only partially frozen, and observe the patterns of freezing and thawing ice and water that decorate the banks like so many chandeliers. The true season for nature lovers, though, is spring. As early as late March snow trilliums (Illinois's smallest and earliest-blooming trillium) occur by the dozens along the wooded bluffs and steep slopes that border the river. They grow with various-colored hepatica in a subtle but nonetheless spectacular wildflower show, especially to those seeking some sign of life after a long, cold winter. As the spring season progresses, Allerton literally "lights up" with wave after wave of showy spring ephemerals. On the floodplain of Willow Branch Creek, near the parking area of the Lost Garden in the southernmost part of the park, acres of Virginia bluebells create a blue lake of flowers during most of April. For perhaps the finest display of blue-eyed Mary in the state, drive to the Sun Singer and take a short hike down the slope to the floodplain of the

Floodplain display of blue-eyed Mary

Sangamon in late April or early May. This unique, diminutive annual (most spring wildflowers are perennials) is related to the garden snapdragon and carpets acres of the floodplain like an undulating blue and white sea. Hiking any of the trails during spring will yield a bounty of other wildflowers as the season progresses—bloodroot, Dutchman's breeches, wild ginger, spring beauty, toothwort, wild geranium—but a special show is reserved for those who brave a mile or two hike (starting at the Lost Garden parking area), heading north toward the Sangamon. Here the trail passes through a beautiful, open forest with large trees and a diverse understory, and it soon heads to bluffs overlooking the Sangamon. On a ridge here, exposed to more sun and thus warmer and drier, find glade-like communities with a different flora—yellow star grass, pussytoes, and displays of prairie shooting star! Most think shooting star to be a prairie plant. It is an important spring component of tallgrass prairie, but it originally was a denizen of open, oak forests. It's like looking in a botanical history book to see it growing so well here.

During summer, on the floodplain where the blue-eyed Mary bloomed, look for bright red cardinal flowers, punctuating the wood nettle, often with ruby-throated hummingbirds dancing above them. As you walk through the upland summer woods and along the edges of prairies, skirted with easily accessible trails, Allerton comes alive with butterflies, including such gems as the northern pearly eye, common wood nymph, giant swal-

Tall bellflower with halictid bee in late summer

lowtail, and great spangled fritillary. Interested in unusual insects? Look for the large but thread-like bodies of pelecinid wasps along the trail edges, seek out large robber flies that mimic bumblebees on the floodplain nettles, or just enjoy the antics of

White-tailed doe and fawn in Sangamon River

green tiger beetles that cavort on the trail, always just ahead of your footsteps.

Visiting Allerton, one of Illinois's Seven Wonders, is like peeling an onion: the outer layers are the traditional haunts of this unique place—mansions, gardens, sculptures—but the real treasures lie beneath the surface, buried in the remoteness of Allerton Park. All a visitor needs is a willingness to walk, perhaps access to a few field guides, and eyes attuned to observation of the natural world. With these simple tools, a day at Allerton is likely to yield a lifetime's worth of memories.

CHAPTER 32

Mason County Sand Areas

With the exception of parts of the sand deposits, of some small swamp areas, of rock outcrops, of ponds and lakes, and of some small tracts of forest, all the original vegetation of Illinois has been destroyed or greatly modified by clearing, planting, or pasturing. The area covered by the last four of these exceptions is very small, but there are still thousands of acres of sand deposits in nearly original condition and available for study. They still contain some virgin prairie that has never been plowed or pastured.

—Henry Allan Gleason, *Vegetation of the Inland Sand Deposits of Illinois,* 1910

BY 1900, ILLINOIS'S tallgrass prairies were significantly diminished, but thousands of acres of sand deposits in nearly unspoiled condition made up some of the largest areas of natural vegetation left in the state. The chief sand areas are located near Havana, Hanover, Oquawka, and in Kankakee and Iroquois Counties, all in the northern half of Illinois. The meltwaters of the Wisconsin glacier deposited and shaped the sand and ultimately the sand prairies and savannas in Illinois. The Havana deposit was formed as meltwater cascaded down the prehistoric course of the Illinois River. This tremendous flood, known as the "Kankakee Torrent," carried a huge volume of sand and gravel downstream at breakneck speed. At present-day Hennepin, the river is narrow and entrenched in bedrock. Here the water lost its velocity, and the sand was deposited in Tazewell, Mason, and Cass Counties. This sand creates a special home for a unique collection of plant and animal species.

The flora here is a combination of tallgrass prairie plants of Illinois and plants usually associated with drier, open habitats farther west. The western species probably arrived in Illinois thousands of years ago, when the climate was warmer and drier. As the region became cooler and moister, these species died out in most areas, but they persisted here because of the special environment provided by the sand.

The vegetation of the dry, sand prairie is strikingly different from that found on the black-soil prairie, although they do share some species, such as common milkweed and little bluestem. Even though the sandy areas receive the same amounts of heat, light, rainfall, and wind as the rest of Illinois, they experience larger variations in temperature from day to night and from surface to subsoil; the water-holding capacity of the sandy soil is also less. In open areas, the surface sand is constantly shifting, sometimes forming dunes or blowouts (areas where the sand and vegetation have been removed by the wind).

To survive the harsh conditions, plants have evolved several strategies. Visitors to the preserve should note that the leaves of many plants are narrow or small, thereby reducing the amount of surface exposed to the sun. Leaves may also have a protective covering of silvery hairs or scales, giving them a grayish-green color. Perennials possess deep roots, seeking the limited supply of surface water. They also frequently grow in tufts or bunches to reduce wind exposure. The thick, succulent pads of prickly pear cactus form mats close to the sand.

Gleason, a renowned botanist, explored the sand areas around Havana in the early 1900s while he was a student at the University of Illinois. One of his main reasons for studying this area was that the sand deposits "constitute the only considerable area of natural vegetation in the state, and because their vegetation is closely related to that of the original prairie. It is also of some general value, since it concerns an area which has received little attention from botanists." During the summers of 1903 and 1904, he carried out fieldwork near Havana in what was to become Sand Ridge State Forest.

Sand Ridge State Forest and Henry Allan Gleason Nature Preserve

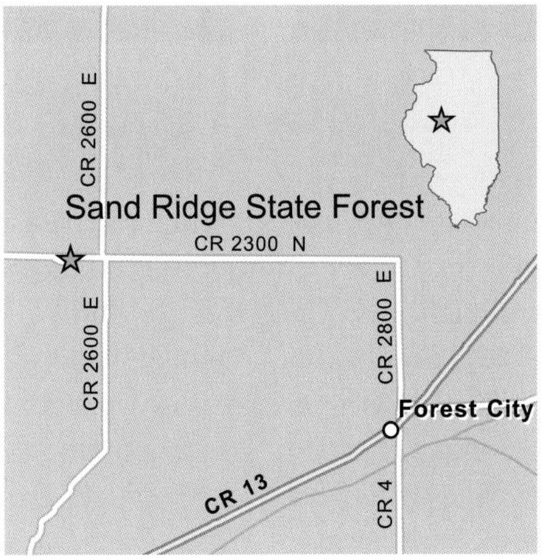

The gently rolling sand dunes, expanses of oak-hickory forest, and stretches of sand prairie found at Sand Ridge State Forest contrast sharply with the blacksoil landscape of central Illinois. The flora here is a combination of plants common to the tallgrass prairie—little bluestem, butterfly weed, and rough blazing star—and western plants usually associated with drier, more open habitats—prickly pear cactus and silvery bladderpod. Sand Ridge State Forest, appropriately, sits on a low bluff or "sand ridge" overlooking the Illinois River. The state began purchasing the submarginal, sandy farmland in 1939 for an experimental forest, and today Sand Ridge is our largest state forest, at seventy-two hundred acres. It is a mix of oak-hickory woodlands, pine plantations, and sand prairie.

During Gleason's visit in 1904 he wrote, "By far the most interesting visit was to the Devil's Neck, a large wild expanse of blow sand, where we found many interesting things, . . . a few plants of *Lesquerella spathulata* [silvery bladderpod] hither-to known only from Northwestern Nebraska and Montana." The area referred to as "Devil's Neck" is now contained within his namesake, the Henry Allan Gleason Nature Preserve located on the western edge of Sand Ridge State Forest.

Any curious individual who is interested in both botany and history can see silvery bladderpod. Though it is not particularly easy to find the plant, each trip seeking it is well worth the effort. Once on the well-worn path into the preserve, you will find a large sand dune around sixty feet high and covered with vegetation—mostly prickly pear cactus that blooms in late June, little bluestem, and scattered blackjack oaks—looming in front and to the north. This dune is the same one Gleason called Devil's Neck. The top of the dune provides a great overlook into the Illinois River valley, and in spring it is likely to be cloaked in masses of bird's-foot violets. If your visit happens to be in May, after the violets have faded, look into the dune's central blowout area; there you will see clumps of small, four-petaled yellow flowers—silvery bladderpod—draped across the bare sand.

Sand Prairie with butterflyweed

Prickly pear cactus blooms in summer

Discovering this bit of botanical history may give you, as it does us, a delightful chill.

Seeking an obscure wildflower, though, is hardly the only reason to visit Sand Ridge State Forest. The area provides a wealth of nature viewing, perhaps topped by the butterflies and dragonflies that occur from March through October. While the area has been "managed" as a state forest for many years, and nonnative pines now make up a significant part of the forest, areas of native sand prairie and sand forest still persist. Most butterflies can be seen by slowly driving the park's roads while looking for activity along the roadside. From late April into early May, a small white butterfly flitting low to the ground and nectaring on various flowers just might turn out to be a true spring ephemeral, the Olympia marble. Easily confused with the more common cabbage white, this species is distinctive on the underside with its gold and brown "marbling" that resembles a tiny slab of Carrara marble. During special years, the park roads come alive with massive explosions of hackberry butterflies, covering moist spots on the land by the hundreds, and sometimes by the thousands. For those interested in a diversity of dragonflies and damselflies, seek out the isolated sand ponds and patrol their edges. You will be rewarded with many species of dragonflies—green darners, spangled skimmers, eastern pondhawks,

Group of gorgone checkspot and pearl crescent butterflies

Bull snake, a denizen of dry habitats

Carolina and black saddlebags—and damselflies, sometimes so numerous that their mating activity animates the shoreline with gleaming threads of green and blue. Because the area is sandy, those small, very active creatures just ahead of you are invariably tiger beetles, very pugnacious predators that patrol the sands in search of their next meal. The reptiles and amphibians seen here are likely to be bull snakes, six-lined racerunner lizards, green frogs around the ponds, and the charismatic eastern box turtle. As you search for insect treasures, you will be accompanied by the sounds of crackly grasshopper wings and the calls of indigo buntings, field sparrows, eastern towhees, and mockingbirds.

Gleason's discovery, the silvery bladderpod, a western plant

The combination of extensive butterfly and dragonfly viewing opportunities, easily experienced from the park roads, and a hike into the Henry Allan Gleason Nature Preserve to experience a bit of Illinois's botanical history and to stretch out those leg muscles is a great way to spend a late spring or early summer day, exploring the ten-thousand-year-old inland sand deposits of Illinois.

Devil's Neck, a large sand dune at Henry A. Gleason Nature Preserve

Sand Prairie–Scrub Oak Nature Preserve

A botanist once stated that locations in Sand Prairie–Scrub Oak Nature Preserve were where an individual could stand on an old sand dune, look in all the cardinal directions, and see a landscape as it was before European settlers colonized Illinois. That's quite a feat in today's world. It is a place in Illinois where you see almost no manmade structures and can watch regal fritillary butterflies dance about the prairie vegetation, all to the background calls of northern bobwhites.

Spring usually comes early to Sand Prairie–Scrub Oak. When they first emerge, the plants are small, and the clumping habit allows the sand to show

Sand prairie at Sand Prairie–Scrub Oak Nature Preserve

through. As a result, the area has a tufted appearance, similar to that of a true desert. The first flowers to appear are those of sand phlox, followed by the pansy-like bird's-foot violet. Each succeeding day adds not only to the floral display but also to the greenery, as bunch grasses begin to cover the sand. Spring is the only season that is truly green in the sand prairie. By late spring the luminous, yellow-orange blossoms of puccoon mingle with the various shades of violet spiderwort; its long, thin leaves help it conserve moisture. Spring also begins the insect showcase, with the first appearance of various butterflies, nymphal grasshoppers and katydids, and various types of bugs. (Note, "bug" is actually a true entomological term denoting members of the insect orders Hemiptera and Homoptera.)

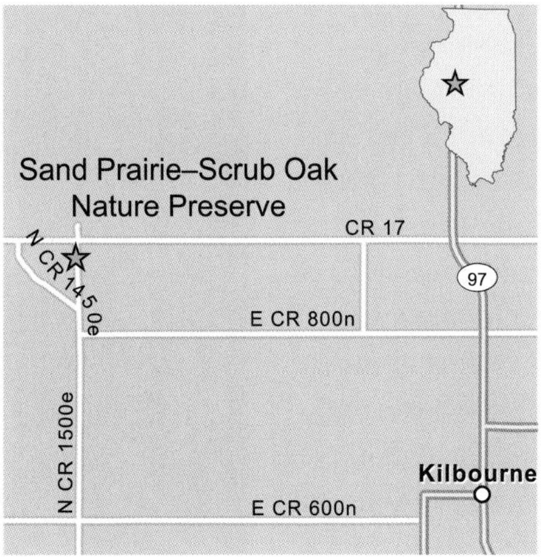

By summer, yellow and orange are the colors of the sand prairie. Dwarf dandelion, coreopsis, western sunflowers, black-eyed Susan, the bright orange of butterfly weed, and the waxy, yellow flowers of prickly pear cactus dominate the landscape. In the northeast corner of the preserve, however, don't overlook a showy display of common milkweed blossoms in early to mid-summer. Perhaps one of the best in Illinois, this area can be literally dripping with butterflies—several species of swallowtails, diminutive hairstreaks, colorful nymphalids and sulfurs, and the always-secretive satyrs. As you search for the butterflies, you will be serenaded by dickcissels echoing their name from stunted trees, and be sure to watch where you step, as camouflaged white-tailed deer fawns may suddenly materialize and bound away. The grasses are now large and obvious, and they include little bluestem, June, grama, and needle grass. By late summer, the dryness of the sand is evident. Grasses are already turning brown, and the sere landscape is broken only by the tall, pink spires of blazing stars. The drone of katydids

Regal fritillary with soldier beetle

Male regal fritillary

Pair of American painted lady butterflies on blazing star

and the hot, summer winds are the only sounds; six-lined racerunners and the occasional bull snake leave sinuous marks in the undulating sands.

The entire area is not just sand prairie but a mosaic of sand savanna and open sand forest. Sand savannas, like other savanna communities, were maintained by fire in presettlement times. The rhythmic dunes and ridges limited the severity of fires and allowed a savanna to develop instead of a sand prairie. The open, scrub-oak forest is largely black oak and blackjack oak, species that can withstand the arid conditions.

Although no formal trails exist in the nearly fifteen-hundred-acre preserve, the area is mostly open and makes for easy walking. While any season here can be a memorable experience, for those who have only a single chance to visit, make it during late June or early July and enjoy a slow, casual hike through one of the greatest butterfly spectacles Illinois has to offer.

SOUTH

CHAPTER 33

Bell Smith Springs Recreation Area

> To cross the stream (Hunting Branch), I abandoned my shoes for water sandals—the water is COLD! Across the creek is a magical world of green moss cushions, plate-sized lichens, a vast sheet of sandstone, and gnarled, twisted trees.
>
> —Susan Post, March 2012

BELL SMITH SPRINGS is in the Shawnee National Forest and is named after its former owner, whose name is etched in a moss-covered canyon wall near the spring. Located in Pope County, the area is about nineteen miles southwest of Harrisburg. It is a world of vertical cliffs, clear, rocky streams, outstanding rock formations, and lush spring flora.

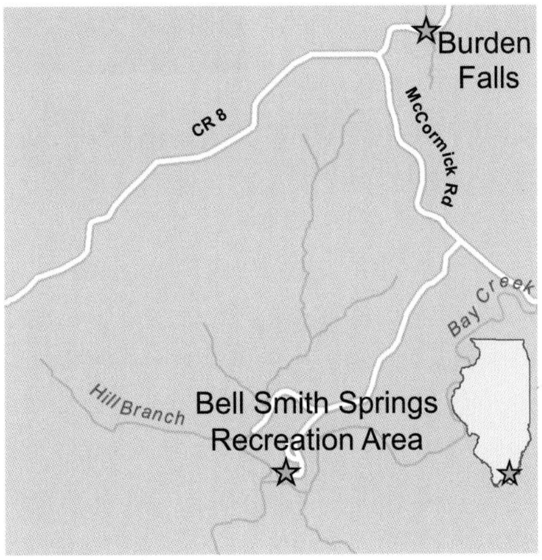

This region is an area of contrasts. Sandstone ledges are windswept and scorched by the midsummer sun, yet blankets of lichens and moss help to insulate portions of the rock against the extremes of heating and cooling. The bare rock ledges have surface temperatures that regularly exceed 120°F and are often 40° warmer than air temperatures only a few feet above. Thus, plants here must be adapted to these extreme conditions. Also, their presence ameliorates the fracturing of the rock by expansion and contraction and retards its breakdown into soil.

Cliff-top vegetation is extremely sensitive and attuned to the violent fluctuations in moisture. Consequently, most rock-ledge plants grow and flower in spring when rainfall is relatively plentiful. Each spring, bluets, false garlic, and yellow stargrass appear in shallow depressions in the ledges and at borders where the sandstone slips beneath the soil of the open oak forest on the bluff tops.

The soil-rock borders on ledges are transition zones, constantly reshaped by the action of wind and water. Dripways originate here as water flows down the gently sloping rock ledges, forming algae-covered wet streaks. In spring, these dripways become a proving ground for delicate, long-legged crane flies. Large, writhing masses, or leks, of male crane flies roll back and forth across the moist ledges, pausing only when a female happens along and dives into the amassed males. After a brief but intense struggle within the lek, the female emerges, attached to a large male. The male uses his six spindly legs to form a cage over the female. This strange pair walks to the nearest dripway, and the female begins laying eggs on the wet, algal mat. For the duration of the egg laying, the male wards off other males that attempt to reach the female by bumping them with his slender body, never relinquishing his claim to the female. In a short time, the eggs hatch into tiny crane fly larvae that travel up the dripways to complete their development under a mat of vegetation in the upland forest. Within weeks, the dripways are only dark, dry streaks on the sandstone, providing few clues to their unique relationship with the crane flies.

Although no single plant seems particularly characteristic of the rock ledges, one insect may be—the lichen grasshopper. This grasshopper is specially suited for living on rock ledges that are encrusted with lichens. Its dark brown, green, and whitish markings make it difficult to see against the mottled surface on which it spends most of its time. When disturbed, the grasshopper usually flies only a short distance, confident in its ability to camouflage itself after landing. Only when it flies, exposing its gaudy, yellow hindwings, can this grasshopper be readily seen. This species is at the northern limit of its range in southern Illinois.

French's shooting star is as unique in the valleys as the crane flies are on the ledges. The species is named after Southern Illinois University entomology professor George Hazen French, who first discovered it in 1871. The plant grows under the driplines of sandstone ledges, where the sandy soil is kept moist during the growing season. In Illinois, French's shooting star is restricted to the Shawneetown Ridge, a sandstone belt approximately ten miles wide across southern Illinois.

Canyon with cardinal flower

Although smaller than the prairie shooting star, its real difference can't be seen by the naked eye: it has twice as many chromosomes as the prairie species. French's shooting star blooms in late April under a dripline near the stone steps that descend into the canyon.

The most unusual geological feature of the area is a natural bridge, carved by water erosion. The bridge spans about 125 feet, is nearly twenty-five feet wide, and stands thirty-eight feet high. The rock is eight feet thick at the apex of the arch. The forces of water have also caused great blocks of sandstone to separate from the canyon walls and

Spring leafout of American beech in canyon

Bay Creek winter ice and snow patterns

Natural bridge in canyon floor

French's shooting star

create blind alleys and narrow passages within the forest. On top of these blocks are isolated islands of wildflowers, mostly two species of waterleaf.

A network of hiking trails helps visitors discover the riches of Bell Smith Springs. The trail leaving from Hunting Branch Picnic Area follows an ever-narrowing valley to a spectacular gorge carved by the erosive action of a tributary of Bay Creek. Upstream, the water soon becomes only a meandering trickle, eroding unique, circular holes (called moulins) into a vast, sandstone shelf. The longest trail is Sentry Bluff, which runs along the bluff tops of Bay Creek, crosses the creek, and traverses Sentry Bluff and Boulder Falls.

While hiking and exploring in the fall, take time to enjoy the sluggish, leaf-strewn stream called Bay Creek. The beech-lined banks, set against the rocky bluffs with a brilliant blue sky for a backdrop, can only be found at Bell Smith Springs, one of the last great wild places in Illinois.

Sandstone glade panorama

Outside the park proper, other areas of interest are the allee-reminiscent, narrow roads that lead to and from Bell Smith Springs. These are lined in spring with redbud and dogwood and are home to such spring butterflies as the falcate orangetip and elusive pine elfin. Only a few miles away, Forest Road 402 fords a small creek. While most, in their zeal to reach Bell Smith Springs, might pass by this area, it's a good idea to stop at a small parking lot near the ford and enjoy one of the most scenic waterfalls in Illinois. Burden Falls is a seasonal, one-hundred-foot waterfall (made up of two terraces) that plunges into a deep canyon that cuts a swath through the sandstone into Burden Falls Wilderness Area. Navigate the creek and falls with caution, as the trails are narrow and often slippery. The waterfall dries to a trickle by midsummer.

Road to Burden Falls and Bell Smith Springs

Burden Falls (upper)

CHAPTER 34

The Cache River Ecosystem

The Cache is a café-au-lait brown, muddy river surrounded by an intense, deep-green swamp . . . a place for all seasons, for all hues, for each and every possible color in the arc of an ephemeral rainbow.
—Michael Jeffords, 2008

WHILE THIS ACCURATE yet brief quote does describe the landscape, it falls far short of the indescribable palette of colors that is the Cache. No modern paint store, no artist's paint box can approach the myriad hues observed during every visit to the Cache. Spring is a cacophony of subtle shades of green—soft, ephemeral, pastel greens. Summer is also green, but a humid, dense, sweat-soaked bevy of heavy greens. Fall is a rusty, golden, clean, clear set of earth tones, mimicking the colors of the layered, red-rock country of Utah. And finally, there is winter. Few see this extraordinary southern landscape after the glory of an ice storm or following the wet, clinging fury of a fast-moving blizzard. Here the colors tend toward the grays, subtle blues, and, if you are lucky, the incredible peach color of a dying winter sun setting across the face of the swamp.

Deep in southern Illinois, occupying the old streambed of the Ohio River, lies a landscape so atypical of Illinois that few citizens have discovered its multitude of wonders. The Cache River basin marks the geographic point where the last invasion of the sea into the Midwest reached its northernmost limit and lies only a few miles from the southernmost extent of the continental glaciers of the Pleistocene. The area is a true melting pot for nature. While this area originally consisted of approximately 250,000 acres of dense, primeval, cypress-tupelo swamp and lowland forest, much has been changed over the years, a fact that this landscape shares with the rest of Illinois. Even though most of the wet forest and swamps were logged in the early part of the last century, and many streams were channelized or straightened to drain the swamps, much still remains. A visit to the Cache River involves a treasure hunt of sorts. To experience the Cache, seek out access points along its sinuous track, from its origin in the Shawnee Hills to the mouth just north and east of Cairo. Fortunately, an outstanding visitors' center, south of Cypress on Route 37 (the Henry N. Barkhausen Wetlands Center), provides an excellent introduction to the area.

Over thousands of years, the Cache River has twisted, turned, and meandered through the flat terrain that made up its watershed. Because the land was so flat, numerous sloughs, swamps, and other types of wetlands dotted the river's course. What was once contiguous is now fragmented, largely because of agricultural development, and forms a complicated corridor running across southern Illinois. Yet the Cache River basin still supports a diverse mixture of forests, grasslands, wetlands, shallow lakes, and streams, and it is the northern limit for cypress-tupelo swamps in the Mississippi River valley. Today, conservation and restoration efforts are the goal of the Illinois Department of Natural Resources, the U.S. Fish and Wildlife Service, private organizations, and individuals who make up the Cache River Joint Partnership. Even efforts to reconnect the Cache—it was literally divided in half during the early part of the last century—are underway. During the early part of the twentieth century, the Post Creek Cutoff, a drainage ditch that starts in the middle of the river's watershed and leads directly to the Ohio River, has caused many negative issues for the river over the last century. The Cache is now divided into two parts—the Upper Cache and the Lower Cache. During periods of high water, the Lower Cache actually flows backward to the Cutoff and into the Ohio. During low water periods, the Lower Cache does not flow at all.

The Cache River and adjoining Cypress Creek wetlands were designated a Wetland of International Importance and a Natural National Landmark, notable for their rich diversity of waterfowl and varied plant and animal communities. This area supports some of the largest and oldest living trees east of the Mississippi River and harbors more than 90 percent of Illinois's high-quality swamp habitat. The Cache lies at a biological midpoint of North America—one of only six areas in the United States where four or more physiographic regions overlap. As a result, the area is bounded on the west by the Ozark Hills, on the north by the Central Plateau, on the east by the Interior Low Plateau, and on the south by the Gulf Coastal Plain. This mixture of bedrock, soils, and climate provides a diversity of habitats seldom matched in the Midwest.

Cache River State Natural Area consists of more than fourteen thousand acres of swamp, meandering floodplain and river forest, and upland cliff and glade communities. By visiting the various sites with evocative names like Little Black Slough, Heron Pond, Wildcat Bluff, and Cave Creek Glade, you begin to gain a sense of the past and an appreciation of the area. Cypress Creek National Wildlife Refuge was literally created, beginning in 1990, from farmland that was once a vast complex of lowland forest centered on Cypress Creek. The refuge provides homes for immense numbers of waterfowl, but it also gives visitors a look at the historic landscape through trails that lead to places with descriptive names of Limekiln Springs and Hickory Bottoms. The refuge's nearly seventeen thousand acres under protection are just the beginning of a much larger effort that will protect lands along the entire length of the river.

"This river is hidden," said a French adventurer credited with naming the Cache when he spotted its log-jammed mouth on the Ohio in 1702. His words are still true today because the natural features, the hidden treasures of the Cache, the remnants of its past, must be actively sought out to be experienced. The gems are the living landscapes and organisms waiting to be discovered by anyone with a little skill at map reading, a willingness to walk, and a healthy dose of curiosity. So, obtain an *Illinois Atlas & Gazetteer*, get off the interstates, and explore unique sites located near tiny towns with charming names such as Cypress, Belknap, Perks, Karnak, and Ullin. As noted above, access to the Cache and its wetlands requires a bit of effort. It can involve paddling a canoe or kayak to a state-champion bald cypress over one thousand years old, hiking a short distance on a boardwalk to view a nearly primeval wet woods, or climbing to an overlook to see an uninterrupted expanse of forest with the brown ribbon of the Cache winding through it. Add the diversity of the plants and animals that call this place home to the truly beautiful landscape and you have the makings of a day, a week, a month, or a lifetime of exploration.

Max Hutchison, a third-generation resident of the area, sums up much of the Rodney Dangerfield–like attitude the Cache has experienced over the years. "Although I grew up on the Cache, I never really appreciated its wildness and the diversity of its natural features until I left the area and saw some of the rest of the world." Although the Cache may have gotten little respect over the course of its history, it certainly appears to be coming into its own as one of the great wild places left in Illinois.

Henry N. Barkhausen Wetlands Center

The Henry N. Barkhausen Wetlands Center is the best place to begin your journey of discovery. The center is named after Barkhausen, a conservationist, Cache supporter, and former director of the Illinois Department of Conservation. The center provides maps, informational exhibits, an audiovisual presentation, and a computerized virtual tour of the Cache. These give the visitor a preview of what they might encounter. Look out the window of the center's observation room—mink, muskrat, river otter, ruby-throated hummingbirds, American goldfinch, and various water snakes are just a few of the organisms that stop by.

Restored wetland at Barkhausen Wetlands Center

Summer gathering of great white egrets

Sunning diamondback water snake

Take time to explore the trails surrounding the center. Depending on the season, the paved path may be embellished with coyote scat, remnants of turtle eggs, or eastern pondhawk dragonflies. Listen for the "sleigh-bell-like" call of spring peepers, the "running-the-finger-over-a-comb" call of the chorus frog, or the "marbles-clacking-together" call of the cricket frog. Try to identify the sparrows as they keep a step ahead; field, song, Savannah, and swamp sparrows occur here. The "*keer keer*" of a red-shouldered hawk and the "crow with a cold" call of the fish crow can usually be heard near the center. The Barkhausen Wetlands Center hiking trail connects to the Tunnel Hill State Trail, where you should take a few moments to stop at the bridge over the Cache. River otters are frequently seen here, as are numbers of turtles, shingled on a log. In spring, be on the lookout for the courting behavior of the prothonotary warbler.

Heron Pond Nature Preserve

Heron Pond Nature Preserve, a bald cypress swamp, is part of the Cache River State Natural Area. The trail to Heron Pond crosses the confluence of the Cache River and Dutchman Creek on an arched footbridge, passes through a bottomland forest, and soon enters the world of the swamp. Coming off the bridge, you feel as if you have entered a different land. Many times you will be greeted by a symphony of sound, frogs and birds all competing for "air time." In spring, the forest trail is lined with wildflowers and the swamp is full of lemon-yellow, male prothonotary warblers, little bits of swamp sunshine claiming their space. In late spring, if it has been dry, look left into the swamp for American featherfoil. These miniature, inverted, botanical chandeliers "hang" from a ceiling of duckweed. By August, the huge white blossoms of spider lily have opened, creating patches of white in the unrelenting green. In late fall, the cypress trees discard their needles to litter the duckweed around each base with a golden halo. Infrequent winter snows perform the same function, only in bright white. As the trail winds alongside the Cache, silent hikers may be rewarded with a sighting of skittish hooded mergansers, a basking softshell turtle, or a playful mink or muskrat.

The adventure into the swamp is greatly aided by a long boardwalk. Once on the boardwalk you

Fall at Heron Pond

Cypress knees for tree support

Woodland phlox along the Cache River

Heron Pond after winter snowstorm

Green tree frog

will be surrounded by bald cypress with feathery foliage; duckweed, complete with hidden frogs and their high-pitched pips; and the swishes and squeaks of birds. Step carefully, as sometimes a cypress katydid, a denizen of bald cypress canopies, has been dislodged and lands on the boardwalk. At the end of the boardwalk listen for the raucous squawks of great blue herons; a rookery is just barely visible through the trees. Look for sinuous trails in the duckweed, created by swimming snakes, the gnawed workings of beavers, or the futzing behavior of wrens. After the boardwalk, proceed onward, skirting the swamp and ending at the state-champion cherry bark oak, a massive, dark-trunked behemoth of a tree, some twenty-three feet around.

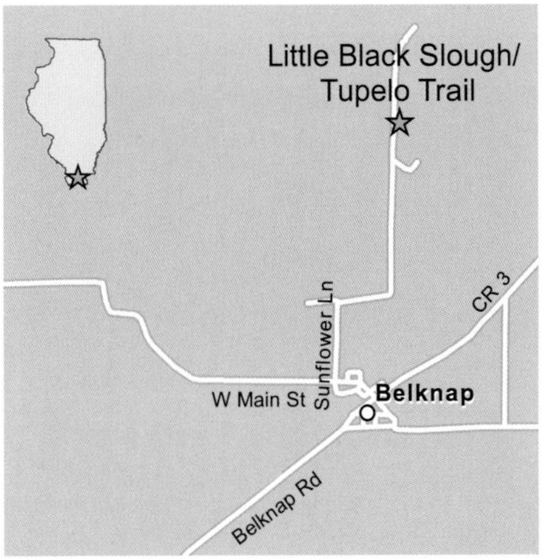

Little Black Slough Nature Preserve

Little Black Slough—part of the Cache River State Natural Area—is well known for its cypress-tupelo swamp, but it also has floodplain forests, upland woods, and small patches of limestone barrens. Some of the finest timber in the state was once found here. Forested areas were cut in the 1870s and the wood shipped to Chicago to help rebuild the city after the great fire. But if you view these trees only in terms of board feet, your vision of the world is too narrow.

To explore Little Black Slough, take advantage of the Tupelo Trail. This trail winds through an oak-hickory forest, where it's like walking on ball bearings during the fall of an excellent nut crop year! In early winter,

Swamp marigold at Little Black Slough

Little Black Slough in fall

the wide-buttressed tupelo trees are gray-green with lichens and surrounded by duckweed. To the naked eye, it appears as if the lichens are slowly moving up the tupelo trunks. With the aid of binoculars, however, they are revealed as well-camouflaged brown creepers. During spring on the trail that leads into the swamp, small rock outcrops are covered with pale yellow corydalis, while cricket frogs stay one step ahead of you. Yet, perhaps fall is the best time to explore this trail: the leaves of the tall trees glisten against the backdrop of an incredibly blue sky, and the swamp may experience a "swamp marigold bloom"—an unexpected treat and perhaps one of the best wildflower displays anywhere. Viewing this spectacle is a once-in-a-lifetime thrill.

Brown creepers

It's as if the swamp is on fire, with every available surface consumed by bright yellow flames. Red-headed woodpeckers fly from tree hole to tree hole, while pileated woodpeckers dart from tupelo to tupelo. A sharp eye may also spy isolated, bright green tree frogs. Even if you encounter no wildlife, the tupelo-cypress swamp at the end of the trail offers one of the truly primeval landscapes found in Illinois.

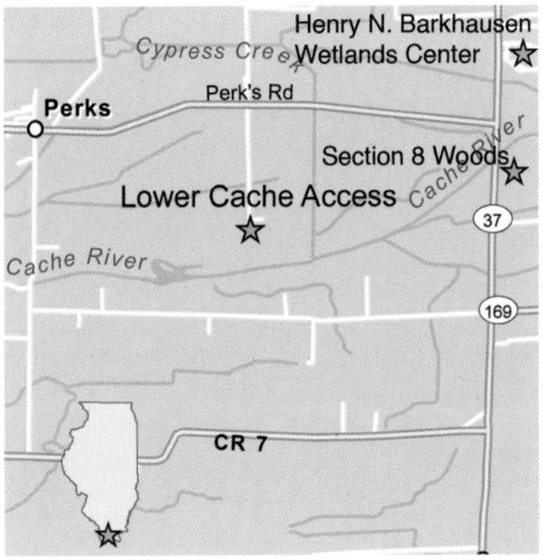

Lower Cache River Access Area

The Lower Cache River swamps, part of the Cypress Creek National Wildlife Refuge and the Cache River State Natural Area, form a contiguous, forested corridor. Measuring 9.25 miles long by about a half-mile wide, it is one of the largest, most significant natural areas in the state. One of the best ways to view this area is via canoe. With only arm power, journey through duckweed and buttonbush to explore eight-hundred-year-old cypress trees at Eagle Pond—one specimen has more than two hundred knees! The highlight of the trip is a stop at the state-champion bald cypress. Because the tree is hollow, its actual age is unknown, but it is certainly more than one thousand years old. It is also the largest tree in Illinois. While here don't forget to look up for chattering groups of chimney swifts that nest in the cypress, or a bald eagle with a fish in its talons, food for a juvenile in a nearby nest. Buttonbush lines the canoe trail; its dangling, Christmas tree-ornament-like blooms appear in June and July.

Buttonland Swamp at Lower Cache Access

Waterline at Buttonland Swamp

Buttonbush in bloom

Limekiln Springs cypress

Limekiln Springs

An interesting trail through the Lower Cache heads to Limekiln Springs, located in the Cypress Creek National Wildlife Refuge. During spring, a wooden boardwalk is littered with the seeds of pumpkin ash, while the forest floor is scattered with wildflowers. The trail passes several of the springs that flow from the limestone bedrock. These springs help maintain the water in the swamp during droughts and provide a unique habitat for uncommon aquatic species, such as the cypress minnow.

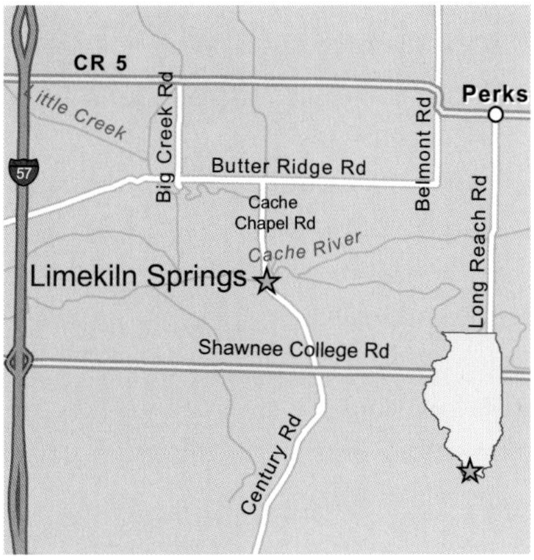

The springs flow into Limekiln Slough, a biologically significant Illinois stream. During mid-May, an abundance of Indian pink wildflowers occur along the trail. Each tubular, scarlet flower has a yellow center, reminiscent of the prothonotary warblers skittering about overhead. Eastern musk turtles occasionally emerge on the shoreline of the slough. The dusty trail is a magnet for wild turkeys; look for their scratchings and dust bath depressions. In early July, gaze north from the boardwalk into a sea of American lotus blooms.

Big Tree Access

Very early into this short walk, a noble pin oak, towering on the right side of the trail, whets one's appetite for big trees. A few feet farther, a truly dramatic grove of bald cypress, each tree more than a thousand years old, comes into view. Reaching over one hundred feet tall and some in excess of forty feet around at their buttressed bases, these have been dubbed the "Winnie the Pooh" trees, because all are hollow. Nearly one hundred examples of these immense cypresses are scattered through the woods. Take note, also, of the gargoyle-like knees scattered around the trees. The function of these knees is much like the outrigger on a canoe—stabilization of the tree in the moist soil. Be aware that in spring you may need rubber boots, because these trees occupy the ancestral bed of Cypress Creek. Each tree, located in the Cache River State Natural Area, provides a vivid impression of the past.

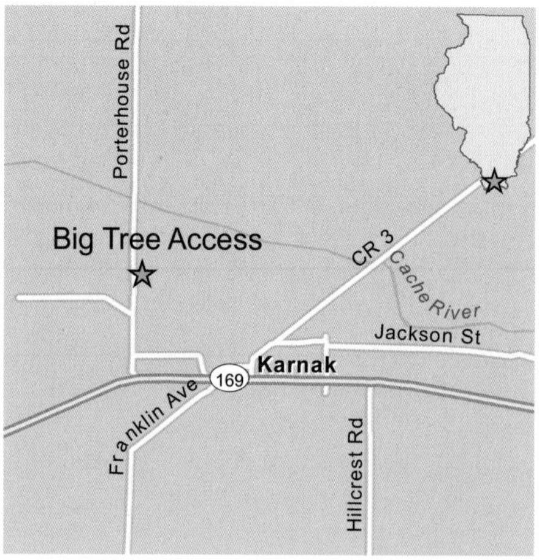

Frank Bellrose Waterfowl Reserve

A cursory, first view from the observation deck at Bellrose, especially in spring and summer, reveals little more than a grassy field backed by dark trees on the horizon. Periodically, though, large wading birds such as great egrets, little blue herons, and great blue herons are seen stalking the wetlands. On late afternoons in winter, Bellrose becomes a cacophony of sounds and sights as thousands of mallards, pintails, blue-winged teal, and greater white-fronted geese erupt from the marsh at the slightest provocation. At dusk, waterfowl come to roost by the hundreds, by the thousands, sometimes the tens of thousands, in a show that is not to be missed.

The Frank Bellrose Waterfowl Reserve, located in the Cypress Creek National Wildlife Refuge, honors Bellrose, a waterfowl biologist at the Illinois Natural History Survey. His work, spanning more than sixty years, led to a better understanding of wetland resources, included the first practical, artificial housing for wood ducks, and documented the effects of season length and shooting hours on waterfowl populations. It appears that the preserve is a success. What began as twenty-one hundred acres of swampy, marginal farmland validates the adage, "If you build it, they will come." Access to the Bellrose Reserve is somewhat limited, but a viewing platform is found on the eastern edge, and further access may be granted. Visit the site headquarters on the campus of Shawnee Community College for more information.

Ancient bald cypress trees

Greater white-fronted geese at Bellrose

Nesting barn owl at Bellrose

Large giant cane thicket in fall

Hickory Bottoms

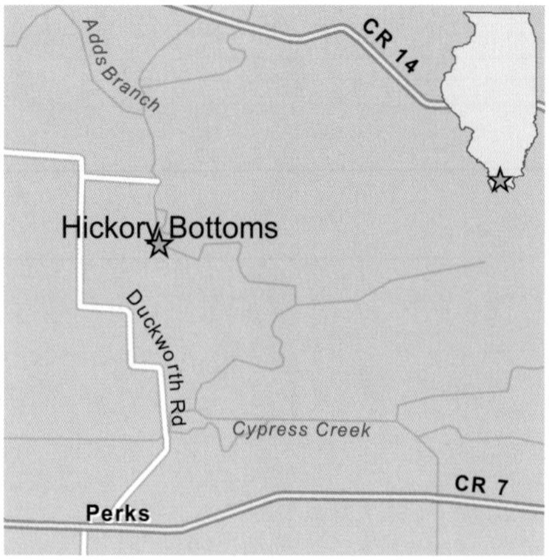

If you enjoy a primeval-looking forest that offers large, columnar trees, a multitude of cypress knees along the winding channel of Cypress Creek, and an assortment of little things—southern leopard frogs, bird-voiced tree frogs, Appalachian eyed brown butterflies, long, skinny brentid weevils, and stinging rose caterpillars—then Hickory Bottoms is your choice. Located a few miles north of Perks off Duckworth Road, this remote location within Cypress Creek National Wildlife Refuge will make you feel the joy of total isolation. The winding dirt and gravel road leads to an old barn and parking area. Follow the trail across the bridge and turn left. The major forest is on your left, and the trail enters to wind around through massive oaks—Shumard, swamp white, overcup, and swamp chestnut. Bring tree and insect field guides to help interpret this unique stretch of lowland forest.

Wildcat Bluff

Few names evoke a greater sense of wildness than Wildcat Bluff, located in the Cache River State Natural Area. A mile hike along the top of this three-hundred-foot bluff that separates the Shawnee Hills Natural Division from the Coastal Plain Natural Division will provide views of the upland forest, falling away on the steep slope. At trail's end, a small hill prairie provides an interesting display

Primeval forest along tributary of Cypress Creek

Appalachian eyed brown butterfly

of prairie plants in this mainly forested landscape. The real draw, however, is the panoramic view into the valley of the Cache. The river, seen as an umber ribbon in winter and early spring, disappears into a sea of green foliage in spring and summer. From here, nothing is visible but an uninterrupted forest with no sign of human habitation. For the adventurous, a faint trail near the parking area leads below the bluff to a series of sandstone overhangs. Follow these for several hundred yards and enter the world not of wildcats but of lions. Cone-shaped pits in the dry sand are the homes and traps of the elusive antlion. Tracks in the dust provide clues to who has recently visited—lizards, mice, snakes, and opossums. For a fortunate few, bobcats—a ghostly glance, then gone—can still be seen here.

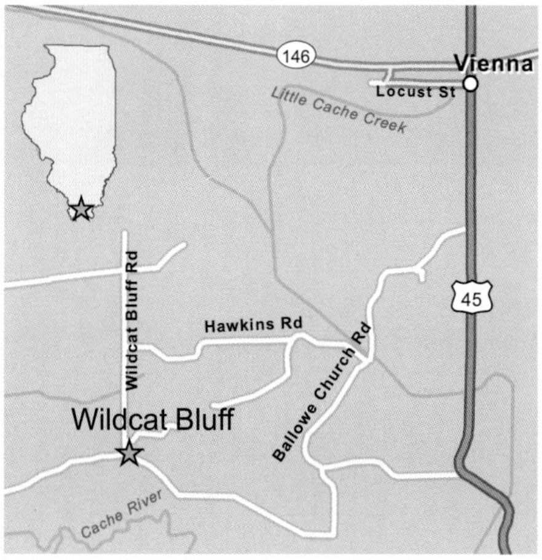

Section 8 Woods Nature Preserve

Don't let the boring name fool you. Section 8 Woods, located in the Cache River State Natural Area, is a place not to be missed. A short hike along the boardwalk away from busy Highway 37 leads into a flooded, primeval forest of tupelo and cypress. Along the way, experience unusual trees such as overcup oak, water hickory, water elm, and Drummond's red maple. At the end of the trail, look south to the state-champion water tupelo. Each spring the surrounding forest echoes with the twittering calls of prothonotary warblers, flashing yellow through the pale green vegetation. Lucky visitors may experience the courting displays of yellow-crowned night herons. The hollow hammering of woodpeckers resonates throughout the Cache, and this is an excellent site to see them. Observe the black-and-white wings of a distant pileated or note the nearby downy and hairy woodpeckers that often nest near the boardwalk. During winter all seven species of Illinois woodpeckers may be seen here.

In fall, the boardwalk is littered with the dark, oval fruits of tupelo trees. Take time to study the plum-like fruits as they appear to have the starry, night sky etched on their skin. Don't forget to observe the surroundings very closely—the boardwalk railing may harbor a migration of spiderlings, wheel bugs sunning themselves before a final frost, or graduated, dripping icicles on a cold winter day.

Cave Creek Glade Nature Preserve

Cave Creek Glade, located on top of a steep, limestone-strewn slope, is a piece of the Shawnee Hills adjacent to the Cache. Boxed in by forest on three sides, this prairie opening is a challenge for flatland legs. During a good year, the early and late

Wildcat Bluff

Young cottonmouth with yellow tail used as a prey lure

Ant lion pits in dry soil

Panorama from Wildcat Bluff

An ant lion larva waits at bottom of each pit

Roosting black vulture

Foggy Cache River at Section 8 Woods

spring wildflower displays are noteworthy. Wild hyacinth's pale lavender wands highlight the bottom of the glade in early spring; in late spring the glade is dominated by pale purple coneflowers. If viewed from a distance, the glade, with its coneflowers, is reminiscent of a strawberry sundae—a green mound of prairie "ice cream," topped with bright pink, concentrated at the top and dripping down the sides. Also blooming along the wooded slopes in late spring is American colombo, a tall gentian with odd, green flowers. As you examine the colombo, small brown butterflies—little wood satyrs—dart in and out of the woods. The parking area for the glade is across Route 45. Near here is a small tributary of the Cache that contains many of the area's "signature" organisms—prothonotory warblers, wood ducks, and American featherfoil.

Courting prothonotary warblers

Section 8 Woods Nature Preserve

Shingled turtles

Cave Creek Glade coneflower bloom

In summary, the Cache is a treasure trove of biological wonders that never fails to mystify and entertain. The place is a balm for work-weary souls. Whether it's a cottonmouth snake eating a periodical cicada, newly emerged luna moths drying their wings on a cypress, a misdirected snowy owl perched along a roadside during winter, or the lush, feathery foliage of spring cypress, the Cache is ever changing. Who can anticipate what adventures the next visit will yield? The Cache never disappoints and always surprises. Even a "bad day" in the Cache, where you haven't seen anything new, is still one of the best experiences to have.

CHAPTER 35

Cedar Lake

A visit here is like exploring an Illinois version of the Boundary Waters of Minnesota. Endless coves and a sinuous shoreline beg for exploration, by foot, by canoe, or by kayak. A day at Cedar Lake will always surprise.
—Michael Jeffords, May 2011

MOST NATURALISTS ARE not particularly fond of impoundments, especially in a state as flat as Illinois. They are generally featureless expanses of brown water, with eroded, muddy or rip-rapped shorelines that reflect the differing water levels during wet and dry periods. Other than expanses of open water, they have little to offer in the way of scenic beauty. Any wetlands, potentially rife with charismatic vegetation and wildlife, are usually only found at the upper end, away from the dam, and often inaccessible by foot or boat. On the plus side, reservoirs do often attract large numbers of migratory waterfowl, gulls, and certainly plenty of fast-moving pleasure boats, jet skis, and fishing boats. Given all those factors, an impoundment deep in southern Illinois, surrounded by forest (more than half contained within the Shawnee National Forest) and created in a highly dissected landscape, certainly piques the curiosity. Cedar Lake, built in the 1970s, is a beautiful lake bordered by imposing bluffs and traversed by trails with evocative names like Wolf Den Hollow and Cove Hollow. The 1,750-acre lake, which resembles lakes from the Canadian north woods, is divided into two sections separated by a rocky terrace—Cedar Lake and Little Cedar Lake. If you are not aquatically inclined, the best way to experience this intriguing landscape is by hiking the Cove Hollow Trail to Wolf Den Hollow (come during the week and you will likely be alone) that provides great overlooks of Cedar Lake. Walk the less popular but still scenic Little Cedar Lake Trail in the southern part of the area to experience wetlands, lowland forests, and wildlife openings. Sightings here can range from wood ducks to woodcocks, trapdoor spiders to ten-spot dragonflies. Both trailheads are accessed by entry

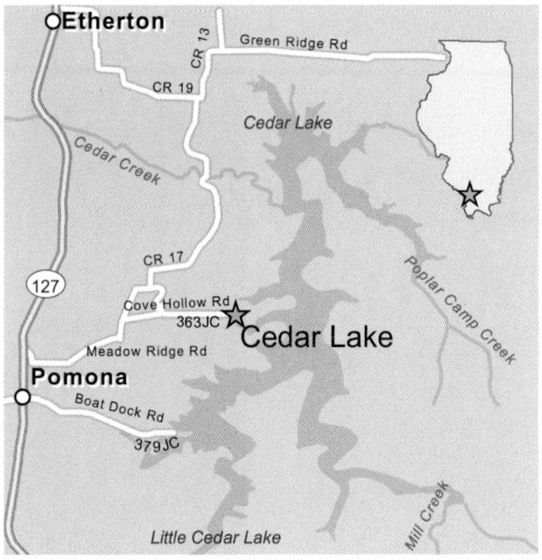

Cedar Lake shoreline

roads from Route 127, a road many consider to be one of the most scenic in Illinois.

While the wildlife may be typical of most of Illinois—white-tailed deer, fox and gray squirrels, and even the occasional beaver—the landscape is rugged, diverse, and can be a challenging excursion for flatlanders. Sandstone outcrops line the trails, connecting numerous deep, cool shelter bluffs. The moister, north- or east-facing walls often support interesting colonies of ferns, mosses, and the primitive liverworts. In fact, Cove Hollow is a massive shelter cave, formed by the erosion of rocks of varying hardness. A small waterfall is active each spring. The trees are large and straight trunked; tulip poplars tower above the valley floor as they reach for the sunlight, and American beeches lend their gray, canvas-like bark to the otherwise dark boles of the ravine forest. At the numerous

Goldenseal in bloom

Great blue heron along shoreline

stream crossings, check carefully, as small colonies of black-winged damselflies patrol the shoreline. The metallic green bodies of the males contrast sharply with the bronze females. Spring brings a cadre of wildflowers, including yellow trout lilies often growing in small clusters among the rock ledges. Unusual flowers include relatively large clusters of tiny, white-flowered goldenseal, perhaps more attractive in late summer when the bright red berries decorate the forest floor. The unique French's shooting star occurs here in some numbers. The species, first identified by Southern Illinois University entomologist George Hazen French in the early part of the last century, lives only at the driplines under sandstone ledges. Here the soil is perpetually moist, and this diminutive

Trapdoor spider

member of the shooting stars usually occurs in rows that reflect the outline pattern of the cliff above. The species blooms in April and May.

One doesn't often associate butterflies with deep, ravine forests, but the falcate orange tip is the exception. These small, white butterflies (superficially resembling the ubiquitous cabbage white of our gardens) cavort along the trails each spring. A true spring ephemeral, the females of this species are white with black markings, but the males, should one land long enough to allow a good view, have bright orange tips on their forewings. If it's just the right time in spring, you may note courting behavior when one or several males dance in the air above a resting female. Strolling through the forests is an adventure, as many of the trees are massive, at least by Illinois standards, and the forest, growing on slopes of varying steepness, has a pleasing openness. In spring, when the leaves are a pale green, the airy forest is a great place for birding, as the targets of your search are easily visible. The trails lead up slopes, down ravines, around massive sandstone outcrops, but perhaps the most interesting areas are when the trail follows the bluff tops and crosses sandstone glades. The view of the lake is impressive, while the flowers and plants of the glades provide a much different perspective on the flora. Here grow species adapted for dry, nearly soil-less conditions: tiny four-petaled bluets, yellow stargrass, a minute member of the amaryllis family, pink sedum, and even prickly pear cactus, sometimes blooming in late June with bright yellow, showy flowers that are a magnet for native bees of the region. Only the imagination, good field guides, and a curiosity for the unexpected are needed to make a visit to Cedar Lake a memorable experience.

CHAPTER 36

Devil's Kitchen Lake—Rocky Bluff Trail

> A perfect spring day—the wildflowers are in peak bloom. Celandine poppy provides glints of sunshine, while blue-eyed Marys engulf trees like floodwaters. Above, the tall trees support not only ephemeral leaves, but an assortment of warblers—Kentucky, worm-eating, hooded, blue-winged, and northern parula—a treat for eyes and ears.
>
> —Susan Post, April 2009

WHEN GEOLOGICAL features excite us, it is usually not a term like *geological sapping* that causes the heart to flutter. Yet when this obscure geological process—groundwater seeping out from a cliff face, undermining a cliff, and causing the subsequent collapse of the saturated soil and rock—creates an immense, overhanging cliff over which a stream flows, we take note. Waterfalls have always been considered some of nature's great wonders, and this one, especially after a heavy downpour, can be truly dramatic. The falls are just a few yards from the start of the Rocky Bluff Trail, located on the northeast corner of Devil's Kitchen Lake, south of the larger Crab Orchard Lake. Called Rocky Bluff Falls, the locals know it as an intermittent waterfall, one that only has a significant amount of flow just after a heavy rain event. The falls, nearly fifty feet in height, has two tiers, and the filmy flow gurgles along a rocky streambed that soon intersects with nearby Grassy Creek. When water is abundant, the small stream has enough force that the second tier is bypassed, and the water tumbles from the top of the cliff in a roaring cascade. For most visits, though, the falls are a mere trickle, and the main attraction is the undercut and the realization that this site has enormous potential for a future visit.

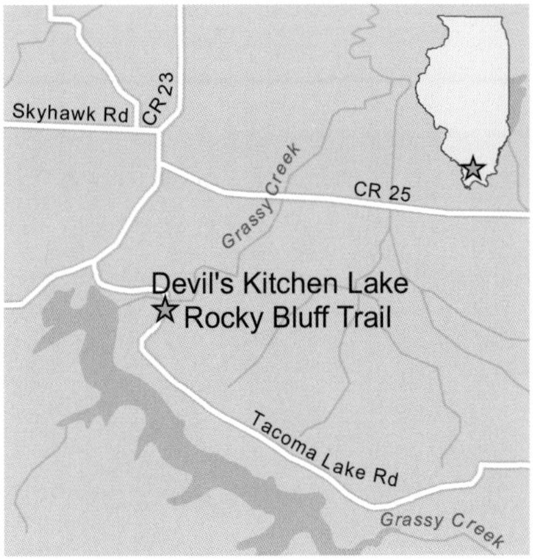

After the steep, rocky trail (a series of stone steps) has wound its way down to the base of the falls and crossed the stream, it soon heads off between the cliff base and Grassy Creek, through a forest that is a carpet of wildflowers in spring. To the left on the floodplain, find large expanses (several acres) of blue-eyed Marys and Virginia bluebells interspersed with bright yellow celandine poppies. While these species are relatively common, their occurrence together makes

Falls at Rocky Branch

Tiger swallowtails at puddle club

White trillium and celandine poppy

for an unusually showy display. To the right, on the lower, rock-strewn slopes of the creek, find large numbers of both great white and white trillium, their porcelain and green threesomes (three petals, three sepals, three leaves) a startling contrast to the moist, fern-and-moss-covered sandstone. Note the flat spirals of maidenhair ferns growing on black, wire-like stems. Add patches of Dutchman's breeches, squirrel corn, spring beauty, blue phlox, and wild geranium, and you have one of the best flower shows in southern Illinois.

Your exploration is not yet complete, though, as the trail heads to the left and soon skirts Grassy Creek. The cliff approaches the trail on the right side and is laced with another geological structure with an equally obtuse name (Liesegang rings) but one that exploits the infinite palette of natural colors deposited when groundwater flows through sandstone. The earth-toned mineral deposits left behind in the concentric rings would be the envy of any potter. The large overhang has a sandy bottom, and if not too many of your peers have hiked this way, large numbers of conical pits decorate the sand. Each is a different size and a closer inspection will reveal a very alien-looking creature buried in the bottom of each. The size of the pit is proportional to the size of its inhabitant, the larva of the ant lion. The adults look somewhat like damselflies with antennae, but the larvae are ice-tong–jawed, ruthless predators that sit in the apex of the pit, waiting for prey to tumble in so they can be skewered and sucked dry—savage nature on display, but on a relatively minute scale.

After escaping the antlion pits, the trail leads to a unique overlook of Grassy Creek and soon heads around a corner and up a series of steep steps into the drier forest above the moist valley. Along the way, note that the understory plants now consist of purple larkspur, mayapple, and fragile fern. On cold winter days, look down at the base of dry plant stems. Here, oddly shaped formations of ice that resemble lacy, inverted cones often develop as moist air, rising from the underlying cavities in the rock, encounters the cold of winter. The trail winds back along the bluff top through an oak-hickory forest and is a good place to view wild turkeys and enjoy the rolling, forested topography of the Shawnee Hills. Accompanying you along the trail during

Frost formation

spring and summer may be a small, brown butterfly—the gemmed satyr—dancing along, just above the dead leaves, only to disappear quickly when it lands. Soon the trail crosses over a rocky creek bed, usually very slick when wet but easily traversed on a newly constructed bridge. This is the creek that forms Rocky Bluff Falls, so tread carefully and stay away from the treacherous edge. If you choose, as you reenter the parking area, take a short trip down the stairs to the base of the falls. It may have rained during your short hike, increasing the flow, but more important, it's another opportunity to take a last look at one of the truly memorable locations in Illinois.

CHAPTER 37

Ferne Clyffe State Park

> Ferne Clyffe is where I go in spring for butterflies and nightjars; in summer, it's for the coolness of the blind canyon that ends in a waterfall and to experience massive Hawk's Cave. Fall is for golden color, while winter is always full of surprises—a gathering of bluebirds, multitudes of dripping icicles, or a bobcat crossing my path.
>
> —Susan Post, December 2012

JUST SOUTH OF WHERE the Illinoian glacier halted, the escarpments of the greater Shawnee Hills, with massive sandstone and shale bedrock, stand ancient, weathered and exposed. Most prominent is the Pennsylvanian sandstone, deposited by a warm sea some 270 million to 310 million years ago. It survived burial by glacial soil and rock deposits that filled in much of the landscape to the north. The land was untouched by the ice, but not unaffected. Canyons that were originally cut by torrential glacial meltwaters have, over time, been widened and deepened by the meandering of clear, rock-bottomed streams. These slow reminders of the past have also carved out shelves, steps, and the so-called "caves" or shelter bluffs in the canyon walls. The caves are actually undercuts in the sandstone with large, over-hanging ledges forming the ceilings. The plant assemblages that developed here are the result of the geological conditions that dictated their character. Ferne Clyffe State Park in Johnson County has excellent examples of sandstone canyon, ledge, and cliff communities. The park covers twenty-four hundred acres and contains unique rock formations, gorges, canyons, shady dells, shelter bluffs (caves), fern-laden cliffs, and even an intriguing, intermittent waterfall.

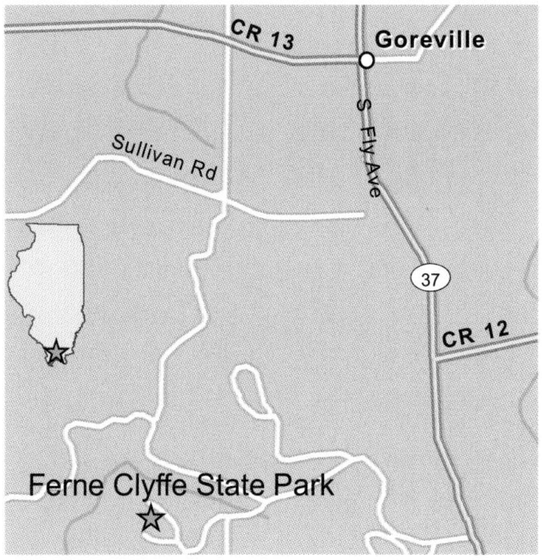

By the early 1900s Ferne Clyffe was already a popular place to visit. Celebrated as a natural scenic spot, it was named for its abundance of ferns located in the box canyon near the waterfall. On Sundays, twenty cents would buy transportation on the morning train from Goreville and admission to the park. At that time, the 140-acre park was owned by Emma Rebman, a schoolteacher and Johnson County school superintendent. By 1949, the state had purchased

Ferns along Round Bluff

the original 140 acres from Rebman. During her stewardship, she took great pleasure in naming various points in the park, including Hawk's Cave and Round Bluff.

Hewn by wind and water, the sheer cliff of Hawk's Cave forms a vast overhang 150 feet long and nearly as high, with excellent acoustics. From the cave one is afforded a fine view of the early-spring upland forest community of Ferne Clyffe State Park. The floor of the overhang may appear to be nothing more than a layer of fine dust, something to linger in without shoes and socks. Close observation of the dust, however, reveals patterns of life. Circular depressions are antlion pits dug by larvae of the insect family Myrmeleontidae. Each pit has a predatory antlion larva covered by dust and lying in wait at the base. Small insects fall into the pit, cannot climb out because of the loose soil, and become a meal for the large-jawed antlion. Sinuous patterns on the floor indicate the passing of various species of snakes that spend winter in the cave. Today, the snakes are much less numerous and the migration is evident only by a few sinuous patterns in the fine dust.

At the base of the cliff, where water dripping from the overhang has formed a ribbon of moisture, may be found an uncommon relative of the prairie shooting star—French's shooting star. Named for George Hazen French, an early entomologist at Southern Illinois University, this diminutive plant was originally thought to exist in a band only ten miles wide across southern Illinois, but isolated populations have since been found in Indiana, Missouri, Arkansas, and Kentucky.

Olive hairstreak butterfly

Male falcate orangetip butterfly

A massive sandstone outlier named Round Bluff by Emma Rebman stands like an island, separated from the other bluffs of the park. Round Bluff, an Illinois Nature Preserve, contains many of the seven hundred species of plants found in the park. A mile trail around the bluff base provides an excellent glimpse of the preserve. In the spring, as one descends into the ravine on the northern side of the bluff, groupings of wildflowers and ferns line the trail—mayapple, yellow trout lily, larkspur, and squirrel corn. The latter covers the wood's floor with lush, feathery foliage. Perhaps the greatest concentration of blooming Jack-in-the-pulpits in the state occurs here. Large sandstone blocks have separated from the canyon walls and create blind alleys and narrow passages within the forest. Each imperceptibly slides toward the valley floor, assisted by gravity, the push of freezing ice, and growing tree roots. The tops of these blocks are isolated islands, many never experiencing human footprints. Saxifrages, mosses, and various species of ferns clothe the face of the bluff in a verdant carpet. Farkleberry, red cedar, and stunted blackjack oaks are the common woody species on the dry, desert-like bluff tops, while spicebush and sassafras are found in the moister areas at its base. During late spring, red accents to the lush green are blooming columbine on the moist side (north) and fire pink on the dry side (south).

While the most common butterflies here are spicebush and eastern tiger swallowtails, for a butterfly enthusiast a spring trip here is a must. Look for olive hairstreaks twirling above the red cedars, goatweed butterflies cruising up and down the

Round Bluff Trail

trail, and falcate orangetips flitting through the forest like spent dogwood petals. Spring tent camping is a treat, as your 5 AM wakeup call is likely the call of a whip-poor-will or a Chuck-will's-widow, two species of nightjars that are fairly rare in Illinois. Visitors with a sharp eye and ear may notice an unusual, bumblebee-mimicking robber fly on the vegetation, blue-throated eastern fence lizards scampering over fallen trees, or the slow rustling of an eastern box turtle through the dry leaves.

Ferne Clyffe State Park, with its valleys, dells, canyons, brooks, ferns, flowers, insects, reptiles, and birds, offers the outdoor visitor infinite variety. In winter, while Starved Rock and Matthiessen State Park have massive icefalls, the ice here is more subtle but equally impressive. Every cliff edge is rimmed with icicles, like a lacy collar, and the dripping waterfall may resemble nothing so much as a large, blue-white stalactite, escaped from the darkness of a cave.

CHAPTER 38

Fults Hill Prairie Nature Preserve

> The rocky hills jut out to the highway; the white rock reflects the hot, afternoon sun. Relief occurs only when we pass an open cave. Where the trees and viney plants are able to grow, columbine litters the rocks with its brilliant, orange-red blossoms dangling on graceful, curved stems. On top of the bluffs are the hill prairies; here, new shoots of prairie clovers and grasses cover the hillside with a fresh green. The delicate blossoms of white, blue-eyed grass interrupt the pattern of green forbs. Dangerously clinging on the rocky overhangs, coreopsis and blue vervain grow, adding much-needed color to the harsh rocks.
>
> —Susan Post, May 2008

TO MOST PEOPLE, prairies are flat grasslands. It is not only the topography, however, that distinguishes a prairie, but the vegetation. Prairies growing on pronounced slopes are called hill prairies. Located high on a west-facing bluff overlooking the Mississippi River valley, Fults Hill Prairie is one of those unique prairies. This small sliver of Illinois, reminiscent of the Missouri Ozarks, is more closely related to the southwestern United States.

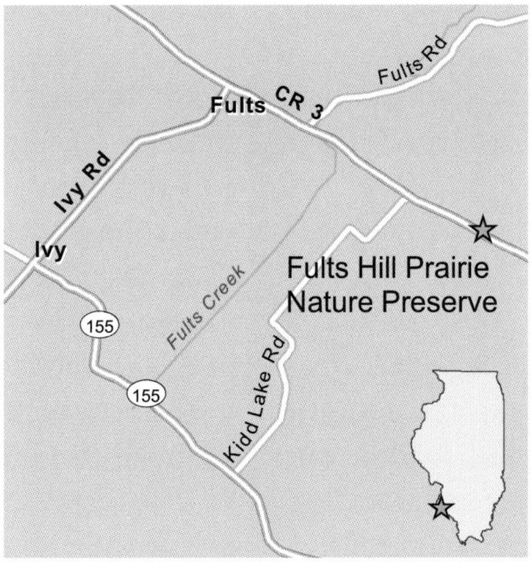

This prairie is part of the old French land grants (long, thin properties) common in St. Clair, Monroe, and Randoph Counties, the boundaries of which were at right angles to the bank of the Mississippi River. The bluff that includes Fults Hill Prairie is tall, towering more than three hundred feet above the bottomlands, and consists of limestone, with a blanket of loess capping the bedrock. For those unfamiliar with the term *loess*, this material is a direct product of glaciation (finely pulverized rock) and is the parent material for much of Illinois's incredibly fertile soil. Loess is sediment formed by the accumulation of silt (in this case, ground up rocks with the texture of flour), picked up by air currents during the dry winters at the edge of recently glaciated land, and deposited downwind. Over time, this material accumulated in layers anywhere from a few inches to many feet thick.

Fults is classified as a loess hill prairie and has two types of vegetation—the slope supports a deciduous forest; during spring, phacelia blankets the slopes. The other type of vegetation is prairie, and while hill prairie bota-

Fults Hill Prairie Nature Preserve

nist Robert A. Evers called the prairie "not rich in species," it is the rare or semi-rare species that makes this hill prairie important.

To explore Fults, use the two hundred wooden steps to climb upward. At the top, wind your way through various overlooks and woods; and within a mile, the prairie appears, and the view is dramatic. The distant hills to the west are the Missouri Ozarks, and elements of their fauna and flora call Fults home. Little bluestem, Indian grass, and big bluestem are the dominant grasses. The purples of leadplant, purple prairie clover, purple coneflower, blue vervain, and the yellows of puccoon and coreopsis break up the green carpet, depending on the season. There is no "official trail" to explore, just narrow, steep paths that lead to moments of discovery. In the spring, look for the white-flowered species of blue-eyed grass, a diminutive relative of the iris. In the fall, the pink blossoms of autumn wild onion grace the path. A look down may reveal a large tiger beetle with a green head and a red-brown body. These are called splendid tiger beetles and occur only along Illinois's western edge and in far southern Illinois. They, and the unusual prairie scorpions that inhabit the steep, rocky slopes, are part of the western fauna. In open, sunny areas, look for gatherings of nectaring butterflies—checkered white, dainty dwarf, buckeye, pearl crescents, and monarchs. If the season is right, you could wonder through a veritable small storm of them dancing around your feet. In early summer, when the vervain blooms, note relatively large numbers

Splendid tiger beetle

Plains scorpion at Fults

of nectaring Nessus sphinx, an uncommon Illinois moth. If you are a close observer, the long, sinuous, bright green shape of a rough green snake may materialize where the prairie meets the woods, visible only because it chose that moment to move. Fults Hill Prairie was dedicated as the state's thirtieth nature preserve in 1970, and in 1986 it was designated a National Natural Landmark by the U.S. Department of the Interior.

Enjoy the view across the wide floodplain of the Mississippi River, feel the ever-blowing wind in your hair, look down to see the nearby Kidd Lake Marsh Nature Preserve at the base of the bluff and its contingent of blooming American lotus in midsummer, and you have an afternoon nature-viewing experience at its absolute finest.

CHAPTER 39

Garden of the Gods Recreation Area

I am on a geology field trip at Garden of the Gods, and I am supposed to be looking at Camel Rock, learning how it came to be. I don't even make it to the lookout, though, as I am mesmerized by a pair of rough green snakes, entwined in a shrubby tree—camouflaged, counter-shaded, bobbing and weaving, a life snake for me.

—Susan Post, October 2005

A TRIP TO Garden of the Gods Recreation Area in the Shawnee Hills without viewing Camel Rock is like going to Yellowstone National Park and not seeing Old Faithful. Don't be like most people at Yellowstone, however, and fail to get off the "main drag" to experience the geological wonders of this landscape firsthand. Anyone with a taste for geology, or those who just like to "climb around on rocks," will find this area most provocative. After viewing the famous Camel Rock formation, visit the nearby wilderness area. Step onto rock ledges clothed with lichens, gaze over untrammeled forest vistas, and create your own names for the fantastic rock formations. Wind your way through the woods to encounter bizarre sandstone bluffs, huge boulders, and eroded sandstone knuckles. View the forest color provided by huge, old-growth oaks, maples, and tulip trees. As expected,

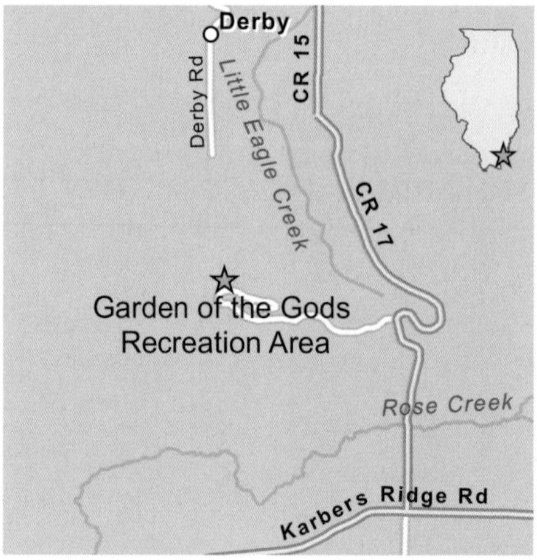

the landscape is spectacular in the fall, but it is equally stunning, albeit more subtle, in the spring. Spring colors are a mix of infinite shades of green, especially when viewed from a rock pinnacle, as the canopy stretches, unbroken, to the horizon. If visiting during a misty or foggy morning, even better, as the moisture will intensify the red, gray, and green of the rocks, lichens, and moss.

The massive Pennsylvanian sandstone escarpments of Garden of the Gods stand ancient, weathered, and exposed for all to see. A visit during a southern Illinois summer will have you craving water. Although none is obvious (except for a hand-pump drinking fountain near the parking area), evidence that water has influenced these formations is everywhere. The sandstone was deposited by a warm sea some 270 million to 310 million years ago. Water, in the form of ancient glacial meltwater and

Face formation

recurring rain, sleet, snow, and ice, over thousands of years has moved along the joints and planes of the sandstone, expanding crevices into fissures, turning fissures into clefts, and eventually creating pinnacles, curiously carved boulders, rock shelters, tunnels, and deep valleys.

The rocks are stacked or eroded into bizarre shapes and have within them odd formations—moulins (weathered holes in the rock), and Liesegang rings (concentric circles of eroded rock with vibrant colors). The Liesegang rings, composed of iron, appear on cliff faces as dark reddish swirls and raised designs with target-like patterns. Chemical changes caused the iron to solidify as iron oxides (rust) between the rock particles; the sandstone is held together by these raised, dark bands of iron and has resisted weathering. The formation takes its name from Raphael Eduard Liesegang, a German chemist. The area is also one of the best places to stand on and view a cuesta, a long, symmetrical ridge with a steep slope on the south side and a long, gentle back slope that inclines toward the north. This continuous ridge of massive, erosion-resistant sandstones extends from Battery Rock, overlooking the Ohio River, to Horseshoe Bluff, overlooking the Mississippi Valley.

Begin to explore the area by taking the short, paved observation trail. Although this walk won't be a "real" wilderness experience, the scenery is well worth it. Along the trail, see formations such as Table Rock, bedrock that has been ground down to a perfectly flat surface; Devil's Smokestack, a huge pillar that formed when the softer sandstone around it washed away; and Camel Rock, the poster child of southern Illinois. Sandstone glades are a prominent feature of the bluff tops. These are openings in the forest that usually feature a mixture of stunted, wind-shaped trees—blackjack oak, post oak, and red cedar—and open, rocky terrain with scattered vegetation. Plants include bluets, pussytoes, shooting stars, and pink oxalis. Near Camel Rock look for farkleberry (a relative of blueberry), a bushy evergreen that bears small, black berries. This plant is restricted to the southern third of Illinois and grows on sandstone cliffs.

Within a half-mile's distance, you will have seen and experienced the most prominent features of Garden of the Gods and warmed your leg mus-

Garden of the Gods Wilderness Area

Liesegang rings

cles for the more challenging feature of the landscape, the Wilderness Trail. The recreation area is bounded on three sides by the Garden of the Gods Wilderness Area, a relatively undisturbed thirty-three-hundred-acre rocky, forested expanse of intriguing terrain. For a unique, intimate experience, hike a few miles in this fortress of solitude. What you will see will delight, challenge those flatland leg muscles, give you a chance to put a name to the various rock formations, and provide a glimpse into the biological and geological past that helped shape southern Illinois.

Camel Rock at Garden of the Gods

CHAPTER 40

Giant City State Park—Trillium Trail

Giant blocks of sandstone, of controversial origin,
Civil War era graffiti encrusted with green moss,
and massive cliffs that beg to be scaled, all pale
in comparison to the spring wildflower show.
—Michael Jeffords, April 2012

SOME ASCRIBE TO THE geological theory that the large blocks of sandstone that form the signature feature of the park eroded away from the cliff and slipped downhill due to gravity; others propose that the seams between the blocks merely eroded away, leaving the maze of clefts that form the "giant city." Whichever theory seems most plausible to you, or even if you simply don't care and just want to enjoy the cool, moss-coated, vertical walls of the sandstone maze on a hot summer day, Giant City State Park is a great place to explore. Civil War soldiers, taking refuge here, carved information high on a vertical wall, leaving their timeless graffiti in an elegant font. But for nature lovers, perhaps the best place to experience the area is near the Makanda entrance to the park on the aptly named Trillium Trail. In fall, during early evening or morning, search the large trees across the road from the parking area, as they may be festooned with numbers of vultures (black and turkey) silhouetted against a colorful sky. These are the inspiration for the esoteric "Vulture Fest" that occurs each summer in nearby Makanda.

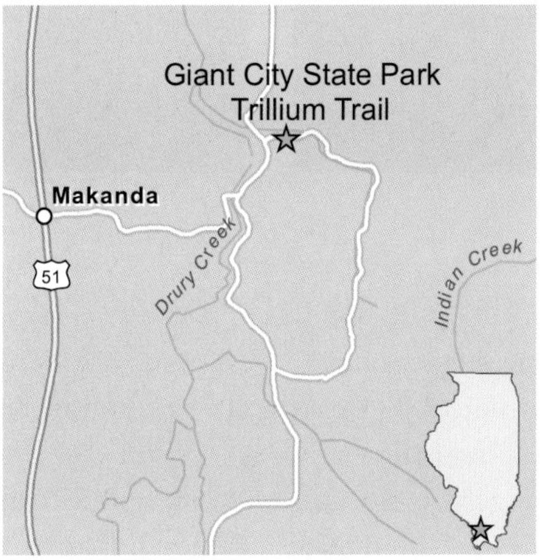

The best time to visit, though, is during April, to hike along the base of the sandstone cliff, through the detached, sandstone blocks that surround the Trillium Trail. The path eventually angles up a series of primitive steps to cross the drier topside. Soon it heads downward and you return to the parking area. This brief description does little, however, to highlight the grand display of wildflowers that occurs here. Trilliums are the stars, with two species, the familiar magenta prairie trillium, scattered in moist pockets of soil, and the less familiar, white trillium, occurring in large numbers. Formerly

Sandstone blocks

Group of white trilliums

called Gleason's trillium, this large, showy species follows the traditional trillium pattern—three petals, three sepals, three leaves—and the flowers have a decided slant to one side when in full bloom. In the northern United States the flower often droops below the leaves, but in southern Illinois they mostly remain erect. While trilliums tend to grow in clumps, here they can be found interspersed with a wide variety of other spring ephemerals. Trilliums are found in the eastern United States, the far western United States, and in eastern Asia, a most odd distribution pattern for this unique group of plants.

Perhaps the showiest display is made up of white trillium and celandine poppy. The bright yellow poppy flowers rival the trilliums in size and can grow to eighteen inches tall in rich sites on the forest floor. Their sap is yellow and will stain your fingers when the stem is broken. In some areas of southern Illinois, celandine poppies create lavish, hillside displays, but here they merely add accent color to the wildflower carpet. Speaking of

Yellow trout lilies

White trillium flowers

carpets, imagine a soft, filmy, blue-green layer of leaves, growing in a flat plane several inches off the ground, and you have a fourth notable species along the Trillium Trail: squirrel corn. A relative of the familiar bleeding hearts of our gardens, the white flowers, growing on erect stems above the filmy canopy, shine with a fine porcelain texture. When viewed close up, they resemble miniature hearts. Growing in the same habitat, but seldom in the same grouping, is a close relative of squirrel corn, Dutchman's breeches. The flowers have a similar color, texture, and growth habit, but these flowers resemble inverted Dutch pantaloons. In addition to the wildflowers, look for bumblebees and the bumblebee sphinx moth. These two species form a mimicry complex—the stinging bumblebee is the model; the harmless moth is its mimic. Both model and mimic occur together on the abundant larkspur and Dutchman's breeches. Heading up the stairs a little earlier in the season may lead to a discovery of yellow trout lilies along the path, their glowing, yellow flowers like miniature Easter lilies.

Vulture roost

Three species of trout lilies call Illinois home—the prairie trout lily (rare and seldom observed), the white trout lily, and the yellow trout lily. In northern and central Illinois white trout lilies predominate with a smattering of yellows in select locations. In southern Illinois, the yellow trout lily is dominant, and the white form becomes uncommon.

The top of the bluff is radically different than the fecund flower show below. A dry forest of oaks and hickories grows nearly to the edge of the bluff, interspersed with desert-like sandstone glades, their only vegetation consisting of mosses, lichens, occasional clumps of bluets, yellow star grass, and colonies of prickly pear cactus. Bright green tiger beetles run and flit ahead on the trail, always just out of reach of the aspiring photographer, and zebra swallowtails add a final touch of magic to this out-of-the-way corner of Giant City State Park.

CHAPTER 41

Horseshoe Lake State Fish and Wildlife Area

> Even before we turn into the park, we have had memorable wildlife sightings—a mother otter with three kits crossing the road, a dozen Mississippi kites taking advantage of overhead thermals, and a distant skein of geese, tiny against the afternoon sky.
>
> —Susan Post, August 2008

IMAGINE A LANDSCAPE that could be from the bayous of Louisiana, a place of striking bald cypress in a pea-green, crescent-shaped lake, rife with waterfowl, American lotus, wading birds, and southern solitude, and you have Horseshoe Lake. A cutoff remnant of the lower Mississippi River, known as an ox-bow lake, the cypress trees reflect the nearness of the river and its propensity to flood. When viewed from a distance, the near-yearly flood cycle is recorded on trunks—the lime green lichens that decorate each trunk do not fare well under the muddy waters of the mighty Mississippi. Thus, a distinct waterline is visible, especially during the winter months, when visitors to the area have the place pretty much to themselves. During the cold season, thousands of Canada geese, greater white-fronted geese, and snow geese spend time feeding in the nearby fields and decorate the swamp with their black, white, and grey bodies. While a common site in most of Illinois, seeing Canada geese swimming among the cypress is actually quite striking and presents enormous opportunities for the photographer. The area can be experienced from the comfort of your car, as a road leads around the periphery of the lake and good views can be had during just about any season. Stops at various overlooks, some that feature short boardwalks into the swamp, provide easy access to the buttressed, cypress trees. Look for wood ducks, ring-necked ducks, and hooded mergansers in late winter. Though skittish, they can easily be viewed from the confines of your car. In spring, various woodpeckers, prothonotary warblers, and great blue herons are frequently seen in the nearshore shallows. Summer is the time to experience the American lotus in full bloom: the great ivory

Fall color at Horseshoe Lake

Canada geese in swamp

American lotus flower

flowers decorate the quiet, southwest corner of the lake, and they are quite near the road. Here numbers of red-winged blackbirds, with the territorial tinkling calls of males, nest from late spring into summer. For a more rigorous experience, a parking lot on the north end leads to a causeway that crosses the lake onto an island. The hiking/biking trail follows the shoreline of Horseshoe Island (the round-trip is nearly six miles) and eventually leads to Horseshoe Lake Nature Preserve, a near virgin forest of beech, sugar maple, swamp chestnut oak, and American elm.

Fall here is unique, as the cypress are deciduous conifers, and before they lose their needles, they turn a glorious golden-yellow, creating a scene of southern splendor on crisp, blue-sky days. As noted above, visiting here in winter features solitude, the decorative boles of the cypress reflected in the gunmetal grays and blues of the quiet waters, and the birds—masses of birds.

Located in the most southern tip of Illinois, just a few miles north of the confluence of the Ohio River with the Mississippi, the area is easily reached from I-57, a mere four hundred miles south of Chicago. Even though Louisiana may feature New Orleans, for those seeking a swamp and wetlands experience, they need travel no farther south to spend a few days in a place where "in the quiet and solitude, the bayous of the Deep South come to mind."

CHAPTER 42

LaRue–Pine Hills Research Natural Area

Hiking here is like traversing an endless, linear florist shop. The constants are blankets of purple larkspur, filler for the multiple arrangements, and bouquets of trilliums, white phacelia, bluebells, and ragwort, all interspersed along the trail—a wildflower parade that stays put as I move along.

—Michael Jeffords, April 2011

IF A TRIP TO Great Smoky Mountain National Park is not an option, don't despair, as a little bit of the Smokies can be found in Illinois at LaRue–Pine Hills, dubbed *Illinois's Biological Garden of Eden*. The area rivals the Smoky Mountains in plant diversity but cannot compete with its sheer numbers of salamanders, as the Appalachians are the salamander capital of the world. But then, the national park doesn't close a road for the annual snake migrations, as does LaRue–Pine Hills!

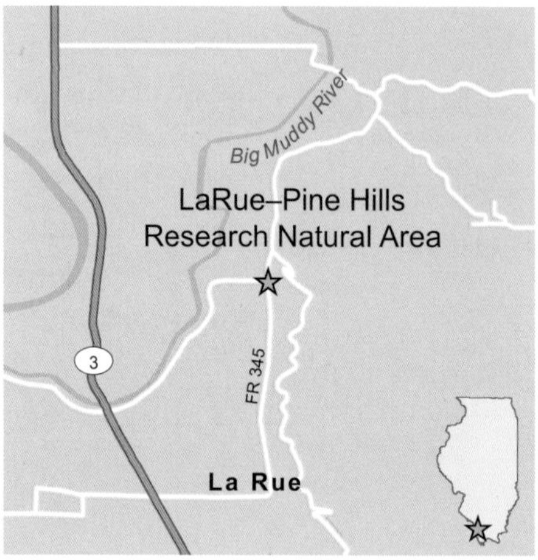

La Rue–Pine Hills Research Natural Area is a five-mile-long by two-mile-wide strip of land running north-south along the western edge of the Shawnee National Forest in Union County in the Ozark Natural Division. Designated in 1970 as the National Forest Service's first Ecological Area, and in 1991 as a National Research Natural Area by the Department of the Interior, LaRue–Pine Hills is an enticing melting pot of widely different habitats. Limestone cliffs, like those in the Missouri Ozarks, abut swamplands reminiscent of Louisiana. Densely wooded coves, similar to those of the Appalachians, also are a prominent feature of the landscape. In a four-square-mile area, twelve hundred plant species occur—40 percent of all the known Illinois plant species and half of all plants native to Illinois. Ninety percent of the state's known mammal species live here, including the elusive bobcat, which routinely ranges over the rugged forest ridges, and the rare eastern woodrat, a species of pack rat that lives at the base of the bluffs and creates large middens (mounds of debris and artifacts collected by many generations of rats).

The area's reptiles and amphibians have a special place of honor here—the road at the base of the bluff, between the cliffs and the swamp, is closed

Celandine poppy expanse in cove forest

Cricket frog with unusual green color

Copperhead crossing the "road"

for their migration from bluff to swamp and back again, for two months during spring and fall. It is the only road in the United States that is closed biannually for snake migration—a favorable and memorable occurrence in the annals of human relationships with snakes.

Sixty-five species of snakes, frogs, turtles, skinks, salamanders, and lizards are known to live here. At LaRue–Pine Hills, the limestone bluffs of the Mississippi River are adjacent to extensive swamps that occupy the old river channel of the Big Muddy River. Walking the road means you can have one foot in the Ozark Division and the other in the Lower Mississippi River Division! Rarely is the transition of these natural divisions so abrupt, and the juxtaposition of habitat types provide the amphibian and reptile species with all of their life cycle requirements—foraging and reproduction in the swamps and over-wintering sites in the bluffs. Whether the road is so flooded or muddy that you walk it in knee boots, or so dusty that your shoes kick up miniature dust devils, hundreds of tiny frogs will celebrate your presence as they hop along

Larkspur growing on rocky slope

in front of you. So remember why the road is closed and watch your step!

The area is not just a haven for reptiles and amphibians; each spring the talus slopes along the base of the bluff become carpets of wildflowers, and a two-mile walk along the road will yield significant displays of some very unusual species. Any large white patch on the upper slopes near the bluff base is likely a mass of cleft phlox, a spring ephemeral that prefers dry habitats, and the talus slopes seem to perfectly suit cleft phlox. The dry bluff tops can also be cloaked with this species. Walking the road is like traveling through a narrow botanical garden, with celandine poppy, white trillium,

Bluffs of Pine Hills

Virginia bluebell, woodland phlox, and, perhaps the most numerous of all, vast colonies of purple larkspur that seem to flow up the steep slopes. Watercress grows in the adjacent ponds; while phacelia, an eastern species, clusters along in the low areas between road and cliff. The uncommon sessile trillium is sometimes encountered, interspersed with the more common prairie trilliums. With the abundance of flowers comes a diversity of butterflies and moths. Look for hummingbird moths, the uncommon Nessus sphinx, various swallowtails, and even fifty species of stinkbugs!

Hiking along the bluff tops, with views of old-growth, cove forests below, will help you appreciate the diversity of this landscape and the breadth of the lower Mississippi River floodplain that stretches to the far horizon. In spring, bring your binoculars, for the forest is alive with spring warblers—hooded, yellow, worm-eating, Kentucky, and Louisiana waterthrushes. You may even encounter the rare pink azalea, a denizen of the eastern mountains, and short leaf pine. Collectively, for anyone interested in seeing the most biological and habitat diversity in the shortest time, LaRue–Pine Hills, located in Union County, is the place to go. No other location in Illinois can potentially yield the wealth of species found in this very charismatic strip of our biological heritage.

CHAPTER 43

Little Grand Canyon

As you descend the canyon in spring, listen for the Louisiana waterthrush's loud, ringing call, and look for the tail-bobbing and swaying antics of the bird. They seem to be able to rush down the slick, moss-laden terraces. We, however, will take our time.
—Susan Post, April 2012

NO MORE ICONIC SITE exists in North America than the Grand Canyon of the Colorado River. A billion years of geological history are showcased in this mile-deep, erosional slash across northern Arizona. Because this is one of the driest areas in the country, the geological layer cake is on full display.

Illinois, too, has such an iconic canyon embedded on the far western edge of the Shawnee National Forest. Although not quite so large or well known as its namesake, for a state characterized as "flat and uninteresting" by many, a visit to Little Grand Canyon can be quite an adventure. Unlike the Arizona version, Illinois's Little Grand Canyon is cloaked with vegetation, ranging from upland, oak-hickory forests on the ridges to American beech, maples, and sycamore growing along the canyon floor. Its geology is also revealed, although somewhat more subtly. Eroded sandstone, courtesy of Cedar Creek and its tributaries, created this unique box canyon. The canyon opens onto the Mississippi River floodplain near Turkey Bayou, and the Big Muddy River flows across the entrance. During the epic floods of 1993, the Little Grand Canyon was inundated for several weeks during the summer by the flooded Mississippi; this killed many of the very large trees, especially the beeches, resulting in the lower canyon now exhibiting an early successional forest, complete with a much thicker, shrubby understory.

Hiking the three-mile trail that follows the canyon, created by the Civilian Conservation Corps (CCC) during the Great Depression, can be a challenge, especially the section that heads down to the valley floor through an always-slippery, steep-sided side canyon. Stone steps, chiseled from the canyon floor by the CCC, make the descent a little easier, but

Mouth of Little Grand Canyon

when coated with water during spring, or after a summer's growth of moss and algae, the descent can be downright treacherous, so be careful! The canyon floor, especially in spring, is a mosaic of wildflowers, highlighted by colonies of bright yellow celandine poppy, pale blue Jacob's ladder, Dutchman's breeches, and Virginia bluebells. Visitors may also be treated to a show of spring tiger and zebra swallowtail butterflies along the winding trail that follows the valley, crisscrossing Cedar Creek. At the canyon's mouth, the creek empties into the Big Muddy River. Side trips to the sculpted, sandstone canyon walls may yield several seasonal waterfalls, the swirls of Liesegang rings, or just a nice place to relax under the massive, cool, sandy-bottomed sandstone overhangs. Look for both American and Fowler's toads hopping about. American toads have dark spots that contain one or two warts and a mottled chest, while Fowler's toads have three or more small warts in the spots and, if their chest has spots, it's limited to one in the center.

Leaving the lush floor of the canyon for the nearly four-hundred-foot climb out requires a bit of rock scrambling at the Three Sisters Waterfall. A series of switchbacks leads to a lookout point with a sweeping view of the other side of the canyon and the Mississippi River floodplain. The sinuous course of the Big Muddy parallels the ridge leading back to the parking lot and mimics the several species of snakes that use the canyon as a winter hibernacula. The trail follows the ridge top through a dry forest, and it is lined with flowers in the spring—wild blue phlox and the occasional

Ravine entrance into Canyon floor

Large puddle club of male swallowtails

colony of shooting star. This area is a preferred feeding and mating territory for large numbers of swallowtail butterflies. Keep your eyes peeled for spring migrants, unusual insects, perhaps even sightings of male eastern fence lizards that showcase their metallic-blue neck patches while doing female-attracting pushups on tree trunks. While perhaps the hike is not as grueling as the one down and up the "other" Grand Canyon, the three to four hours spent here is well worth the effort and provides an intimate encounter with the diverse landscape that resides, and sometimes hides, within Illinois.

Fowler's toad

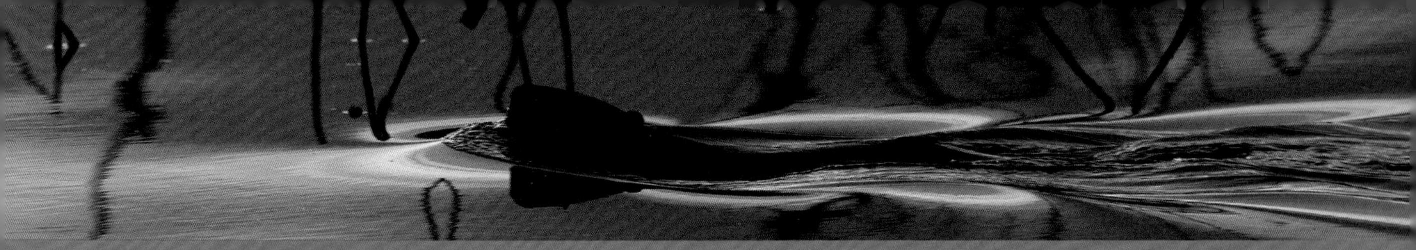

CHAPTER 44

Mermet Lake Conservation Area

Just when we were thinking, "This is the first time we haven't 'seen' something at Mermet," I spy a black and white tussle on the pavement—two jakes (young male turkeys), nails scraping the asphalt, beaks down each other's throats, and feathers fluffed and ruffled, like two high school guys fighting over a girl—oh wait, that's what they are doing!

—Susan Post, October 2012

THE AREA SURROUNDING Mermet Lake Conservation Area in Massac County was settled much later than the other areas along the Ohio River due to the deep water of its cypress swamp. The swampland, referred to as the Mermet Bottoms, even prevented the original land surveyors from mapping parts of it. The small town of Mermet began as a campsite for the construction workers of the Chicago, Burlington and Quincy Railroad, completed in 1910. With the formation of the Cache River Drainage District in 1911, attempts were made to drain the lowlands, but the Mermet Bottoms remained low and swampy. Remnants of the swamp that once blanketed much of the Coastal Plain Division can be seen as a few old cypress trees standing in the middle of the lake.

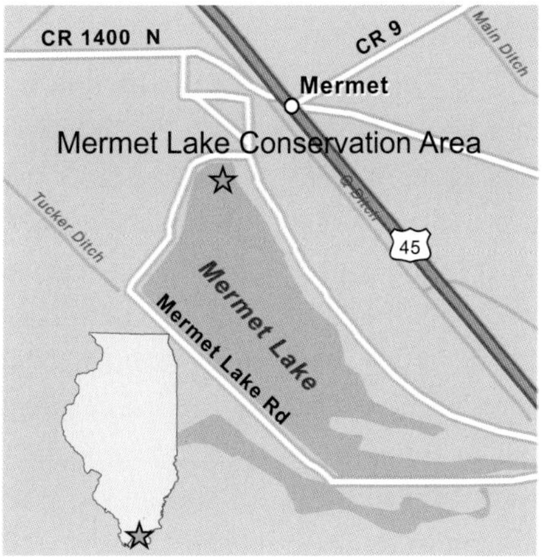

The state purchased the land in the early 1940s for development as a wildlife refuge. During 1962, a system of levees was constructed, creating a lake for duck hunting. Each fall, the level of the lake is lowered to accommodate hunters. After the hunting season has passed, the water level is restored, and in the spring, over two hundred acres of open fields are planted to various grains to attract waterfowl. Even though Mermet was developed for hunting, more than 90 percent of the visitors are area fishermen angling for largemouth bass, channel catfish, and sunfish, and there are wildlife viewers who hope to catch a glimpse of a beaver, a bald eagle, or an American bittern. Mermet Lake is perhaps the premier wildlife viewing area in Illinois, and you never have to leave the comfort of your car.

A drive or walk around the five-mile perimeter road at Mermet is reminiscent of Florida, especially in the summer when the heat and humidity mimic the Deep South. Double-crested cormorants cluster

Tupelo reflections

on a dead cypress, their wings outstretched, drying after a bout of fishing. Great blue herons stalk the shadows created by the gray stumps of downed cypress, while a great white egret flies overhead.

Begin your journey by following the one-way levee road around the lake. Take advantage of the first few pull-offs to admire the American lotus and to look for birds and turtles. To the right, along part of the levy, each spring you may encounter large beds of copper iris, a plant that reaches its furthest extent north in this area. The flowers, ranging in color from copper to red-violet to merlot, form quite a display, and during some years, a purple form appears, likely a hybrid between the copper and equally stunning blue iris. During July, the northeast corner of the lake is covered with the large, cream-yellow blossoms of American lotus; and by late summer, hundreds of red-winged blackbirds start to gather here, perching on the lotus seedpods, giving the impression the pods are alive. Also during summer, other areas around the levee road feature stands of lizard's tail, an unusual plant with white, curved flower clusters that project above the leaves.

Check the levees and adjacent open fields for eastern wild turkeys, especially around dusk, and also for deer, as both favor the area between the woods and the lake. In August, the wet areas feature the bright red blooms of cardinal flower. The ponds usually have Canada geese with goslings in the spring and early summer, and look for turtles poking their snouts through the water. Investigate the various boat ramps, for at times, these are places to view egrets roosting in the large, skeletal cypress trees. A look down at the water may reveal a grass pickerel, silently fanning its tail among the moss and debris, hoping to elude the wading birds. Multitudes of whirligig beetles often form dizzying patterns on the water's quiet surface, while first-instar water striders try out their new, hydrophobic skates near the lake's edge. Hairs on their feet allow them to "walk" on water.

At the south end of the lake, encounter one of the better areas for turtle viewing. Every available log is often crammed with red-eared sliders; dozens of them stretch out their back legs in seeming ecstasy as they bask. As reptiles, turtles maintain their body temperature by relying on external sources of heat.

Grouping of copper iris

Jousting young male turkeys (jakes)

Great blue heron at swamp's edge

Notice that as some of them bask they extend their extremities; this encourages any parasites, such as leeches, to drop off. Snakes, primarily northern water snakes, are visible along the shore as they swim among the partially submerged rocks.

Along parts of the road, the lake appears more open, and on your right is a ditch formed by the construction of the levee road. Don't fail to check here for muskrat and beaver. During spring, the ponds within the swamp area harbor mallards, wood ducks, pied-billed grebes, and blue-winged teal. Various mergansers and even rafts of white pelicans sometimes make a appearance. Scan the open water for giant rafts of coots; look for large cypress in the middle of the lake (remnants of the old swamp)—bald eagles and ospreys often perch here. Take advantage of the many pull-offs to scan the lake and the surrounding area. Check for excitable belted kingfishers, aggressive birds that express displeasure by giving a rattling call that has been compared to a New Year's Eve noisemaker.

Any season, and any time of day, is a good time to visit Mermet Lake Conservation Area. Unfortunately, from November to the end of waterfowl-hunting season, the area is closed to the general public to allow hunting. Don't let this deter you, though, and visit often to enjoy the wildlife spectacle.

Sunset over Mermet Lake

CHAPTER 45

Piney Creek Ravine Nature Preserve

While the rock art is a fascinating find, if you are entomologically inclined, the mud dauber tubes that share the rock art's canvas are equally interesting. These tubes are nests for the wasp's larvae and have been provisioned with paralyzed spiders. Today they hold only mummified remains in a twenty-first-century sarcophagus.

—Susan Post, October 2007

NESTLED ALONG THE western edge of the Shawnee National Forest lies a landscape more indicative of the Missouri Ozarks than of Illinois. It extends in a thin, rugged band just east of the floodplain of the Mississippi River in far southwestern Illinois. The landscape is characterized by very steep bluffs, mostly clothed in forests, with a spotting of hill prairies on exposed bluff tops. The plants found here are a combination of northern species such as sphagnum moss, and Ozarkian species such as Bradley's spleenwort (a rare fern). Piney Creek Ravine Nature Preserve, straddling the Randolph County–Jackson County line, is representative of this natural division and is one of only two places in Illinois where the shortleaf pine grows naturally. Shortleaf pines have slender, drooping branches and trunks covered by a light, cinnamon-red bark that is broken into large, scaly plates.

They have two to three thin needles in a cluster and are less than three inches long.

Given the eons that Piney Creek has had to work on the landscape, it has produced an impressive bevy of troughs, overhangs, waterfalls, and rocky pools, perhaps most notable because this area differs so dramatically from the surrounding agricultural landscape. The valley developed as part of a drainage system following the retreat of the Illinoian Glacier some one hundred thousand years ago.

Although not easy to find, the preserve is well worth a visit during any season, but spring, fall, and even winter provide great viewing opportunities and nearly absolute, sandstone-encased solitude. A loop trail meanders along the bluff top through a forest of post and blackjack oak, with occasional examples of the aforementioned shortleaf pine. The trail eventually crosses scenic Piney

Piney Creek Ravine in fall

Rocky forest with shortleaf pine

Fall mushroom display

Creek that cascades down a series of sandstone shelves before wending its way down the valley. In spring, a great diversity of wildflowers populate the rich forest, including trilliums, spring beauty, and pussytoes, a plant with fuzzy leaves resembling a cat's paw. If it's a wet spring, a scenic waterfall is present near the beginning of the trail (where you walk over the top) and near the end of the trail (where you pass by in the valley below). If you have a hand lens and are botanically inclined, the moist sandstone walls support a variety of nonflowering plants (remember those beginning lectures in your college botany class?) such as liverworts and mosses. Most rock surfaces have a thin coating of some botanical marvel, with an especially creative group of rock-loving lichens on the drier surfaces. Along the valley floor, the streambed is often only a sheet of pure sandstone, so be careful, as it can be coated with a slick film of algae. Look for various insects along the shoreline, including the attractive black-winged damselfly.

While enjoying the eminently photographable scenery of Piney Creek, keep your eyes open for its animals, including the large American millipede, up to six inches long with a multitude of legs supporting a cylindrical body. For a lesson in coordination and choreography, spend a few moments watching the creature move about the landscape, its legs moving in a sinuous synchrony worthy of any New York chorus line. A few hours spent exploring may also yield sightings of the eastern fence lizard (in spring note the bright blue neck patch of courting males), American toads, garter snakes, and, if you are lucky, the occasional rough green snake, and perhaps a fleeting glimpse of a blue racer.

Even though this might be your first visit to Piney Creek, humans have actually lived here for eons, evidenced by their artwork. This area has the largest concentration of prehistoric rock art in Illinois, represented by nearly two hundred designs that date from 500–1000 A.D. (called the Late Woodland Period) and 1000–1500 A.D. (the Mississippian Period). The rock art is of two types: petroglyphs, created by pecking or grinding designs into the rock surface, and pictographs, paintings produced by grinding various minerals, such as limestone, into a yellow or red powder, mixing it with animal fats, and painting designs onto the surface of the rocks. Petroglyphs visible here include depictions of humans, deer, serpents, and crosses. The various pictographs show human figures, deer, birds, human hands, and even a canoe. While they are not always easy to distinguish, take your time and enjoy this artful legacy from the distant past. In 2001, the rock art of Piney Creek Ravine was placed on the National Register of Historic Places.

A final note: the fall colors here can be spectacular, so time your visit for late October to enjoy the show. If the year has been dry, the colors may be somewhat dampened, but the early leaf fall does not detract from your visit—it only reveals the splendor of the sandstone canyon, the life's work of meandering Piney Creek.

CHAPTER 46

Rim Rock/Pounds Hollow

> Columbine perch precariously on slabs of slick sandstone, their flowers dangle and dance in the breeze on the edge of the abyss. No close look for me.
>
> —Susan Post, April 2011

PICTURE AN UNUSUALLY scenic trail that climbs up the rear of a sandstone escarpment, past a mysterious, ancient wall built millennia ago by native peoples, and you have the teaser for a day of exploration at Rim Rock/Pounds Hollow Recreation Area. Embedded deep in the wilds of Pope County, the area is so distinctive that it was designated a National Recreation Trail in 1980. The trail soon skirts the edge of an impressive valley, dubbed by early settlers as *the pounds*, an *old country* term that means *some sort of enclosure*. Thus, the rock escarpment is called Rim Rock and the valley below is named Pounds Hollow; both have enough unique landscape and natural history features to appeal to the casual visitor and certainly to those interested in delving deeper into the natural history of this fascinating area.

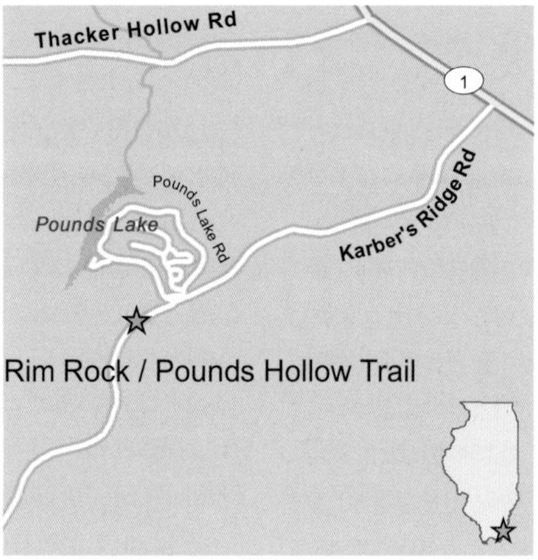

On Rim Rock, early attempts at farming met with limited success, and the land was reclaimed and planted to various trees, including the large cedar grove planted by the Civilian Conservation Corps (CCC) during the 1930s. The real stars, though, of this dry, upland forest reside along the cliff edges bordering the deep valley below. Here, the 300-million-year-old Pounds Sandstone emerges from the forest and ends abruptly in sheer cliffs, creating distinctive, sandstone glade communities for several hundred yards between the trail and the cliff edge. If you desire a closer look, tread carefully, as the vegetation is fragile and the wet rocks can be very slippery, especially in spring and winter. A slip, and the hundred-foot drop to the valley floor will be very unforgiving!

Plants of the glades have adapted to the harsh conditions—little water, except from runoff and seepage from the nearby forest, and almost no

Pounds Hollow

soil, except in the numerous cracks and crevices that have eroded into the sandstone. First note the cadre of massive, gnarled cedar trees, windswept and craggy, Illinois's version of bristlecone pines. Some may be four hundred years old. Surrounding the cedars find cushions of mosses, growing like green powder puffs on the rock. The wildflowers of the glades include common blue violet, tiny, four-petaled bluets with a propensity for soil-filled cracks, dwarf dandelion, pussytoes, violet wood sorrel, false garlic, yellow star grass, and prickly pear cactus. The latter's presence should remove any doubt about the dryness of this habitat. The nearby dry oak forest is dominated by black and white oaks, and each spring an expansive display of shooting stars lines the trail.

After exploring the uplands, head down via a series of wooden platforms and stone steps into the valley below. Perhaps the claustrophobic or those worried about earthquakes that might cause a slight shift in the geological features should remain above; but, for most, the trip down is quite an adventure. The trail, sometimes outfitted with wooden steps, leads between huge blocks of moist sandstone. A look skyward will reveal only a narrow sliver of blue, and in most places the clefts are only an arm's width across. Underfoot, primitive stone steps (compliments of the CCC) can be treacherous, and after a rainstorm, the trail actually becomes a small streambed for a time, so boots might be advisable in spring. The walls are cloaked with a thin layer of moss and interesting

Columbines growing on cliff top

Slots through sandstone blocks

ferns, including the unusual walking fern, a species that calls cracks and crevices in the dark, cool cliff recesses home. Even the occasional salamander—slimy, two-lined, or zig-zag—may be seen skittering about on the clammy walls. All too soon the trail emerges onto a talus slope and leads into the valley—Pounds Hollow. The forest here is moist, open, and dominated by large American beech, tulip tree, sugar maple, and various oaks. It doesn't take much imagination to note that a return trip in fall is a necessity. Unlike most forests in Illinois that have a dearth of flowers come fall, the forests and sandstone glades here boast several species of goldenrod, asters, and sunflowers that just add to the already showy canopy color.

Spring wildflowers are abundant and include squirrel corn, dwarf larkspur, Jacob's ladder, prairie trillium, and colonies of white trillium, whose large, showy, tri-petaled flowers accent the verdant trailside leading up and out of the valley. Many species of ferns also call the hollow home. Rattlesnake, Christmas, marginal shield, and common polypody keep the understory green, even after the demise of the spring blooms. A visit in spring

Mating wheel bugs

Spring form of luna moth

when the redbud and dogwood are in full bloom and the beech canopy is a filmy, ephemeral green is nothing short of spectacular. Look closely at trees and small shrubs, as luna moths frequent the hollow and are often encountered unexpectedly. For most visitors, this is a once-in-a-lifetime experience, even though the giant, pale-green, long-tailed beauty of a moth is really the most common of the giant silkmoths found in Illinois.

North of the valley floor, the Beaver Trail leads to Pounds Lake. While plenty of evidence exists of these mammals along the trail, encounters are rare. Instead, look for their dams, gnawings, scent-marking mounds, and tracks. A final treat for some, and maybe a shock for others, is that the area seems to be a congregating area for the large, lethal (at least to other insects), ominous-looking wheel bug. This largest of the assassin bugs in Illinois has a large, cog-shaped protuberance on its thorax and is quite distinctive. Although usually solitary, they occasionally congregate here by the hundreds, so look for them, enjoy them from a distance (they have a painful bite), and consider their presence an added bonus to this unique area of the Shawnee National Forest.

CHAPTER 47

Simpson Township Barrens Natural Area

> Large areas of barrens were converted into forests "as if by magic" when the anthropogenic fires that maintained them were stopped and the oak sprouts became trees.
>
> —Henry Allan Gleason, *Annals of the Association of American Geographers*, 1922

IF A SINGLE WORD could define the Shawnee National Forest, *diversity* would be most appropriate. The Shawnee occupies an area of Illinois just south of where the Illinoian Glacier stopped during the Pleistocene Epoch (about 120,000 years ago). Here, massive sandstone, limestone, and shale escarpments form the dominant landscape feature—ancient and eroded. Today, a mantle of trees covers most of the landscape, but not all. Glades are open areas in the forest where the bedrock is at or near the surface. Rock ledges are windswept, inhospitable places; trees grow only around the edges and in the ever-widening cracks and faults in the rock. The deep, steep-sided ravines are verdant jungles of American beech, maple, and a host of other tree species. The dominant landscape feature, though, is the forest, mostly of oak and hickory, that supports great tree diversity across the varied topography.

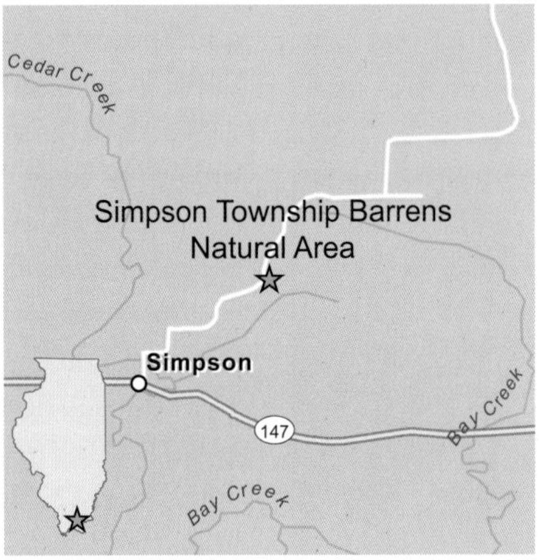

Barrens occur within this landscape as unique, open habitats that, while not exactly pretty to the eye, are important components of the forest ecosystem. The term "barrens" may provide an impression that would deter a visitor into thinking the site is not worth visiting, but nothing could be further from the truth. While they may be barren of typical forest vegetation, these communities are rich in life and complex in structure. Barrens occur on sandstone, limestone, or shale, and they owe their existence to a balance of natural forces, including periodic fires, that prevent them from becoming a forest. Unlike forests, where trees dominate, in a barrens community the herbaceous layer is equally as important as the scant trees. The landscape has many vines, lichens, and mosses scattered about in patches of open ground. Surface rocks contribute to the unstable, often poor soil

Simpson Township Barrens in late spring

conditions. The plant communities, however, remain very diverse with white, post, and blackjack oaks common (although all are scattered, stunted, and limby). The herb layer has farkleberry, little bluestem, Venus' looking glass, purple milkweed, Indian pink, pale purple coneflower, New Jersey tea, and a host of other species. Animals include Ozark Baltimore checkerspot butterflies and eastern hognose snakes.

While many barrens are scattered throughout the Shawnee National Forest, Simpson Township Barrens is easily accessible, located a few miles north of the small community of Simpson, along Trigg Tower Road. A small pull-off on the gravel road and an interpretive sign designate when you have arrived. Note the different "look" of the place; slabs of limestone dot the surface, making the soils alkaline, and support a combination of forest and prairie plants that create a diverse expanse of landscape. During the warm season, prepare to be surprised by the flora and fauna of Simpson Barrens. In late spring, when the purple milkweed blooms, their giant, purple globes of flowers can be dripping with butterflies, especially the large and showy great spangled fritillaries. But look closely, as those smaller but equally showy butterflies, black with orange, white, and yellow spots, are Ozark Baltimore checkerspots. They sip nectar from many flowers, but they may also be found imbibing various environmental fluids,

Ozark Baltimore checkerspot feeding on fluids from a dead box turtle

Eastern hognose snake

such as those found on the carcass of a decaying box turtle! Other butterfly residents include silvery checkerspots, the occasional sleepy orange, and a diversity of large swallowtails. The fringes of the barrens, where it grades into the surrounding forest, support a significant population of Indian pinks, a plant originally thought by early settlers to cure intestinal worms. Plants growing here that are more typical of the tallgrass prairies to the north include rattlesnake master, pale purple coneflower, bird's-foot violet, and even the brilliant yellow hoary puccoon. In summer, butterfly milkweed provides nectar islands for native bees, wasps, and various skippers. The avian serenade includes numbers of indigo buntings, cardinals, and perhaps even the occasional yet elusive scarlet and summer tanagers.

Encounters with herpetofauna may include an eastern hognose snake. If it is aware of your presence, it may run through its repertoire of defensive

Indian pinks against limestone

Mating periodical cicadas

strategies, starting with coiling up and inflating its body and head to resemble an Old World cobra. And if that doesn't frighten you away, then perhaps regurgitating its last meal and secreting foul-smelling musk from its anal glands will do the trick. A final ruse is simply to roll over, complete with open mouth and forked-tongue lolling on the dry soil, and play dead. The eastern hognose is a most entertaining reptile. Be aware that while the eastern hognose is harmless, the barrens community is also home to the nonaggressive yet venomous copperhead, so watch where you step, as the copperhead is a master of disguise, resembling a cluster of fallen leaves. In late summer, numbers of grasshoppers complete the faunal picture that is Simpson Barrens; come prepared with camera, curiosity, and enjoy a stroll through a barrens that is certainly not barren at all. Be warned, though, that tick and chigger repellent is a necessity for any visit here.

CHAPTER 48

Trail of Tears State Forest

Whenever I walk the fire roads here, the Robert Frost poem *The Road Not Taken* goes through my mind. I wonder, as the trail winds through the woods, did I take the right path. What am I missing . . . ?

—Susan Post, October 2010

SOUTHERN ILLINOIS HAS more kinds of trees than does all of Europe. A visitor can get a glimpse of this arboreal variety at Trail of Tears State Forest—huge American beeches in ravine forests, dry hilltop forests of black and white oak, and isolated clumps of the uncommon red buckeye in the adjoining Ozark Hills Nature Preserve. More than 620 species of flowering plants, ferns, and trees occur at Trail of Tears, including nearly every species of tree found in southern Illinois.

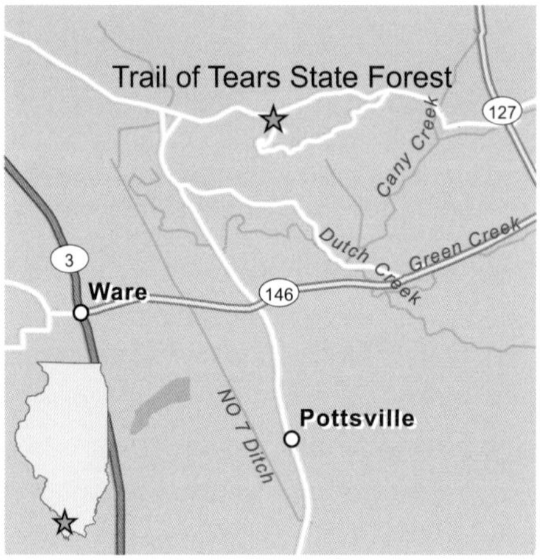

Originally known as the Turkey Farm, Trail of Tears was established in 1929 as the Kohn-Jackson forest. The forest's purpose was to set aside lands for the growing of timber for forest products, watershed protection, and outdoor recreation. In conjunction with the state forest is Union State Nursery, which produces up to 3 million seedlings a year. More than forty fire roads (trails that access the interior of the forest in case of a forest fire) are open for hiking and exploration of this five-thousand-acre forest.

The forest's present name memorializes the tragic time when Native Americans from the Cherokee, Creek, and Chickasaw nations were displaced from their reservations in the Southeast and forced to move to Oklahoma. They overwintered in makeshift camps four miles south of the forest's boundary. Hundreds of lives were lost, and their trek became known as the "Trail of Tears."

In spring, everything you encounter and everywhere you look is interesting. The main public access point on the road through the forest contains a small parking lot with various picnic facilities and trailheads. Many trails were constructed by the Civilian Conservation Corps in the 1930s to provide easy access to the forest. Slopes that rise abruptly on

Forestry planting

all sides of the parking area are cloaked with celandine poppies and squirrel corn, often encasing the bases of the large beech and oaks like Christmas tree skirts. The early blooming harbinger of spring occurs along the sinuous creek banks. The bird watching here is superb, though a good pair of binoculars is a necessity because the canopy is high and the trees grow on steep slopes. This is a good spot to look for warblers, blue grosbeaks, and broadwing hawks. Redbuds and dogwoods lend a colorful, airy feeling to the open forest, and zebra and tiger swallowtails exploit the redbud flowers, creating a truly iconic spring scene. Here, look for the unusual understory tree, red buckeye, native to the southern and eastern United States but occurring frequently at Trail of Tears. The bright red and pink flowers lend a very different look to the shrub layer of the forest. Streams in the area support various salamanders—zig-zag, long-tailed, and cave—while Louisiana waterthrushes patrol the rocky streambeds. Note, also, that this is a place where trees are produced, and during spring the plantations are quite attractive and dramatic, with the dark boles of trees contrasting sharply with the yellow flowers of the weedy understory.

Each fall this same area has a great color show. The golden yellow of the American beeches provides a wonderful contrast to the russets and ambers of the many species of oaks. Hiking the backcountry of the forest entails following the many forest roads that lace the park, and the landscape soon becomes very hilly, with many ridgetops and

Forest panorama

deep, cool ravines to test your hiking mettle. Some of the largest American beeches in Illinois regularly materialize from the shaded forest.

Like many places in Illinois, Trail of Tears State Forest is an out-of-the-way location, nestled in lightly populated Union County. It may take a little effort to get here, but a visit is well worth the time. No one feature stands out, but the accumulated splendor of large trees, a beautiful forest, unusual plants, and the likelihood of encountering seldom-seen wildlife make for a great opportunity to venture into a truly wild area of Illinois. Explore with a camera, with binoculars, with a notebook for recording your observations, or just stroll through the remarkable landscape that is Trail of Tears.

Large American beech trunk

Red buckeye flowers

Cave salamander

CHAPTER 49

War Bluff Valley Sanctuary

. . . a dancing, gemmed satyr, never taking a break;
a loggerhead shrike flies in, and just as quickly,
leaves; a dozen wood ducks at a pond, no time
for photos, I just watched them fly; a sighting of a
bright, sleepy orange butterfly ends the day.
—Susan Post, October 2011

WAR BLUFF VALLEY Sanctuary, located deep in the Shawnee National Forest in Pope County, is a biological reserve maintained strictly for its creatures. The nearly five-hundred-acre site was the former home of legendary Illinois Natural History Survey ornithologists Dick and Jean Graber. The pair donated their home and land to the Illinois Audubon Society in 1990. A late-summer visit will likely require the use of a butterfly field guide, as red admirals, tiger swallowtails, little yellows, and buckeyes will commonly flit about. Butterfly treasures, those seldom seen by most observers, include the gemmed and Carolina satyrs; both species merrily bounce through the sun-dappled forest. The Carolina satyr was first recorded in Illinois at War Bluff in 1994.

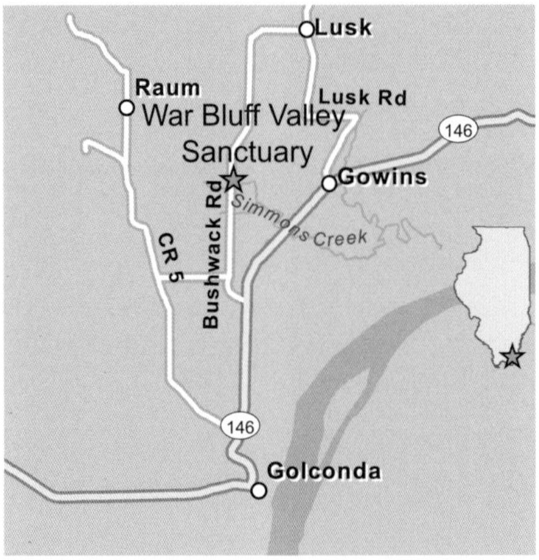

While War Bluff now appears to be the perfect wildlife habitat, including forty-five species of reptiles and amphibians, numerous species of breeding birds, and countless numbers of insects, it wasn't always so. When the Grabers purchased the first tract of land in 1965, it had been farmed with mules and horses for more than one hundred years. Jean commented, "The land was so worn out that it wouldn't even grow lichens." Concerned about the loss of habitat and its effect on birds and other wildlife, they managed the property for wildlife, allowing the natural reforestation of the old farm fields. Today, these fields have reverted to native shrubs—sumac, winged elm, and blackberry, while tulip trees, sycamores, and river birches grow along the creek. Large oaks still occur, and seven ponds have been constructed and naturalized with cattails and other vegetation. One of these, Dragonfly Pond, has no fish, and this allows the eggs and tadpoles of various frogs to thrive,

The ever-changing landscape of War Bluff

as well as the immature stages of toads and dragonflies. A walk along the shoreline is a constant chorus of peeps and splashes, while the air can be literally filled with the antics of dragonflies—eastern pondhawks, Carolina and red saddlebags, spangled skimmers, and green darners.

The sanctuary, with its dense streamside and raspberry thickets, young, regenerating deciduous woodlands, brushy clearings, and impenetrable, weedy tangles is the perfect habitat for wildlife. Bobcats routinely walk through the caretaker's front yard, while spring is a chorus of frogs, including the uncommon crayfish frog. Because the area is such a great place to view insects, since 1994 the local Shawnee Audubon Society holds an insect awareness and appreciation day in late August. All are welcome to the unique event that features butterfly and dragonfly walks and evening black-lighting (a UV light and a white sheet are set up to attract insects at night) for the myriad seldom-seen nocturnal beetles, bugs, and moths.

War Bluff Sanctuary is managed by the Shawnee Audubon Society and is open every day from dawn to dusk. At the entrance, find a small parking area and a trail board with the most recent newsletter and trail maps. You will need to use trail maps, as this is not a manicured, state-park-type setting, but it is rather a place where wild creatures are placed above all else. Six miles of trails with names such as Parula Path, Turkey Trot, Flicker Woods, and Creek Trail explore the landscape. These trails intersect, are not always well-marked, and explore

Twelve-spot dragonfly

Gemmed satyr

Cricket frog on water clover

various habitat types while crossing over several creeks. Depending on the season, these may be stepped across with dry feet or may require a bit of "negotiating" on stepping stones or logs. For those who prefer that wildlife come to them, benches are arranged within view of several bird feeders. As many as fifteen pairs of rose-breasted grosbeaks have been observed at the feeders. The best part about a visit to War Bluff Sanctuary is the surprise factor. It is a place for the true naturalist to explore with field guides, notebooks, and a camera. Dragonflies, frogs, toads, butterflies, and, of course, birds, all blend into the cacophony of sight and sound that characterizes the nature of this recovering landscape.

EPILOGUE

Your Own Backyard

MOST PEOPLE BELIEVE that exploration, particularly of nature, requires travel, often hiking to remote spots, or visiting sites well known for their wildlife spectacles. While this is certainly true, and travel is the basic premise of this book, it is not the only way to see nature in today's world. For those of us who live in towns and cities, simply walking the streets can yield a plethora of unique experiences and observations. We live in Champaign, Illinois, and we routinely walk the two miles to work, trek the one-and-a-half miles to downtown for a weekend lunch, or simply walk the various neighborhoods for exercise. Over the past several years we have encountered some remarkable wildlife and nature events, all within the confines of our urban environment. Walking downtown to lunch we passed an isolated box elder tree, sequestered between a drive-through bank and a line of retail stores. At its base, on a branch that had recently fallen and along the pavement edges of a nearby parking lot we found aggregations of hundreds, thousands, even tens of thousands of box elder bugs. The brilliant, red-and-black of their amassed bodies were clustered together, all stages from tiny red nymphs to the large, winged adults. They remained there all summer and into the fall. Each time we passed yielded a different configuration. The mystery of this aggregation continues to intrigue our entomological psyches.

That same season, a local playground, complete with swings and newfangled play structures in brilliant, rubber-coated colors, beckoned to us. What was most interesting, though, was the hardwood mulch that carpeted the play area, all contained within a railroad tie polygon. The park district adds new mulch each year as it decays, and it forms a soft cushion for rowdy children. Remarkably, the mulch had developed into a perfect habitat for an unusual insect, the false stag beetle (a.k.a., pinching bugs), quite a large beetle that is occasionally observed at city porch lights on warm summer nights. Here, though, the number of beetles was staggeringly large. Hundreds of individuals were emerging from the composting mulch. Their larvae feed on this decaying wood and have obviously found a habitat suited to all their needs. The numbers were so numerous that the children playing about, and their adult caretakers, were noticing them. A quick inspection revealed that the nearby trees and shrubs were laden with both males and females. The males were lined up in military precision on horizontal branches, jousting and fighting for dominance and the right to mate with the watching females. We spent several afternoons ob-

Mass of box elder bugs

serving and photographing this miniature Serengeti. The children noticed our presence and were extremely curious to know about the beetles, and perhaps more astonished, to meet a group of scientists who actually made a living doing, well, science. A bicyclist also happened by, wondered what a group of adults were doing clustered around the base of a tree with cameras and notebooks in hand. Upon learning we were scientists, he exclaimed, "Damn, I knew such people existed (Champaign is the home of the University of Illinois), but I never expected to meet any of them!" Even at work on the University of Illinois campus, nature emerges. The crabapple trees adjacent to our office building are alive with interesting insects. Mealybugs coat the shrubby stems that look like they are clad in polar fleece; only when you touch the branches do the bugs begin to scatter—slowly, but en masse. The tip of each mealy bug has a glistening globule of honeydew, a prize for visiting bees and wasps. Cicada-killer wasps, large and lethal-looking (they capture cicadas to feed their young), buzz around,

Juvenile, sibling Cooper's hawks in authors' backyard

Male false stag beetles fighting over a nearby female

Face of young jumping spider

three to four at a spot, imbibing the sweet honeydew. Several species of mystery wasps and native bees also scour the leaves, always probing for a taste of mealybug nectar.

A final note is to those who have yards. Your little slice of heaven can be a haven for wildlife. Garden less formally; messy edges are good. Use native plants, pile up sticks into a brush pile in a remote corner of your lot, mow less frequently, use no pesticides, feed the birds and squirrels, and who knows what ostentatious displays of nature may result. Over the years we've seen upwards of thirty gray squirrels in our backyard at one time, all feeding, cavorting, and interacting in ways totally unexpected from this often-maligned backyard "vermin." One year we noted a squirrel with a large, puffy jaw and assumed it had some tooth problem or other squirrel malady. Well, it certainly did, for a few days later we found and photographed a most unusual and rare insect, a rodent bot fly. Its size and appearance were reminiscent of a large bumblebee, although with no sting, no mouthparts, and only two wings. This rarely seen behemoth of a parasite had emerged from the squirrel's jaw!

Our squirrel-proof backyard bird feeder has yielded many species of birds, including four types of woodpeckers. It has also attracted the attention of Cooper's hawks, who routinely nest and perch in the tall trees in our neighborhood. Adults will even train their young in hunting techniques in our backyard! Our front yard features a one-oak-tree savanna that supports many native prairie plants. Add in the butterflies, carpenter bees, and other bugs that call our yard home and it's quite a little ecosystem that has developed in a few hundred square feet of urban turf.

The list of nature-viewing opportunities, while seemingly boundless as one's perspective changes, is not infinite. During the years we have been interested in nature, both as children, students, and ultimately professional biologists, the world has changed. Fewer and fewer places remain where nature can thrive in its "pristine" state, if such a scenario still exists, yet the land continues to support a unique cadre of wildlife viewing opportunities and experiences. So our message to you is a simple one: Get out, explore, observe, be infinitely curious, and enjoy the natural world that still exists in Illinois.

Assemblage of American crows on Assembly Hall, University of Illinois

APPENDIX A

Directions to Sites

APPLE RIVER CANYON STATE PARK—The park is located three miles from the Wisconsin border in northwestern Illinois. From Route 78, take East Canyon Road west into the park.

AYERS SAND PRAIRIE NATURE PRESERVE—From Savanna at the junction of Routes 52 and 84, take Route 84 south 2.7 miles to Airport Road; turn and go east 0.5 miles. The nature preserve is north of the road.

BALLARD NATURE CENTER—From Altamont, take US 40 east approximately 2.25 miles to the entrance on the right. From Effingham, take US 40 west approximately 8.75 miles to the entrance on the left. The nature center's sign is at the entrance road.

BEALL WOODS STATE PARK AND NATURAL AREA—Beall Woods is in southeastern Illinois off Route 1 near Keensburg, about 10 miles north of I-64. From Keensburg, take County Road 900N 1.5 miles east to the park.

BELL SMITH SPRINGS & BURDEN FALLS—Drive south from Harrisburg on Route 145 and turn right (west) on Forest Route (FR) 402 at Delwood. Burden Falls is located approximately 3 miles from Delwood, with a small parking area just past the stream ford. After visiting the falls, proceed to a T-junction with FR 447. Turn left and head south past Teal Pond to FR 848. Turn right onto FR 848. At the park entrance sign, go 1.6 miles farther to a right turn that leads down to Hunting Branch Picnic Area. To reach the main parking area for Bell Smith Springs, continue to the end of FR 848.

BIG TREE ACCESS AREA—The access is located northwest of Karnak. From Route 169, just west of Karnak, turn north on Porter House Road and proceed approximately 1 mile to a small parking area on the right. A short trail leads to the large trees.

BLUFF SPRING FEN NATURE PRESERVE—Take US 20 to the southeast side of Elgin. At the intersection (stoplight) of US 20 and Bluff City Blvd. (also known as Shales Parkway), turn south. Follow Bluff City Blvd. as it curves to the east. Go 1 mile to the main entrance of Bluff City Cemetery. Turn left and follow the signs through the cemetery (Central Ave.) to a small parking area at the entrance to the fen on the cemetery's southern edge.

CEDAR LAKE & LITTLE CEDAR LAKE—Cedar Lake is 11 miles south of Murphysboro. Take Route 127 9 miles south of Murphysboro.

Turn east (left) onto Dutch Ridge Road. After 1.2 miles, turn right onto Cove Hollow Road, which dead ends at the parking area/trailhead. Little Cedar Lake is south of Cedar Lake. Take Route 127 approximately 11 miles south of Murphysboro. Turn east (left) onto Landreth Road and travel about a mile. Unless you have a high-clearance vehicle, the last half-mile is over a steep, deeply rutted road, so proceed with caution, or park here and walk in.

DEVIL'S KITCHEN LAKE–ROCKY BLUFF TRAIL—Devil's Kitchen Lake is located southwest of Carbondale. Take Route 13 east from Carbondale to Refuge/Spillway Road and wind around Crab Orchard Lake for several miles; a park sign will direct you to Devil's Kitchen Lake. Once there, follow the road that skirts the lake. The parking area for the trail will be on your left, just after crossing a small bridge. Note: You must obtain a parking permit at the visitors' center on Highway 148.

EMIQUON PRESERVE—From Havana on Route 136, cross the Illinois River and head north on Route 78/97. The preserve access point is on the east side of the road, approximately 2 miles north.

FERNE CLYFFE STATE PARK—The park is located on Illinois 37, 1 mile south of Goreville, and 12 miles south of Marion. It is also easily accessible from both I-57 and I-24. Take exit 7 from I-24, and head west to Route 37. The park entrance is a short distance south on Route 37. From I-57, take exit 40 and drive east to Route 37 and south to the entrance.

FOREST GLEN PRESERVE–FOREST GLEN SEEP AND RUSSELL M. DUFFIN NATURE PRESERVES—Forest Glen is located in southern Vermilion County and is 7 miles northeast of Georgetown. From the junction of Highway 1 and blacktop road 1200N in Westville, turn east and follow the blacktop road east and south for 5 miles; turn and go east 1.8 miles to the entrance of the preserve. The Duffin preserve is on the east side of the entrance road. Forest Glen Seep is located downhill from the group campground. The road to the group campground is often barricaded, requiring a mile hike to the seep.

FOREST PARK NATURE PRESERVE—From Peoria at the junction of Highways 29 and 150, take Highway 29 north for 3 miles; turn and go west on Gardner Lane 0.5 miles to Forest Park Nature Center. The nature preserve is located to the west of the nature center.

FRANK BELLROSE WATERFOWL RESERVE—Access to the Bellrose Reserve is limited, so check in at Cypress Creek National Wildlife Refuge headquarters before visiting. The refuge headquarters is located on the campus of Shawnee Community College. Take Exit 18 on I-57 and drive east 6 miles on Shawnee College Road. Turn right at Shawnee College and Rustic Campus Drive. The headquarters is on the east side, facing Shawnee Community College. Note: The office is not open on weekends.

FULTS HILL PRAIRIE NATURE PRESERVE—Fults Hill Prairie is located along the Mississippi River bluffs near the town of Fults, about 25 miles south of Belleville. From the north, take Route 3 south to Waterloo. Turn right on Route 156, then take the first left onto Lakeview Road (also called Mayestown Road). After downtown Mayestown, turn left on Bluff Road. The preserve is located on Bluff Road, south of Fults. A small parking area on the left and a brown sign designate the site.

FUNKS GROVE—Take I-55 to the McLean exit. At the end of the exit ramp, turn west. Take a right immediately after passing McDonalds. Turn right at the next stop sign and follow Old Route 66 north. Proceed approximately 4.5 miles to Funks Grove Road. Turn left and proceed over the railroad tracks; take the first left. At this point, there will be signs for Sugar Grove Nature Center. Follow this road. At the dead-end sign, continue straight. The road will open up to prairie and you will see the nature center's buildings on your right. When you come to the gravel lane, turn right and proceed to the parking lot. It's best to start your visit at Sugar Grove Nature Center for trail and site information.

GARDEN OF THE GODS RECREATION AREA—Garden of the Gods is southeast of Harrisburg in Saline County. From Harrisburg, follow Illinois 145/34 to Illinois 34 and turn east. From Route 34 turn east (left) onto Karbers Ridge Road. At 2.8 miles, turn north (left) at 250E (Garden of the Gods Road). At 1.4 miles, take another left into Garden of the Gods Recreation Area. National Forest signs and several brown highway signs indicate the way.

GIANT CITY STATE PARK—Giant City State Park is located 12 miles south of Carbondale. From Carbondale, take US 51 south to Makanda Road; go left (east) and follow the signs to the park. The Trillium Trail parking area is just after rounding the bend.

GENSBURG–MARKHAM PRAIRIE NATURE PRESERVE—From Markham at junction with I-57 (west leg of Dan Ryan Expressway) (exit 348) and Highway 6 (159th Street), take 159th Street east about 1 mile to Whipple Avenue; turn left and go north 2 blocks. The nature preserve is to the north with a small parking area.

GLACIAL PARK CONSERVATION AREA—Glacial Park is located in northeastern Illinois in McHenry County. From Route 31 turn west onto Harts Road at a sign for the park. Follow Harts Road to the various parking areas.

GOOSE LAKE PRAIRIE STATE PARK—From Highway 47 south of Morris, turn east on Pine Bluff–Lorenzo Road and travel 6 miles to Jugtown Road; turn north to the park entrance.

GREEN RIVER STATE WILDLIFE AREA—Head north from the small town of Ohio on Route 26. Turn left (west) on Maytown Road. Proceed to Pump Factory Road and park at the first lot on the right.

HARLEM HILLS NATURE PRESERVE—From the intersection of Highway 51 and Windsor Road on the north side of Loves Park, turn east on Windsor Road and go 1.3 miles to where Windsor Road makes a "T" at Forest Hills Road. Turn north on Forest Hills Road and go a little more than 0.1 miles to Flora Drive. Turn east on Flora Drive and go 0.1 miles; the preserve is on the south side of the road.

HENRY N. BARKHAUSEN WETLANDS CENTER—The center is located south of Cypress on Highway 37, two miles north of the intersection of Highways 169 and 37, or nine miles south of the intersection of Highways 146 and 37.

HERON POND NATURE PRESERVE AND CAVE CREEK GLADE NATURE PRESERVE—Take Highway 45 south from Vienna about 4.5 miles to a small parking area on the right, just before crossing a small creek (Dutchman Creek). Cave Creek Glade is on the east side of the road and is a steep, unforested slope with no trail. For Heron Pond, proceed south on Highway 45 to Belknap Road, turn right (west) and go 1.5 miles to a gravel road (Heron Pond Lane); turn right onto Heron Pond Lane and go north 0.5 miles to a large parking area.

HICKORY BOTTOMS—Travel north on Duckworth Road (just east of Perks), and proceed for 2.5 miles. A brown sign indicates the Hickory Bottoms turnoff from Duckworth Road. Turn right on a narrow gravel road and follow it to the parking area. Note: the road winds around for about a mile.

HORSESHOE LAKE STATE FISH AND WILDLIFE AREA—Horseshoe Lake is in Alexander County and can be reached from Route 3. Heading south, turn right onto Promised Land Road and follow it to Horseshoe Lake. Both East Side and West Side Drives provide great views into the swamp and lake.

ILLINOIS BEACH STATE PARK (NORTH AND SOUTH UNITS)—The south unit of Illinois Beach State Park is located on the shore of Lake Michigan, a few miles south of the Illinois/Wisconsin border. From Zion, take Sheridan Road south about 1 mile to Wadsworth Road; go east to the park. After exiting from the south unit, turn right (north) on Sheridan Road, follow it to Seventeenth Street and turn right into the main entrance for the north unit.

IROQUOIS COUNTY CONSERVATION AREA AND PEMBROKE SAVANNA NATURE PRESERVE—Iroquois County Conservation Area is located 2 miles north and 3 miles east of Beaverville in the extreme northeast corner of Iroquois County. From St. Anne take Highway 1 south for 2 miles, and turn left (east) on County Road 3300 for 9 miles to the parking lot. For Pembroke Savanna, from the intersection of Route 17 and Route 1 go south on Route 1 for approximately 4 miles; turn east on 4000S Rd. Go 5 miles, and then turn north on 12000E Rd. The preserve entrance is approximately 0.5 miles north of 4000S, on the west side of the road. A parking area has space for one or two vehicles by the cabled driveway.

KICKAPOO STATE PARK & MIDDLE FORK WOODS NATURE PRESERVE—Kickapoo State Park is 6 miles west of Danville and can be reached via exit 206 or 210 off I-74. Follow the brown signs along the road to the park. Middlefork Woods is located just east of the Middle Fork of the Vermilion River along Glenburg Creek/Kickapoo Park Road. A parking area is just east of the preserve.

LARUE–PINE HILLS RESEARCH NATURAL AREA—LaRue–Pine Hills is 3 miles north of the small town of Wolf Lake (Union County) and is best reached from Illinois Route 3. There are three entrances to the area; the easiest is the Big Muddy River Levee Road. Turn east and proceed to a large curve in the road where the bluffs of LaRue–Pine Hills spring into view. At the intersection, go right to the base of the bluff trail (Forest Road 345) or left to Inspiration Point Trail and Pine Hills Road. Another access is south of the levee road. Turn east on LaRue Road; this dead-ends at a small parking area. A third access point is via State Forest Road, just south of Wolf Lake. Travel east for about a mile and then north (left) onto Pine Hills Road. In wet weather, this road may be impassable due to a creek that must be forded.

LIMEKILN SPRINGS—To reach Limekiln Springs turn north from Shawnee College Road onto Cache Chapel Road (prior to reaching the college). The parking area is within a mile on the right.

LITTLE BLACK SLOUGH NATURE PRESERVE—Proceed to the Cache River State Natural Area Site Headquarters near Belknap.

From Vienna take Highway 45 south 5 miles to Belknap Road; turn right (west) and go to the town of Belknap. Turn right onto 300N (the Dongola–Belknap Road). In town, turn right (north) at a large white church on the right side of the road. A brown sign points the way. Follow the road 0.9 miles to the park office. To reach the trailhead parking area (Tupelo Trail and others) follow a gravel road through a gate on the north side of the office for 0.6 miles to a large parking area. The Tupelo Trailhead is 0.5 miles further up the road.

LITTLE GRAND CANYON—Little Grand Canyon is 8 miles southwest of Murphysboro, between Illinois 127 and Illinois 3. From Murphysboro, go south on Route 127 for 5 miles. Turn right (west) at Etherton Road and travel 3 miles to Poplar Ridge Road. Turn right onto Little Grand Canyon Road and follow it to the entrance. The route is marked with brown directional signs.

LODA CEMETERY PRAIRIE NATURE PRESERVE—From the center of Loda on US 45, north of Paxton, go west on Madison Street 0.3 miles, then north 0.6 miles on W. Mulberry Street to Pine Ridge Cemetery. The nature preserve is north of the cemetery and parking is along the roadside. Do not park in the cemetery.

LODGE COUNTY PARK—Take exit 166 from I-74 near Monticello. Proceed to North Old Route 47 and turn right. The park entrance is on the left within one mile.

LOWER CACHE RIVER ACCESS AREA—The Lower Cache River Access area is located west of the Barkhausen Wetlands Center. Head south on Route 37 and turn west on Perks Road for 1.5 miles. Turn south (left) onto South Quarry Road. The parking area is in 1 mile.

MATTHIESSEN STATE PARK—Matthiessen State Park is located in central LaSalle County on State Route 178. The park's entrance road is 1 mile south of the junction of Route 71 and 178. It can easily be reached from both Interstates 39 and 80.

MERMET LAKE CONSERVATION AREA—Mermet Lake is just off US 45 in Massac County, 14 miles northwest of Paducah, Kentucky. From the north, take exit 16 off I-24 onto Illinois 146. Illinois 146 quickly intersects with US 45 in Vienna. Go south (left) on US 45 for 9 miles to Mermet Lake. From the south, take I-24 to the Metropolis exit at US 45. Take US 45 north for 11 miles to the lake.

MIDEWIN NATIONAL TALLGRASS PRAIRIE—Midewin National Tallgrass Prairie is located in Will County, south of Joliet. The Midewin Visitors' Center is located 2 miles north of Wilmington on Route 53.

MISSISSIPPI PALISADES STATE PARK—The two main entrances to the park are located north of Savanna on Illinois Route 84. The southern entrance leads to a small parking area for Sentinel Nature Preserve.

MORAINE HILLS STATE PARK—Moraine Hills State Park is located in the northeast corner of Illinois, 3 miles south of McHenry near the Fox River. The park entrance is off River Road.

NACHUSA GRASSLANDS—From Interstate 39, exit at Route 64 west toward Oregon for 16 miles to the traffic light at Daysville Rd./1700E. This junction is just before Oregon. Go left (south) on Daysville Rd. for 2.5 miles to Lowden Rd./1500E (past LaVigna Restaurant). Note a brown sign for Lowden-Miller State Forest. Turn right and continue south on Lowden Rd. for 7 miles (you will pass Flagg and Stonebarn Roads) to the visitors' entrance (on right with kiosk).

PERE MARQUETTE STATE PARK AND LOWER ILLINOIS RIVER VALLEY—The park is 5 miles west of Grafton on Route 100 and approximately 25 miles northwest of Alton. Various access roads and parking areas provide views and access to the Illinois River.

PINEY CREEK RAVINE NATURE PRESERVE—From Highway 4 in Campbell Hill in Randolph County, take Rock Crusher Road 6.5 miles west to Piney Creek Road, turn right and go 1.5 miles to the preserve's parking area.

PRAIRIE RIDGE STATE NATURAL AREA—Driving east from Effingham or west from Newton on State Highway 33, turn south on Bogota Road (990 N 900E) and go 4 miles to first curve in road. Go straight off curve to crossroads (600N 900E); turn left (east) for 1 mile or first crossroad (600N 1000E) then turn right (south) and go 1.75 miles to white house with wire fence.

REVIS HILL PRAIRIE NATURE PRESERVE—From Route 97 south of Havana take County Road 1200N approximately 7 miles to County Road 2650E and turn right (south). Proceed 5 miles to North Revis Springs Road. Turn left on East Revis Bluff Road. Access to the preserve is along this road at various locations. Trails to the top are obscure and parking is usually best along the road.

RIDGWAY LAND NATURE PRESERVE—From Route 33 east of Newton, take County Road N900 south to County Road E400. The preserve is 1.5 miles on the north side and has a small parking area and a kiosk.

RIM ROCK/POUNDS HOLLOW—Rim Rock/Pounds Hollow is southeast of Harrisburg in Saline County. From Harrisburg, follow Illinois 145/34 to Illinois 34; turn east (left) onto Karbers Ridge Road, drive through the town of Karbers Ridge (4 miles from the area), and follow the National Forest signs to the site.

ROBERT ALLERTON PARK—Allerton Park is located off I-72 near Monticello. For the north entrance, from I-72 take exit 164 (Monticello/Bridge Street); turn south toward Monticello; turn right (west) at the first intersection (Old Route 47); drive 2 miles, then turn left on County Road 625E; drive 1 mile to a "T," turn right onto County Farm Road; after 0.5 miles turn left into the Allerton Park entrance through brick columns. Follow the signs to the visitors' center. For the South Entrance, take exit 164 (Monticello/Bridge Street); turn south into Monticello; continue straight into town to the stop light for Market Street and turn right (ignore the brown Allerton Park signs); at the four-way stop sign turn right onto Marion Street, drive to the "T" at the stop sign and turn left onto Allerton Road; continue for 3.5 miles, turning right at the sign for the park.

ROBESON HILLS NATURE PRESERVE—From the junction of Routes 1 and 50 in Lawrenceville, take Route 50 east 8 miles to the Business Route 50 interchange; turn and go south and southeast 2.1 miles; turn and go northeast 1.6 miles on Highway 33. The nature preserve is west of the highway, up a steep, unmarked road.

ROLLINS SAVANNA FOREST PRESERVE—Rollins Savanna is located in central Lake County near Grayslake. The main entrance is located on Washington Street at Atkinson Road, just west of Route 45 and east of Route 83.

SAND PRAIRIE–SCRUB OAK NATURE PRESERVE—From Bath, take County Road 900N east 3.6 miles, then turn and go south on County Road 1500E. The nature preserve is west of the road.

SAND RIDGE STATE FOREST & HENRY ALLAN GLEASON NATURE PRESERVE—Sand Ridge State Forest is located in Mason County, about 25 miles southwest of Peoria. Follow Illinois Route 136 to Mason County Road 2800E and turn north. Continue in a straight line for about 6 miles, through the village of Forest City. This road turns west and becomes Mason County Road 2300N and leads directly into the forest. The Henry A. Gleason preserve is on the western edge of Sand Ridge State Forest with a small parking area off County Road 2300E. The preserve is approximately 0.25 miles from the parking lot.

SECTION 8 WOODS NATURE PRESERVE—Section 8 Woods is located north of the junction of Routes 37 and 169, on Route 37 in Johnson County. A small parking area and kiosk on the east are the entrance point to a boardwalk into the forest.

SIMPSON TOWNSHIP BARRENS NATURAL AREA—From Route 147, take Trigg Tower Road (just past Simpson) and head north about 3 miles to the preserve on the right side of the road. Descriptive signage and a small parking area are provided.

SPRING LAKE WILDLIFE CONSERVATION AREA—Take Route 84 south from Savanna for a few miles. The Spring Lake parking area is on the west side of the road.

STARVED ROCK STATE PARK—The park is located on the south bank of the Illinois River. From I-80 take Route 178 south to the entrance. From I-39 follow Route 71 through Oglesby to the park entrance.

TRAIL OF TEARS STATE FOREST—Trail of Tears State Forest lies in western Union County, 5 miles northwest of Jonesboro. Access to the forest is from Illinois Route 127 on the east and Route 3 from the west. Take Trail of Tears Road from either highway to reach the forest.

UPPER MISSISSIPPI RIVER NATIONAL WILDLIFE AND FISH REFUGE—From Savanna, head south on Route 84 for 3.5 miles; turn right onto Riverview Road. Travel 0.5 miles to the office and visitors' center for information on various access points. To access Pool 13 Lock and Dam, turn east on Lock Road, just north of Fulton on Route 84. A Corps of Engineers sign points the way. Note: the entire length of Route 84, from Rock Island to Savanna, provides prime eagle viewing each winter.

VOLO BOG STATE NATURAL AREA—Volo Bog is located 4 miles east of McHenry. From the intersection of US 12 / IL 59 and IL 120 in the town of Volo, go north on US 12 / IL 59 to Brandenburg Rd.; turn and go west (left) 1.3 miles to the entrance on the left.

WAR BLUFF VALLEY SANCTUARY—From Golconda in Pope County, take State Route 146 north 3.5 miles to Bushwhack Road and turn left. Follow the road approximately 2 miles to the sanctuary entrance (look for brown wildlife viewing signs).

WILDCAT BLUFF—From Route 146 west of Vienna take Oak Grove Road (brown sign for Wildcat Bluff) for about 6 miles to Wildcat Bluff Road. Turn right (south) and the road dead-ends in the parking area.

APPENDIX B

Natural Divisions of Illinois

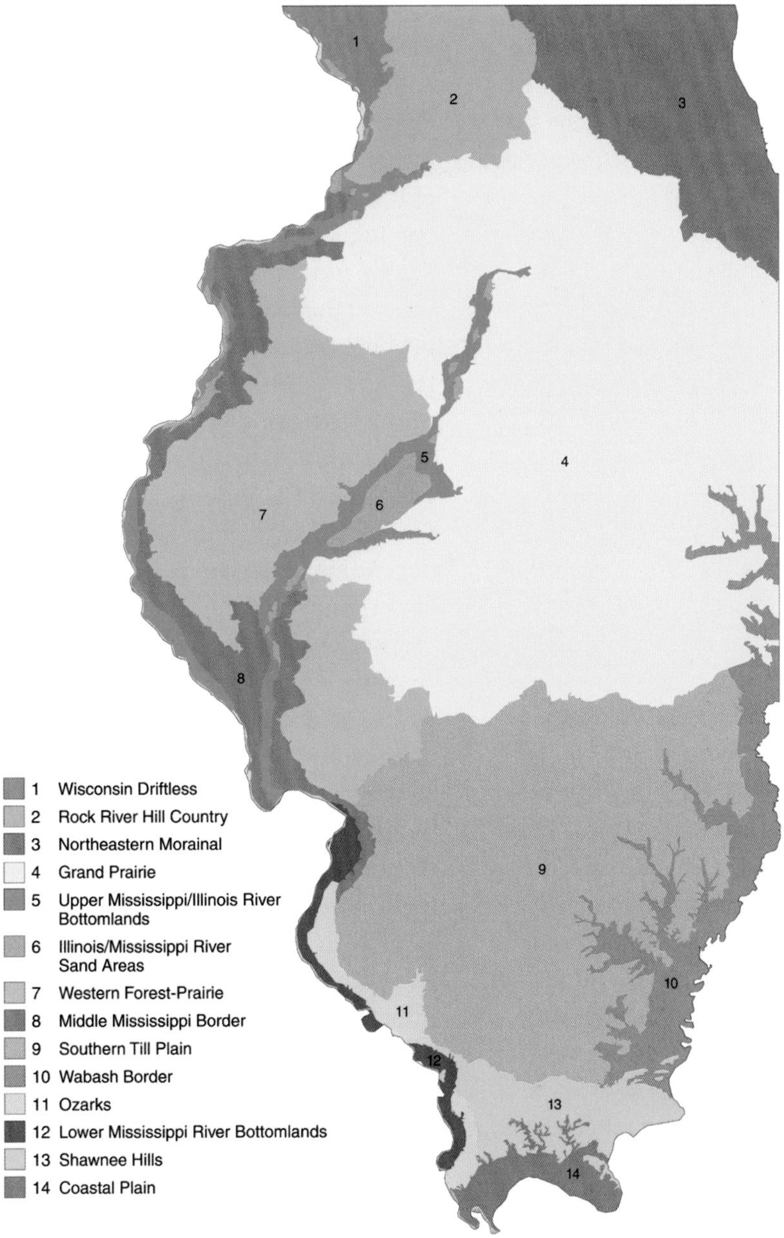

Map of Illinois Natural Divisions

Wisconsin Driftless Division

In 1823, a geologist from Pennsylvania, W. H. Keating, traveled through far northwestern Illinois and observed that the huge granite boulders characteristic of much of the glaciated Midwest were absent. He found ravines and valleys crisscrossing the land in every direction and very few lakes and ponds. From this evidence he deduced that Jo Daviess County and part of Carroll County had escaped the glaciers of the Pleistocene. The Northwestern corner of Illinois may have been an "island" in a Pleistocene sea of ice and became known as the "Driftless Area" (drift is glacially deposited debris).

The Driftless Division has one of the most mature land surfaces in the state. It is characterized by rugged terrain, including loess-capped bluffs (loess is wind-blown sediment), dolomite-capped mounds, and high, rocky palisades. The area has not only the state's coldest winters, but also the highest point—Charles Mound, at 1,235 feet above sea level. The soils are composed of wind-blown loess, disintegrated rock, and, along valley floors, flood-deposited soil. At one time most of the landscape was hardwood forest. Loess hill prairies occur on the steep, south-facing bluffs above the Mississippi River floodplain.

Although the glaciers missed this area, the debris from their melt waters blocked the southeast outlet of Apple River, causing it to cut a new channel. As the river cut through the masses of limestone, dolomite, and shale, it also formed a rugged and picturesque canyon. This iceless region provided a haven that allowed certain plants and animals to survive the glacial periods. Dozens of relict species managed to survive the Pleistocene in the Driftless Area, while their neighbors were forced to extinction. Bird's-eye primrose is one of those relicts found in isolated pockets along the Apple River. Apple River Canyon (Jo Daviess County) and Mississippi Palisades (Carroll County) State Parks are representative sites for this division.

Rock River Hill Country Division

The Rock River Hill Country Division is located in a region of rolling, glaciated topography drained by the Rock River. In 1834, a traveler coming from the prairies of central Illinois to Galena noted the difference in the countryside once he reached the Rock River: "The aspect of the country changes considerably soon after passing Rock River. The prairie is frequently broken by sudden ravines; the number of groves increases; the streams run more rapidly over their pebbly beds; and huge masses of crumbling rock rise like the ruined walls of old castles along the mimic vales through which they take their way."

The soils of this division are thin and are either loess (wind-blown sediment) or glacial till. This division is divided into two sections, depending on the bedrock of the area. One is underlain with dolomite and limestone. Outcrops and "dells" occur along streams. The other section (south-central Ogle County) is underlain with sandstone that has formed bluffs, ridges, and ravines.

Prairie once occupied the larger expanses of upland, while forests were equally abundant along watercourses. White pine, Canada yew, and yellow birch, relict species of the northern forest, can still be found in this division. Prairie knobs (islands of prairie that were either too hilly or troublesome to farm) support downy yellow painted cup and profusions of pale purple coneflower. Nachusa Grasslands (Lee County) is a representative site for this division.

Northeastern Morainal Division

As recently as twelve thousand years ago, the landscape of the Northeastern Morainal Division was covered by glaciers. Evidence of the last glacier is everywhere in this division. Glacial landforms, such as kames (conical mounds of glacial debris), moraines (long ridges of glacial debris), and eskers (ridges of sand and gravel from ancient, embedded glacial streams) are common landscape features. While the glacial landforms provide topography for this division, it also contains the flat, ancestral glacial bed of Lake Chicago (the precursor of Lake Michigan). Sand dunes of varying sizes occur along the Lake Michigan shoreline. The soils are derived from lakebed sediments, peat, beach deposits, and glacial drift rather than loess, and range in texture from sand and gravel to silt-clay loams.

In addition to a variety of prairie and forest communities, this division also has fens (wet prairies with an alkaline [basic] water source associated with calcareous springs and seeps), marshes (common because of the poorly drained soils), sedge meadows, and bogs. Along with having the highest plant diversity in Illinois, the area also features the only true bogs in Illinois, and all of the state's natural glacial lakes. This is also the only division to have a natural beach-and-dunes community. Some interesting plants of this division include tamarack, fringed gentian, lupine, leartherleaf, pitcher plant, grass-of-Parnassus, bearberry, and grass pink, snake-mouth, and small white lady's-slipper orchids. To experience this division, visit Illinois Beach (Lake County) and Moraine Hills (McHenry County) State Parks, Volo Bog State Natural Area (Lake County), or Glacial Park, owned by the McHenry County Conservation District.

Grand Prairie Division

The Grand Prairie Division, the largest natural division, is a vast plain formerly occupied mostly by tallgrass prairie. The grassland was so different that the early travelers had to turn to the sea for analogies, calling the area "a sea of grass" or "a vast ocean of meadowland." In time, this landscape came to be known simply as prairie, a word derived from the French word for meadow. The fertile soils are young and high in organic content. They developed from wind-deposited loess, lakebed sediments, and glacial drift. Natural drainage was poor, resulting in many marshes and prairie potholes. The prairies were a veritable wildflower garden, containing several hundred species of grasses and forbs.

Forests interrupted the landscape on floodplains, on slopes bordering streams, along river bends, and in isolated prairie groves. U.S. Government Geologist David Dale Owen wrote in 1839, "Sometimes the woodland extends along this river for miles continuously, again it stretches in a wide belt off into the country marking the course of some tributary streams and sometimes in vast groves of several miles in extent, standing alone, like islands in the wilderness of grass and flowers." Like their prairie counterparts, prairie groves have a remarkable number of plant species, especially spring blooming herbs.

To experience this division, visit Goose Lake Prairie State Park (Grundy County), Hooper Branch Savanna Nature Preserve (Iroquois County), Green River State Wildlife Area (Lee County), Loda Cemetery Prairie Nature Preserve (Iroquois County), and Funks Grove Nature Preserve (McLean County).

Upper Mississippi River and Illinois River Bottomlands Division

The Upper Mississippi River and Illinois River Bottomlands Division encompasses the rivers and floodplains of the Mississippi River from Wisconsin to where it meets the Missouri River in Calhoun County. It also stretches along the Illinois River and its tributaries, encompassing bottomlands and associated backwater lakes south of LaSalle.

Broad floodplains and gravel terraces, formed by glacial floodwaters, characterize the terrain. Both big rivers have oxbow lakes, but backwater lakes are found only in the Illinois River and its major tributaries south of LaSalle.

Much of this land was originally forested, and forests are still found along the broad floodplains of the rivers. Prairie, marsh, and moist savanna also occurred. A unique habitat here was originally classified as a spring fed bog or a "hanging fen," but it is really a tall shrub fen. This rare natural community, with sloping peat at the edge of a moraine, is also found only in this division. Emiquon Preserve in Fulton County is representative of this division.

Illinois River and Mississippi River Sand Areas Division

The Illinois River and Mississippi River Sand Areas Division encompasses the sand areas and dunes in the bottomlands of the Illinois and Mississippi rivers. Scrub oak forest and dry sand prairie are the natural vegetation of this region. The two principal sand areas of this division are the Havana deposit (Illinois River) and the Hanover-Oquawka deposit (Mississippi River). The meltwaters of the Wisconsin glacier greatly affected the formation of both of these deposits. The Havana deposit was formed as meltwater cascaded down the prehistoric course of the Illinois River. The Hanover-Oquawka deposit occupies an expanse between the bluffs on the east and the Mississippi River on the west. In both of these areas, tremendous floods carried a huge volume of sand and gravel downstream at breakneck speed, depositing material when the water slowed.

Look for prickly-pear cactus, three-awn grass, little bluestem, and Indian grass in Sand Ridge State Forest (Mason County) and Ayers Sand Prairie Nature Preserve (Carroll County).

Western Forest-Prairie Division

The Western Forest-Prairie Division consists of level to rolling uplands between fairly deeply cut rivers, with well-developed floodplains and ravines. This area was covered by Illinoian glaciers. It is a land of deep, forested ravines with intervening flat, prairie openings. Bedrock outcroppings of sandstone, shale, and limestone are common in some locations.

In the area north of the Illinois River valley, both the Spoon and La Moine Rivers drain the landscape. Prior to settlement, prairie almost equaled the amount of forest here. An interesting habitat found here is dry-moist barrens, also known as oak openings. These barrens are transition zones between prairie and forest and once occurred in several parts of the state. Early travelers described the openings as "green groves, arranged with the regularity of art, making shady alleys for the heated traveler."

The area southeast of the Illinois River valley is drained by Macoupin Creek and the Illinois River. The original vegetation of this section was forest, with only 12 percent of the area in prairie.

Although they did not name the forests in this division, early settlers gave names to these presettlement prairies, which existed in large parcels on the uplands. Both String Prairie and Brown's Prairie were found here. Very little prairie or forest remains today in this area.

Middle Mississippi River Border Division

The Middle Mississippi Border Division consists of a narrow band of river bluffs and rugged terrain bordering the Mississippi River floodplain from Rock Island County to St. Clair County, and the lower Illinois River valleys of western Illinois. Bedrock cliffs and outcrops of limestone are common in the river bluffs, with local areas of sandstone. Hill prairies occur atop south- and west-facing bluffs, while oak-hickory forests predominate in the ravines and cooler north- and east-facing slopes.

Deep deposits of loess (windblown silt) are found in this division. Forests along the major river valleys trapped these dust-sized particles, and the material accumulated to form high bluffs. One of the characteristics of loess is its tendency to stand in vertical walls that don't erode. Two peaks in Pere Marquette State Park (Jersey County) are examples of loess—McAdams Peak and Lover's Leap. Another special feature of this division is roosting areas for overwintering bald eagles.

The topography in the eastern part is a result of the Pleistocene glaciers—the Illinoian and pre-Illinoian stages. Limestone underlies most of this section and forms cliffs along the river. Unusual habitats found here include limestone glades, loess hill prairies, and glacial-drift hill prairies. The topography of the western section is more rugged, as the area escaped the Pleistocene glaciers. Limestone and sandstone outcrops frequently occur. Unusual habitats found here include limestone glades and loess hill prairies.

Southern Till Plain Division

The Southern Till Plain Division encompasses the area south of the Shelbyville Moraine and the Sangamon and Macoupin Creek watersheds. The Illinoian Glacial Episode reached its southernmost limit just beyond the limits of this division. The bedrock consists of sandstone, limestone, coal, and shale. A layer of thin soil, usually loess or till, covers the bedrock and has poor internal drainage. Many of the soils have high clay content, leading to "claypan" subsoil. These comparatively light-colored soils lend the name "gray prairie" to the upland prairies. From north to south, the glacial till becomes thinner.

This division is a relatively flat plain, drained by the Kaskaskia River and contained mostly prairie. The more southern areas have rolling, hilly topography and were mostly forested. Found in this division are post oak flatwoods, which occur on the hardpan, clay soil. These flatwoods have the same appearance today as they might have had several hundred years ago. Trees do not live excessively long in a flatwoods. They undergo a regular life cycle of 150 to 200 years, and when they reach a certain size, the trees inevitably blow down because of their shallow root penetration in the clay soil.

Crayfish frogs, ornate box turtles, and a remnant population of greater prairie chickens are characteristic organisms of this division. Post Oak Rest Area along I-57 is a good example of a post oak flatwoods community. Ballard Nature Center (Effingham County) and Ridgway Audubon Sanctuary (Jasper County) are examples of this division as well.

Wabash Border Division

The Wabash Border Division contains the last stronghold of the eastern deciduous forest. Traces of this magnificent forest still remain in the landscape surrounding the loess-covered hills and bottomlands of the Wabash River and the valleys and forests of the Vermilion River. The area is underlain with limestone, sandstone, coal, and shale. Bedrock outcrops are uncommon. The Wisconsin glaciers affected the Vermilion River area, while the entire division was influenced by the earlier Illinoian glaciers. The topography is, for the most part, relatively gentle.

This division is a transition zone between forest and prairie, but lowland and upland forests dominate the landscape. These forests contain a great diversity of trees—American beech, tulip poplar, cottonwood, sycamore, and several species of oaks (pin, overcup, cherrybark, bur, Shumard, and swamp white). The understory is a garden of spring ephemerals. Many of these organisms are geographically restricted—plants and animals more typical of the eastern deciduous forest.

In addition to a large number of tree species, this division contains the state's only National Wild and Scenic River, and it supports several species of fishes found nowhere else in the state, including the bluebreast and harlequin darters.

To experience this division visit the Russell M. Duffin Nature Preserve in Vermilion County and Beall Woods State Park in Wabash County.

Ozark Division

The Ozark Division is a narrow band from northern Monroe County to Alexander County. This sliver of landscape is part of the Ozark Uplift, a domelike geologic structure of exposed, ancient bedrock centered in the Ozark Mountains of Missouri. Massive limestone bluffs, marking the edge of the Mississippi Valley, the sandstone ravines of Randolph County, and the sinkhole region of Monroe County, with its caves and springs, are typical examples of the region.

The northern area was glaciated during the Illinoian Glacial Episode and is underlain with relatively pure limestone. The central area was also glaciated during the same period but is underlain instead with sandstone. The southern part, though, is unglaciated and has cherty limestone, which is more resistant to erosion.

Prior to settlement, most of this division was forested, and a rich assemblage of tree species can still be found here. This is the only division where shortleaf pine occurs naturally. Hill prairies occurred on the river bluffs in the north. While most of the plant species of these prairies are similar to the hill prairies farther north, several Ozark plants, such as Missouri black-eyed Susan, occur here. Unique organisms in this division include the plains scorpion, which hides by day amid the crumbling limestone.

Fults Hill Prairie Nature Preserve in Monroe County, Piney Creek Ravine Nature Preserve in Randolph and Jackson Counties, and Pine Hills Research Natural Area in Union County are representative of this division.

Lower Mississippi River Bottomlands Division

The Lower Mississippi River Bottomlands Division includes the Mississippi River and its floodplain from Alton to the Thebes Gorge. Glacial floodwaters created this vast floodplain ecosystem. The Mississippi River is muddy here due to the silt load brought in by the Missouri River. The soils have developed from this alluvium and are either fine textured and well drained with areas of sand, or clayey with poor drainage.

The northern area contains the American Bottoms, a montage of swales, backwater lakes, ridges, and river terraces. When Charles Dickens visited the area in 1842, all he could hear was the loud chirping of frogs, and all he could see on the "unwholesome, steaming earth" was mud, mire, brake (overgrown marshland), and brush. In the south, forests have pin, overcup, and cherrybark oaks, but also species associated with bottomland swamps. Look for pumpkin ash, swamp cottonwood, and bald cypress in La Rue Swamp, and listen for the calls of green treefrogs.

Shawnee Hills Division

Just south of where the Illinoian glaciers stopped, the massive sandstone and shale escarpments of the Shawnee Hills are exposed. The backbone of Southern Illinois is the Shawnee Hills, which extend across the southern tip of the state from Fountain Bluff on the Mississippi River to the Shawneetown Hills near the mouth of the Wabash River. This division is characterized by high, sandstone cliffs that form the Greater Shawnee Hills. A series of lower hills underlain by limestone and sandstone is known as the Lesser Shawnee Hills.

The topography of this area is rugged, with many bluffs and ravines. The winding courses of clear, rock-bottomed streams widened and deepened the ravines, forming canyons, shelves, steps, and shelter bluffs. A thin layer of loess covers the rocks on the gentler slopes. Where the slopes are steep and erosion rapid, bare rock is exposed.

Most of this division was forested, yet openings occurred—barrens and glades. Barrens are grassy openings found on rocky, south-facing slopes that have only a thin layer of soil covering the rock. Vegetation includes small, gnarled, and twisted blackjack and post oaks, prairie grasses, and the occasional blazing star. Glades are open expanses of bedrock on bluff tops, dominated by red cedar. The ground is likely to be covered with moss, lichens, and sedum.

Ferne Clyffe State Park (Johnson County), Wildcat Bluff (Johnson County), and Garden of the Gods (Pope County) are good examples of the region.

Coastal Plain Division

The Coastal Plain Division is located in the extreme southern tip of the state. South of the Shawnee Hills the land flattens, the drainage is poor, and frequent flooding occurs. Only the sloping knolls and ridges of the Cretaceous Hills break the broad plain of alluvium, consisting of the Cache, the Ohio, and the Mississippi River bottoms. Millennia before human records were kept, this strip of southern Illinois bordered the shoreline of a much larger Gulf of Mexico. Though the seas retreated, the coastal plain of Illinois still resembles plains that surround the present-day Gulf.

The Cretaceous Hills extend in a narrow band from the Mississippi to the Ohio River. They are low hills made of gravel, sand, and clay and are remnants of the more broadly spread Cretaceous deposits in Kentucky and Tennessee. The low, gravelly hills contain acidic seep springs. Plants associated with northern bogs can be found here, including sphagnum moss and a profusion of ferns.

The bottomlands contain the southern swamps at their northernmost limits. Vast stands of bald cypress trees support little colonies of plants on their "knees." Heron Pond—Little Black Slough Nature Preserve (Johnson County), with its boardwalk, is an excellent place to discover this division.

INDEX

Newly retired, **MICHAEL JEFFORDS** was the longtime education/outreach director for the Illinois Natural History Survey (INHS). Jeffords is an entomologist, freelance photographer, writer, and educator. He was staff photographer for the *Illinois Steward* magazine. Also recently retired, **SUSAN POST** was an INHS research scientist and staff writer for the *Illinois Steward* magazine. Post is the author of *Hiking Illinois* (2nd edition, Human Kinetics, 16,000 sold). Jeffords and Post are the co-authors of *Illinois Wilds* (1995, Phoenix Publishing). They are also co-directors of the Illinois Wilds Institute for Nature (IWIN), an INHS program that offers public field courses on Illinois biology.

The University of Illinois Press
is a founding member of the
Association of American University Presses.

Designed by Jim Proefrock
Composed in 11/14 Adobe Minion
with Adrianna Extended display
at the University of Illinois Press
Manufactured by Bang Printing

University of Illinois Press
1325 South Oak Street
Champaign, IL 61820-6903
www.press.uillinois.edu